Yoga inVision 5

dome

frontal
lobe

front kundalini

back kundalini

middle kundalini

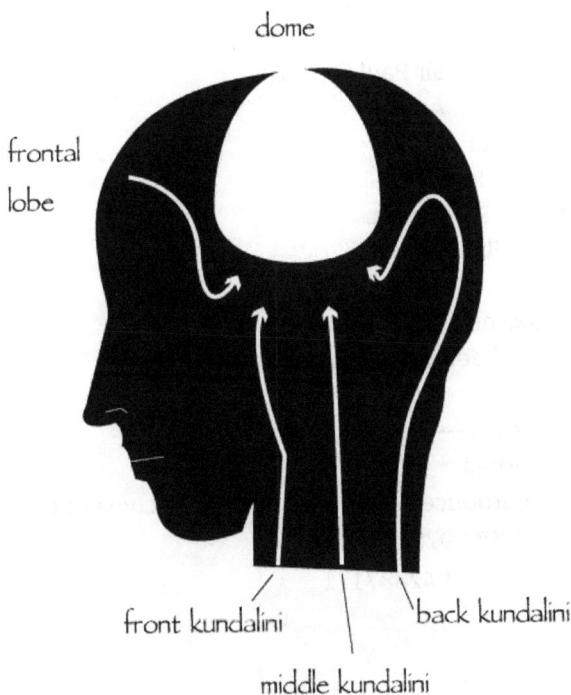

Michael Beloved

Shiva Art: Sir Paul Castagna
Illustrations: Author
Correspondence:
    Michael Beloved
    19311 SW 30th Street
    Miramar FL 33029
    USA
Email: axisnexus@gmail.com
                michaelbelovedbooks@gmail.com

Paperback ISBN: 9781942887164
EBook ISBN: 9781942887171
LCCN: 2018904826

Table of Contents

INTRODUCTION

This is the fifth of the Yoga inVision series. These give beginners ideas of the physical, psychological and spiritual experiences one may have when doing asana postures, pranayama breath-infusion breath methods and pratyahar sensual energy withdrawal. Beyond that is higher yoga, which Patanjali named the *samyama* procedures. He defined *samyama* as a combination of dharana deliberate focus, dhyana spontaneous focus and samadhi continuous spontaneous focus. During practice these progress one into the other. If you are expert at pratyahar sensual energy withdrawal, you will find that you graduate to dharana which is deliberate focus of your attention to a higher concentration force or person. As soon as you master dharana you may slip into dhyana which is an effortless focus on a higher concentration force or person. Once you practice dhyana, samadhi happens as the continuous effortless focus on a higher concentration force or person.

Many persons who take to spiritual life feel that they can construct a path as they advance. This idea denotes failure. After all, if the supernatural and spiritual environment, is not already there, no one will create it now. It is either there or it is not. For instance, if you are moving to a different country, then of course you will fail if the country intended does not exist. It has to be there already. Similarly what you aim at in spiritual life, must be there already, or you will find that your idea is incorrect. This is why I speak of a concentration force or person. I could have said concentration person or divine person, or God. I did not because I do not know how your spiritual path will develop.

You may leave an island in the safest boat and still the vessel may sink. Therefore you have to keep your mind open and be willing to work with providence. In spiritual development, there is providence too. What you desire to have you may not achieve. What you wish to see may never appear to you.

These Yoga inVision journals show how sporadic my course of yoga was. This is after years of practice. It gives some idea of what to expect. Once you get through the lower yoga practice, you will see advancement in a more stable way but it may be incremental, accruing little by little, with bright flashes here and there.

Part 1

Observations were made in meditation in regards to the consumption attitude of the intellect. In the Vedic literature, it is equated to a pecking bird which eats ideas, images and subtle sounds which are presented to it by the memory, the telepathic signals and other sensual intakes. These are used by the imagination orb to create a compelling video in the mind.

The imagination orb is part of the intellect, just as the sharp precise tip of a bird's beak is part of the creature's body.

There is the idea that there are two birds in the psyche, one being the limited coreSelf and the other being the Supreme Being who is unlimited in range and glory. The limited one has a tendency to be curious about the outcome of experiences. The Supreme Being lacks this curiosity and is not subjected to the traumas of much-desired or unpleasant outcomes.

However when we consider the limited spirit and its perception equipment, its adjuncts, the intellect may be regarded as a bird and the coreSelf may be considered as yet another bird which is in the psyche. This would mean there are three birds involved with two of them interlocked to appear as the conjoint limited being in contrast to the Supreme Being.

Because the intellect is oriented towards passion, it is unreliable in its support for the interest of the coreSelf. All the same, the attention of the coreSelf is prejudiced for the intellect. Thus it too is unreliable. The adjuncts are insensitive to the Supreme Being, which means that so long as the core is reliant on the adjuncts, the core itself will be hostile to the Supreme Being. This is problematic.

Atmananda

He showed a concentration force at the top back of the head. This was naad sound resonance. After a time, it faded. He said that grace bestowal to a student by a master yogi, does not stay with the student if the student is resistance to austerities.

Lahiri

He said that there should be the equivalent of eight (8) hours of naad contact practice for three years, for there to be success in making contact with the chit akash sky of consciousness.

January 10, 2006

The subtle body is determined to exploit the bliss content energy. It does this by stirring subtle energies just as the imagination orb generates ideas to stir image producing lust-formatted emotions. A woman I know came to my subtle body. She was desirous of petting because that stirred her bliss energy and caused happy feelings.

The subtle body holds memories of previous bliss enjoyments. These memories are activated from time to time, otherwise they remain in the psyche and become active on occasion even if the next event may not come in a thousand years.

Atmananda

Double concentration force

This was naad and a streak of energy in the top back of the head. Naad sound resonance is used as the base as one is absorbed in the streak of energy.

During this absorption, impressions may form images and may penetrate the focus or even abolish the focus and assume prominence. It depends on the strength of the original impressions which were lodged in memory or which were transmitted telepathically from another person.

I realized that the intellect regularly miscalculates. This is due to lack of full information and deep insight. The coreSelf has this tendency of reliance on the intellect. Thus it endorses the conclusions of the intellect to its detriment.

The intellect unless it is upgraded into the insightful truth-piercing perception (rtambhara buddhi), does not have cosmic grasp. By nature it is error-prone.

To the coreSelf the actions of the intellect are real. The core is impulsively attached to the conclusions of the intellect. When these views prove to be untrue, when they are not honored by nature, the coreSelf becomes depressed because its investment in those conclusions fails to get the support of nature.

At some stage, when a coreSelf realizes these flaws in the intellect and that nature does not have to support ideas, that core no longer invest heavily in the conclusions which are formed in the mind. This frees the self from making costly investment plans. The result is less depression for the core.

Search for the creator-god

Discovering oneself to be conscious in this creation, one may search for a God, for someone who could be held responsible for this cosmic event.

However in the physical world, the search is futile. In the astral domains the search is endless due to infinite split dimensions. If there is a God, he or she must be in a super-dimension. It may be that a limited self cannot reach the territory. It may be that God's dimension is imperceptible such that even if he was before one, one could not detect him.

January 11, 2006

In meditation, I observed that unless the psyche is super-energized, the sense of attention is irresistibly attracted to the imagination orb intellect complex, which in turn is attracted to the memory and sensual intake. The imagination orb is energized by the observational powers of the attention, except that such powers are impulsive.

This observation or insight is the very power which allows a yogi to control the orb and to detach the observational powers from their involuntary operations which imperil the observing self.

January 12, 2006

Yogeshwarananda

He showed that the subtle eyelids block inner light from being thrown out of the psyche. This has value when doing pratyahar sensual energy withdrawal for the conservation of energy and for the cessation of outward interest which results in insight perception within the psyche and development of vision into the chit akash sky of consciousness.

When a yogi ceases interest in exploiting the physical and subtle material energy, he develops insight perception which manifest in various ways according to the dimension the subtle body assumes.

I had an experience of a beam of energy within the psyche. This was transparent and shun through a rectangular opening. I could not direct it. It shun through the rectangular opening out into the subtle atmosphere ahead of me. This type of vision may or may not be directed by a yogi. It may have its own directive energy which shines into a subtle or supernatural dimension on its own. The yogi can see what it illuminated but he may not move it in any direction as desired.

This is similar to the sight of a newborn child, where even if there is vision, the child cannot operate the muscles of cornea, hence the child cannot selectively use the vision but it does have the vision nevertheless.

Navel to imagination orb contact

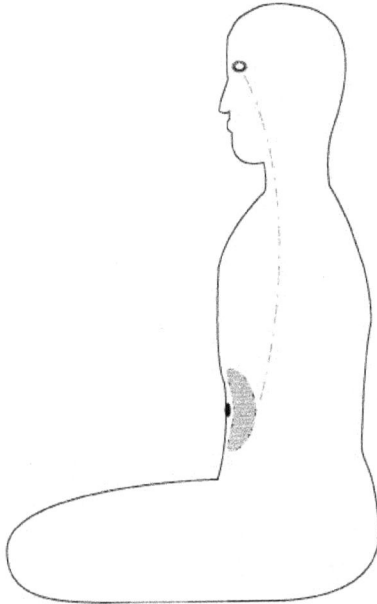

Lahiri

He asked why it was questionable for a man to take a married woman who already has children.

I said that it may be due to unresolved social energy which was due to complexities in the first marriage. The man who wants to be with her, cannot resolve that social energy from her first marriage. Most women would be unsettled because of the previous obligations and the unresolved energies which arise from that.

January 13, 2006

Lahiri

He suggested that the replies given to thoughts should be neglected or redirected. Many thoughts should have no response given to them. Others should be handled in a way which services responsibilities but with an aim that ultimately these should be terminated at least on the physical level. And yet some others should be subjected to bombardment with naad sound resonance energy.

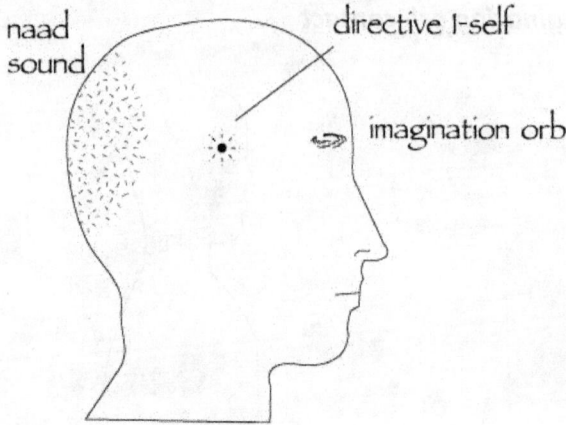

naad sound · directive I-self · imagination orb

Lahiri

He discussed the value of asana yoga postures to retract the kundalini expressions. He stated this.

"The practice of postures is necessary in most cases. Postures should not be derided, minimized or ridiculed."

When he made this remark, I did a stretch back posture and noticed that I could pull muscles in the thigh which I was unable to grip before. Formerly these tendons were mentally out of reach and were resistant to being handled through willpower. These are muscles which are involved in involuntary sexual expression.

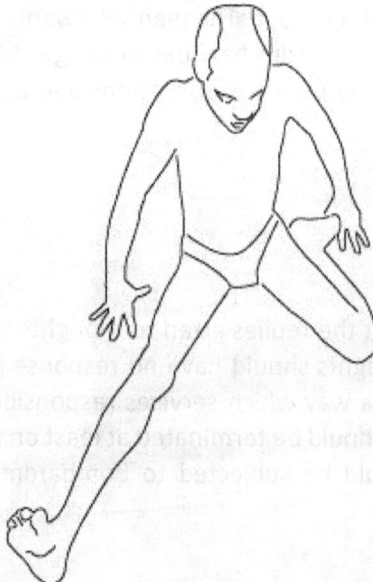

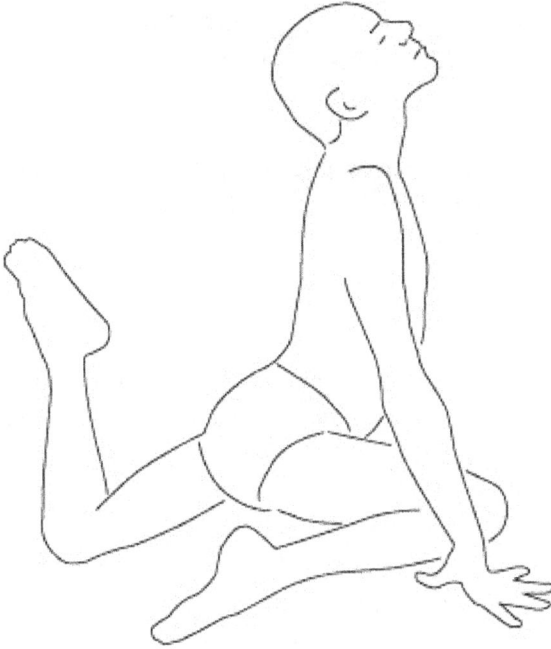

Lahiri suggested that responses to thoughts should be psychic actions which connect the coreSelf to naad. During meditation, one should cease sending thought-replies to anyone. Instead one should be sure to link or relink to naad sound resonance when one realizes that one views a thought energy.

The attention of the coreSelf falls into the space of the frontal lobe. That is its habit. Hence only with effort will naad be connected to the attention. In sleep, in subtle world encounters, in inattentive waking periods, the attention will link with a sensual orb and memory demonstrations through the imagination orb.

January 15, 2006

Involuntary actions of the subtle body

To vent grievances against providence, the subtle bodies meet and quarrel in the astral world. The subtle form is capable of holding a quantity of stress, even energy from many past lives which is stored in its subconscious psychic compartment.

Periodically the subtle body feels the need to vent stress. When this happens if there is no opportunity, it will act by itself without physical support. The persons involved will meet on an astral level and create a circumstance in which the energy is released.

coreSelf enclosure

I realized that the coreSelf is surrounded spherically by an insight suppressing, indiscriminate enthusiasm which surrounds it on all sides.

Yogeshwarananda

Woman celibacy diagram

This diagram shows the lifting of sex hormones in a female body. Sexually charged energy which accumulates in the pubic funnel are pulled up to the navel. From there it is taken through the breasts into the neck.

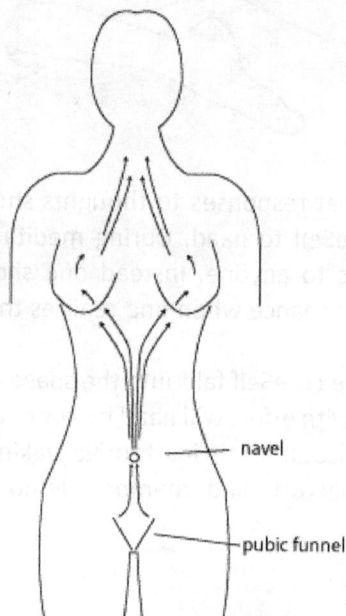

navel

pubic funnel

January 16, 2006

I visited a religiously inclined social leader in a hospital in Guyana. Despite his social contributions to society, this person was an alcoholic. He was in hospital due to heart failure. After the visit during a rest period, I saw him again in an astral hell which is reserved for alcoholic persons. In that place everything, the bodies and the materials, were in a state of abject deterioration. By this I mean the astral bodies and astral materials. Some persons there had pets but the bodies of these animals were in partial deterioration just as well.

One dog attacked me. It bit into my subtle hand and drew energy. This is one of the places where one may find oneself to be hereafter if one is an alcoholic or a drug abuser.

This proves that alcohol abuse leads to deterioration of the energy in the subtle body. Due to that one may go to lower astral dimensions hereafter.

Naad brahma

Naad sound is the pitter patter bombardment spiritual energy on the material energy (brahman on prakriti). A yogi should use naad as the reference, as the basis, as the shelter, as the constant support.

January 17, 2006

Lahiri

The investigative interest manifest as curiosity. It is a small orb in the head of the subtle body. It should be curbed so that it applies itself to naad sound resonance to investigate causal origins.

January 18, 2006

Yogeshwarananda

He said that tratak seems to help with internalizing the vision power. Tratak tires the out-looking sense, causing it to go inward. Tratak is an outward stare into blankness so that the physical eyes tire. The subtle eyes blare and remain unfocused. After a time, there is tiredness in the physical eyes from the staring. This produces a need to tightly close the physical eyelids. The outward coursing subtle vision power spins on itself and retracts into the head of the subtle body. This is a pratyahar sensual energy internalization procedure.

Atmananda

Back of head pull-up

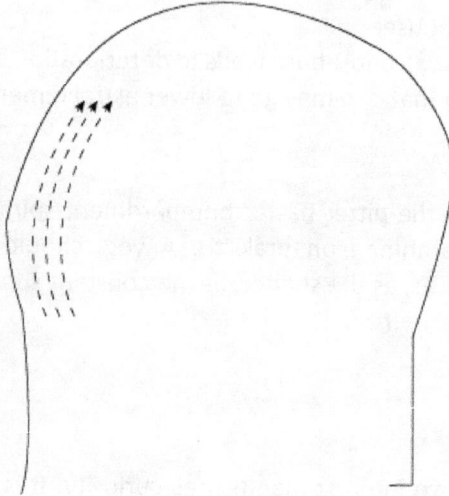

He showed a looking beam which comes from the imagination orb. It is the same energy which configures thoughts and ideas. Even with his assistance I could not operate it. A psychic operation which is involuntary may disappear as soon as one tries to operate it through willpower. For an advanced yogi, that operation may be done easily. This is because there are different categories of coreSelves with differing degrees of psyche control.

January 19, 2006

Atmananda

He said, "Discard the alluring affection force. Give it little or no attention when it is self-stimulated."

This was in reference to my meeting a yoga student with his wife and her father. Activities and energy movements in the subtle body of others is easily seen by a yogi. The breasts of the lady itched. Her sexual organ was excited. In her presence, due to proximity, all males present became sexually alert.

I followed the instruction of Atmananda and discarded a streak of alluring affection force which was in my psyche. Instead I focused on a streak of light in the back of the subtle head.

The alluring force appears in the head of the subtle body where it affects the opinion of the intellect, which in turn influences the coreSelf which donates energy for more development of more allurement. This develops in a flash into a sexual urge.

To facilitate this, the intellect creates a hope energy for sexual fulfillment. This converts into a lust based craving.

Yogeshwarananda

He said that one must practice and struggle to gain mastery, all by oneself. Each person must capture and subdue to unruly portion of the mind.

Atmananda

The intellect which contains the imagination orb, must be subdued by keeping it separate from the indulgent sensuous energy which acts recklessly. The coreSelf must limit its interest in the intellect and forgo some of the benefits it gets from being informed of circumstances by the intellect.

There is a tradeoff between the intellect and the coreSelf where the coreSelf provides energy and the intellect provides sensual experiences which are of interest to the core. However the core must realize that this is not in its interest. It should gradually but surely end the exchange with the intellect.

January 20, 2006

Yogeshwarananda

He taught a method of squeezing the imagination orb and its energy chamber.

One should go wherever the intellect Is mentally located when it imagines during meditation. One should go there boldly without fear. One should grasp and squeeze it directly. No mantras or props should be used. As soon as one finds that the imagination picturizes again, one should repeat the grasping and squeezing action.

There will be a tendency to spare the imagination orb from this control but one should resist that. There will be fear of it and attraction to it, but one should ignore those influences. Even if one feels attracted to its ideas, one should relinquish its dialogue and serial images. The enjoyment which one derives from its images should be rejected. This requires months or years of daily practice. One should practice this even when one is not meditating, even when one interacts with others.

Review of youthful attraction

In meditation, visions from the past, from childhood, in reference to a woman appeared. These were vivid memories. At the time the body I used was thirteen (13) years of age. The woman whom I was attracted to was twenty-two (22) years of age. I felt this attraction even before my body reached puberty which was between thirteen and fourteen.

In retrospect, even before puberty, the attraction was at its root a sexual attraction. In other words even though the physical form had no sexual interest, the psyche expressed that interest. This means that the subtle body retained this interest during the childhood phase of the new physical form.

It did not do that in reference to every female. This was a particularly strong attraction in the subtle body towards this particular person. This attraction energy offers a loan of pleasure enjoyment upon the sight of this person. This is enough to motivate the person being induced to make an effort to complete a sexual liaison.

This system of pleasure motivation is universal. Everyone is afflicted with it. A yogi may study how it operates in his psyche. He may in time gain the insight to reduce it but he cannot eliminate it completely. There are millions and millions of lives which one endured in the past. One carried energies from those experiences in the subconscious. It is likely that anywhere one may go in the physical or astral domains, one will become exposed to someone somewhere with whom one had a sexual relationship. That would cause a related memory to surface either as a coherent recall or as a subconscious instinct.

January 23, 2006

Atmananda

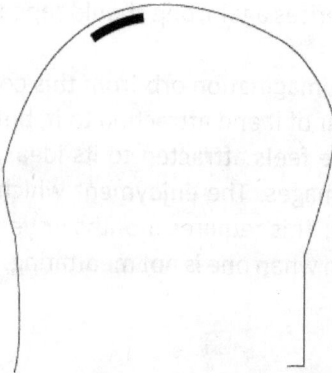

He visited and said that I had not practiced the streak energy back top procedure sufficiently. Then he noted that it was alright since I did some helpful procedures taught by Lahiri. Atmananda gave a ceiling upstick process.

Atmananda / Yogeshwarananda

Within the mind space pratyahar

This is for pulling the imagination orb away from its visualization activity. This is part of the process for completing Patanjali's second sutra. As soon as a visualization begins or as soon as the yogi realizes that one is in progress, he should restrict it. This should happen even if the visualization is invisible. In some experiences the yogi knows that a visualization is being developed even though it is not displayed. Even then the yogi should squelch the imagination orb so that it ceases the invisible activity.

The location of the visualization and that of the imagination orb should be known to the yogi. The orb is for the most part invisible. The visualization becomes visible when its construction causes it to be illustrated as mental pictures and sounds which invoke the curiosity of the coreSelf. Usually the invisible orb is located before the visualization as in this diagram.

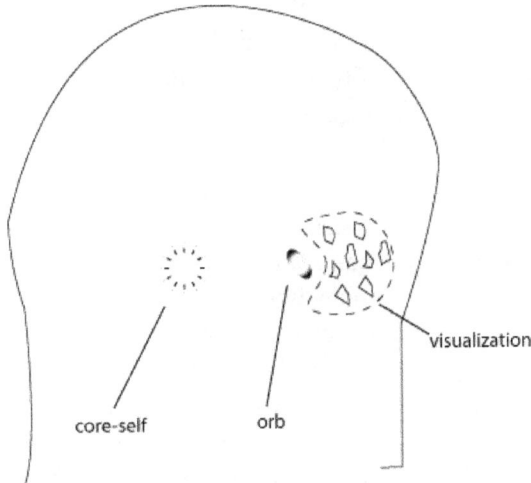

January 24, 2006

Struggle of subtle bodies

The subtle bodies commit themselves to struggle on the astral planes. Violence is played out on the physical level as we observe. However there is another ghastly scene which is in the astral world. This happens with disembodied as well as embodied entities, where one disembodied person may conflict with another or where the subtle body of an embodied person may clash with the subtle form of a disembodied one.

A yogi should become aware of the existential clashes over rights which are due to someone because of the social work they perform. Each of the selves is territorial and wants to carve out a niche for itself where it can improve its conditions and be free from having to endeavor for status.

Two persons who are friendly on the physical side, may be enemies on the subtle planes. This happens because each self is essentially selfish. The self is in this social milieu for its benefit, even at the expense of others. Thus what it cannot play out physically, because of social norms, it will pay out on the subtle planes of consciousness in ghastly psychic warfare.

Atmananda

He instructed that the visualization faculty should be repeatedly taken to the frontal area while the coreSelf should move up to the brahmrandra crown chakra. His emphasis was on persistence. He quoted a verse from Bhagavad Gita.

श्रीभगवानुवाच
असंशयं महाबाहो
मनो दुर्निग्रहं चलम्।
अभ्यासेन तु कौन्तेय
वैराग्येण च गृह्यते ॥६.३५॥

śrībhagavānuvāca
asaṁśayaṁ mahābāho
mano durnigrahaṁ calam
abhyāsena tu kaunteya
vairāgyeṇa ca gṛhyate (6.35)

śrībhagavān — the Blessed Lord; *uvāca* — said; *asaṁśayam* — undoubtedly; *mahābāho* — O powerful man; *mano* = *manah* — the mind; *durnigraham* — difficult to control; *calam* — unsteady; *abhyāsena* — by practice; *tu* — however; *kaunteya* — O son of Kuntī; *vairāgyena* — by the indifference to response; *ca* — and; *gṛhyate* — it is restrained

The Blessed Lord said: Undoubtedly, O powerful man, the mind is difficult to control. It is unsteady. By practice, however, O son of Kuntī, by indifference to its responses, also, it is restrained. (Bhagavad Gita 6.35)

Kundalini yoga value

Kundalini yoga is the method for transforming the unruly parts of the psyche, especially the adjuncts. It causes the psyche to become elevated into higher levels of awareness and removes doubts about the possibility of self elevation. Being anchored in material existence, a self may harbor hesitation about being transferred into the subtle or spiritual environment. This hesitation is removed by gaining transcendental experiences which verify for the particular self that other levels of existence exist and are within reach if sufficient effort is made for relocation.

Kundalini yoga causes

- reform of the physical body
- reform of the subtle motive energy
- reform of the emotional energy
- curtailment of the addiction of the willpower to emotions
- reform of the psychic orbs

As the subtle body discards more and more heavy astral energy, one experiences a higher type of happiness. Eventually one enjoys a bliss force from the highest subtle planes. These events spur the yogi for a tighter more precise practice.

January 25, 2006

Who is she?

I saw a celestial woman and then uttered the question: Who is she? A reply came in the form of an inspiration. She was the goddess of sleep, whose influence is so bewitching that she deters practice. However if she is pleased with an ascetic her presence facilitates practice.

She is a goddess. She is a necessary type of subtle action for resting and recuperating the physical and subtle bodies. It is her stupor influence which is dangerous.

January 27, 2006

Ashoka Vachaspati

He showed internal subtle energy as movement of the imagination orb locking and unlocking on sensual impressions. Usually the willpower is conveyed in this locking and unlocking with no ability to control this. The energy of the willpower is used by this but the willpower is not allowed to control this. Its effort to bring this to order is ineffective.

The attention energy which is the focal point of the sense of identity should situate itself in naad sound resonance. When it is saturated in naad and is confident that it will remain in the influence of naad, it should move forward to kutastha which is the space between the eyebrows.

Some hazy light may be seen there. Or a brilliance may be seen there. This will have a bliss feeling. The locking and unlocking of the imagination orb is indicated by the knitting and relaxing of the eyebrows. When the eyebrows are relaxed that is boredom or relaxation. When they are tense it is a focus on a sensual impression in the mind or in the physical environment.

Acharya Mun

He said, "Naad is the basis of consciousness, its background support.

The psyche steps away from it to pursue illusion. Return the consciousness to naad. This will eventually cause samadhi transcendence. One has to train the frontal adjuncts to abandon images and go to brahmrandra.

February 11, 2006

Acharya Mun

He explained that a yogi must train the frontal mechanisms in the head to abandon images and ideas and go to the upper brahmrandra region where such imaging does not occur.

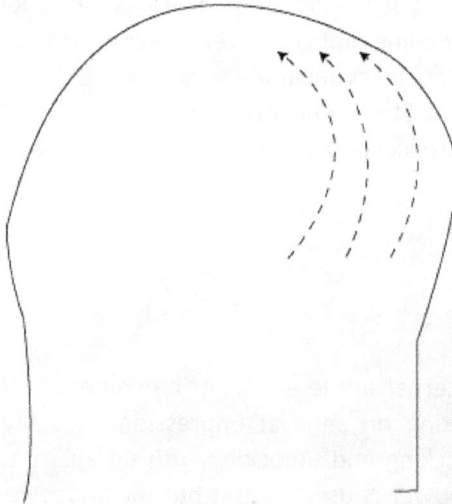

February 17, 2006

Acharya Mun

He said that bhastrika proved to be useful in purification of the intellect mechanism, so that it makes higher selections for focus and becomes resistant to lower motivations.

When kundalini rises through the subtle spine into the brain, it may cause the intellect to spin at a higher rate. The result is higher perception and keen psychic insight, which weans the psyche away from lower astral vibrations and memories having to do with physical existence.

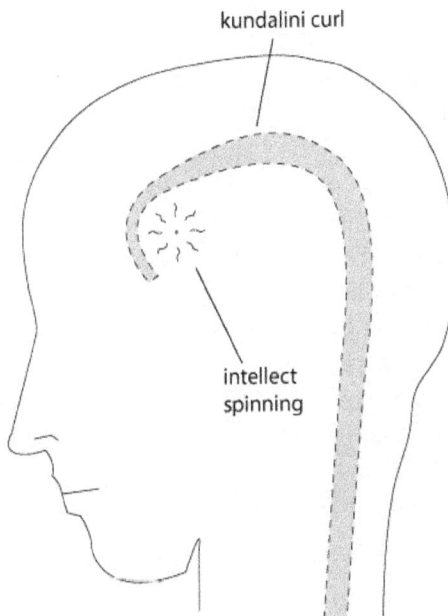

kundalini curl

intellect spinning

February 18, 2006

Supernatural vision development

When the mento-emotional energy cease the regular productions and fluctuations, there is hope for development of the supernatural or spiritual vision. Much meditation must be done to achieve this but it does hinge on stopping the mental constructions which arise in the mind as prompted by memories and sensual perceptions of lower realities.

On occasion without obvious reasons a yogi, or even someone who is not a yogi, may experience supernatural or spiritual vision. That will last for split seconds in most cases. Rarely does that last longer except for advanced yogis.

The problem is that even with practice, the experience of having supernatural or spiritual vision is hard to achieve. Why? Because it does not develop instantly as soon as the yogi can get the mental gyrations to cease. It may take days, weeks, months or even years of meditation for the achievement of having that vision and retaining it.

February 19, 2006

Acharya Mun / Yogeshwarananda

In a meditation after breath infusion I crushed down the imagination orb. It felt like jelly energy. After this it responded to verbal commands in the mind. Its attitude of waywardness disappeared for the time being.

Two yoga teachers mentioned above stated that the orb should always be obedient to the coreSelf, otherwise success will elude the yogi. Their view is that the core should have the power to confront the imagination faculty and should not have to take refuge in the back of the head to escape being dominated by the imagination.

The convention is that by its proximity to the intellect, the core becomes influenced and is circumstantially force to contribute even to the hostile mento-emotional operations. However if the yogi endeavors sufficiently, he will make progress to change the convention, so that in proximity he gains control.

February 20, 2006

Kanda in brahmrandra

A new kanda subtle bulb appeared in the brahmrandra crown chakra. This was the sexual kanda which has the groin area as it default location. This kanda transferred itself into the crown chakra. The imagination orb is attached to the sexual kanda in the groin area. When that kanda moves up to the crown chakra, the imagination orb maintains its attachment just the same.

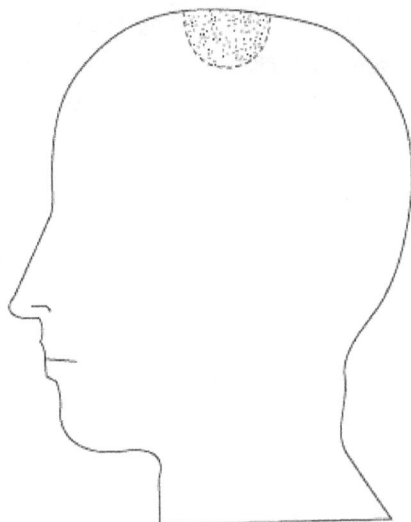

Imagination orb behavior

The imagination orb takes memory impression layers and beads from the right side. It relinquishes these to the left of itself. Some dropped impressions fall into other rising impressions and merge into those memories to create complex ideation.

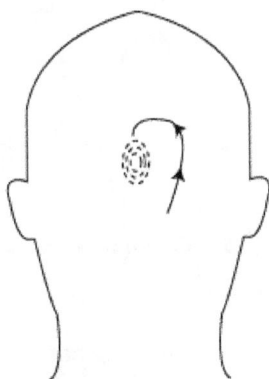

imagination orb
picks up memories

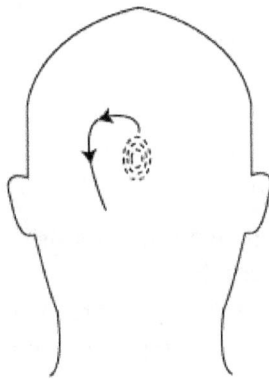

imagination orb
relinquishes reconfigured memories

Thought broadcast

I observed that thoughts from others make contact on the left side of the subtle head. It contacts a membrane of the aura of the intellect. This is a sensitive zone.

When a thought makes contact, it is immediately converted into a picture sound. If this is not squelched, it affects the imagination orb which goes on an expansion rampage. Patanjali (ashtanga) yoga is designed to stop this thought invasion.

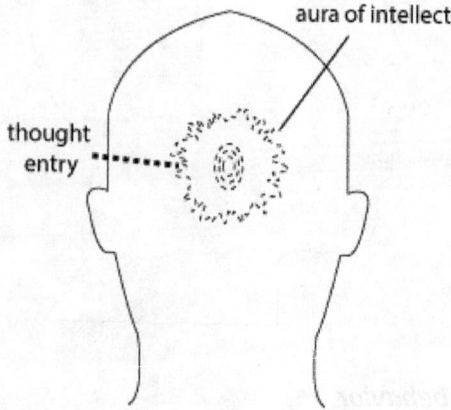

February 21, 2006

Acharya Mun

He said, "Patanjali's system is the key. One should elevate then discipline the intellect if it is still resistant to the aims of transcendence focus. Much practice is necessary."

February 22, 2006

Acharya Mun

He listed two methods using charged subtle energy for curbing the imagination orb:
- top reservoir at crown chakra
- using infused breath energy to twirl the imagination orb

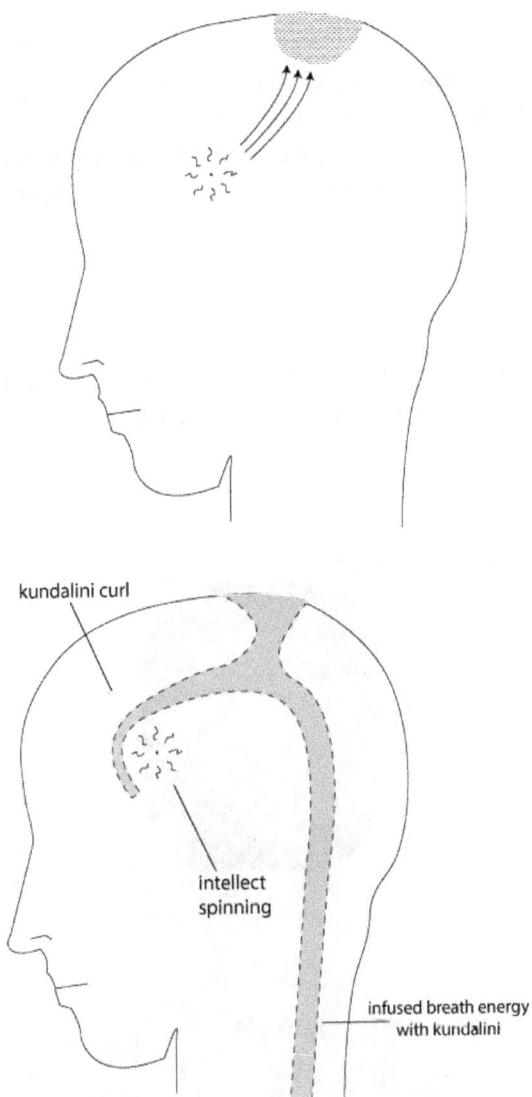

kundalini curl

intellect
spinning

infused breath energy
with kundalini

By the grace of Acharya Mun, I discovered that the imagination orb no longer gyrates at such a high speed. In some meditation, it stops completely for a time, for short periods. This allows one to observe its focusing and defocusing behavior which is like a heartbeat which keeps the throbbing action on and on through the life of a body.

The conventional behavior of rapid displays based on sensual intake and memory is sponsored by low level energy and contact with low level reality. That promotes stupor, drowsiness and sleep.

Checking the behavior of the mind during the waking hours when not meditating, is important. The yogi must gage the progress in that way, to see if the meditation efforts affect conventional consciousness. One should gage the progress to be sure that there is improvement in non-meditative states, even if such progress is incremental.

February 24, 2006

There was a bright light, whitish. It lasted for four (4) seconds only. It was steady. It did not drift. It was ahead in the space between the eyebrows, in the brow chakra.

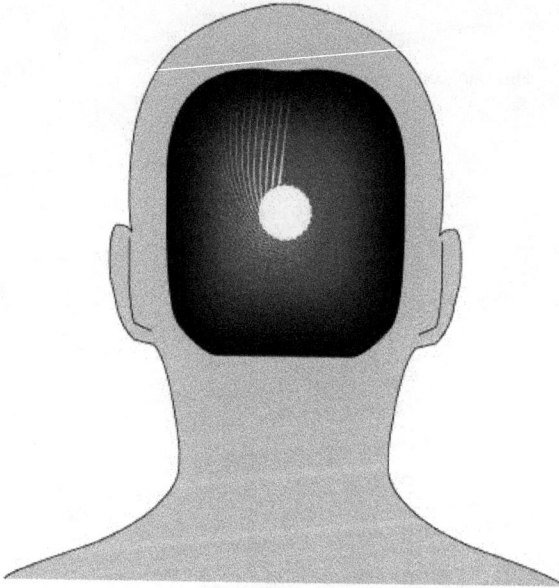

Sleep sensations travel from the brain to the skin of the body. The arrival of the sleep inclination at the skin, influences one to recline the body. During meditation the stupor energy should either be suppressed and it should be absent for the time being. To achieve this the sure way is to do breath infusion before sitting to meditate. The infusion surcharges the energy in the subtle body. It vacates the sluggish stupor energy for the time being.

The presence of Acharya Mun for four days prior caused the intellect to behave nicely. With the departure of this yogin, the intellect feels as it is desires to resume some lower behaviors. However I will challenge it and prohibit its assumption of mental habits which destroy practice.

February 25, 2006

Suppression of thoughts for the purpose of freeing the coreSelf from being preoccupied with thought constructions which are drummed up by the intellect imagination mechanism, is necessary in the initial sage of trying to control the thought production mechanism. After some success one may directly squeeze the thought producing function of the mind and cause it to abandon development of a thought sequence. Ramakrishna used to explain pinching the mind to command it to cease its random activity and its memory abduction for the purpose of bewildering the coreSelf.

Jñānadīpena a key term from Bhagavad Gita.

तेषामेवानुकम्पार्थम्
अहमज्ञानजं तमः ।
नाशयाम्यात्मभावस्थो
ज्ञानदीपेन भास्वता ॥१०.११॥

teṣāmevānukampārtham
ahamajñānajaṁ tamaḥ
nāśayāmyātmabhāvastho
jñānadīpena bhāsvatā (10.11)

teṣām — of them; evānukampārtham = eva — indeed + anukampā — assistance + artham — interest; aham — I; ajñānajam — ignorance produced; tamaḥ — stupifying influence of material nature; nāśayāmy = nāśayāmi — I caused to be banished; ātmabhāvastho = ātmabhāvasthaḥ — situated in the self; jñānadīpena = jñāna — knowledge, realized + dīpena — with light, with insight (jñānadīpena — with realized insight); bhāsvatā — clear, shining, clarity of consciousness

In the interest of assisting them, I who am situated within their beings, cause the ignorance produced by the stupefying influence of material nature, to be banished by their clear realized insight. (Bhagavad Gita 10.11)

Jñānadīpena occurs when the imagination orb is not used on this side of existence but that is not observed because of the rapidity of haphazard spontaneous vision.

One has to think of it while taking help from Patanjali. The mind cannot be squeezed when it is saturated with lower sensual energy. Then it is empowered to resist the coreSelf. Eventually after sufficient practice, attempting to control the thought producing mechanism, the core can suppress mental activity directly. Use of mantras, aphorisms or positive assertions may be expressed mentally but if they are in a foreign language they may not have the intended effect because the mind is language conditioned. It is not just the sound of the word but the meaning which the mind has for it as it was conditioned for word meaning relationship

External thoughts coming from others, hit the membrane of the mind and then create interpretation ripples which surge through the mind. These are illustrated by the imagination orb (intellect) and are then seen in the mind as ideas, sounds and images. The mind responds more readily to commands in a native language rather than in a foreign one such as Sanskrit. Whatever the native sound is for a particular action; that may cause the mind to be more responsive. If someone speaks Sanskrit as the native expression, a sound in the mind in that language may cause more immediate and effective response. When a sound impacts the mind, it causes a wrinkle in the membrane of the mind.

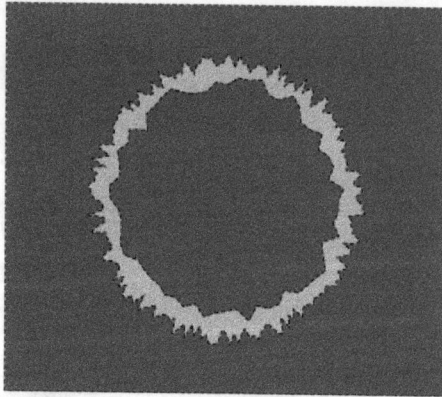

It is a task for the yogi to stop the sensitivity of the reception outer layer of the mind, as well as the sensitivity of the intellect to memory releases within the mind. By the application of a mental or psychic muscle, one may stop it but for some the muscle has to be developed. Keen observation is necessary. First one must recognize the sensitivity. Then one can make the effort to control it. Initially there may be little or no control but if the yogi persist, gradually over time he will develop the ability.

When the inner part of the intellect is suppressed properly, it seems that the membrane response layer develops a resistance where it seems to stiffen when there is provocation. It loses the enthusiasm to react to incoming media from those whose ideas are destructive to yoga. This allows the self to experience some peace within the mind chamber which encourages the yogi to practice more astutely.

February 27, 2006

Yogeshwarananda

He explained that the contact point of the attention energy is charmed by the imagination orb. This causes one to subscribe to the illustrations imagined. It is definite that the imagination orb must be controlled, or there cannot be deep meditation. The yogi should cease denying that the attention is addicted to the imagination faculty. Admittance of this will in time cause deeper insight and development of resistance to the orb.

The attention energy is raw supernatural power. It converts into being willpower. It surrounds the coreSelf spherically as the sense of identity. Stated differently around the coreSelf is a supernatural energy which is the self's sense of identity. This is experienced by the core as its attention or focusing power. Depending on how it is used it is called focus, attention or willpower.

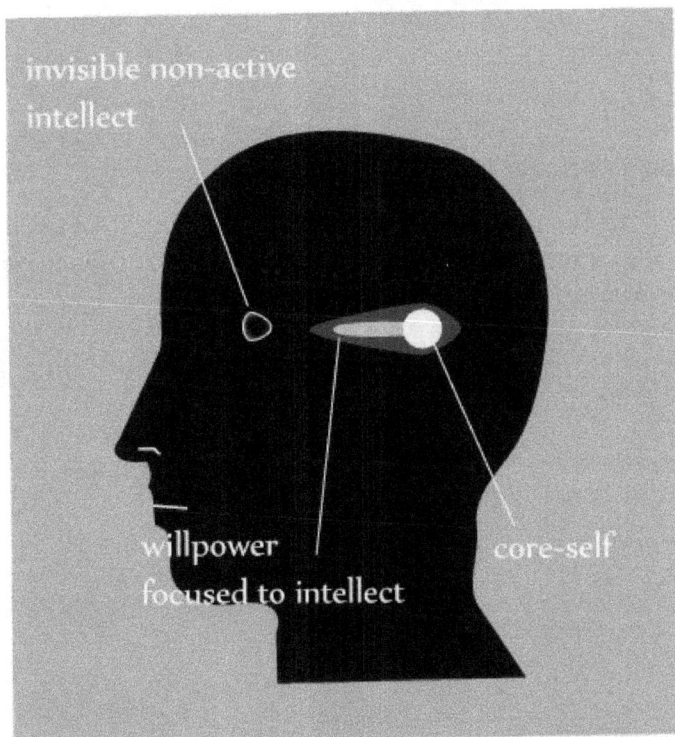

invisible non-active intellect

willpower focused to intellect

core-self

This attention energy has attachment to the imagination faculty which is also called the intellect. Because the attention energy is prejudiced to the intellect, that attention abandons the interest of the coreSelf. The core for its part is attached to the attention energy. Hence it has this tendency to endorse whatever is proposed by the attention except that the attention is influenced by the intellect.

The intellect for its part is attached to the sensual energies which have an outlay as feelings. These may be pleasant or unpleasant but the intellect is assaulted by these. The traumatic adjustments which occur in the intellect come about by the influence of the sensual energies. Thus the attention is affected and the core is affected in turn.

Naad contacts the imagination orb

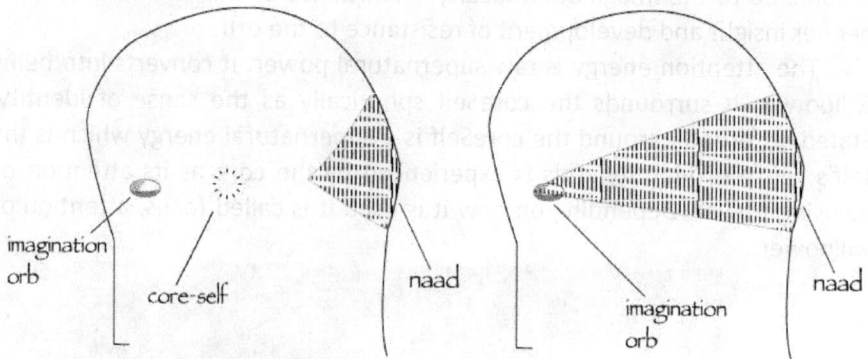

Yogananda / Acharya Mun

Yogananda appeared in a miniature form in my subtle head. He said he did the naad spread into the frontal part of the head and that it was necessary to thwart worldly association.

When he left, Acharya Mun appeared and asked about Yogananda. I explained that Yogananda was a famous yoga teacher and writer from a kriya lineage. Acharya Mun said that he heard of him in Thailand.

Part 2

On this date, I realized that no matter what, no matter the potential for supernatural and spiritual perception, the observational power of the self is limited by its reliance on the imagination orb. The self's reliance on the orb is inversely proportional to its divine vision. Stated otherwise, the more it is reliant on the imagination orb, the less will be its divine perception.

Acharya Mun

He explained that the supernatural perception occurs when the intellect ceases conventional operations as explained by Patanjali in the second verse of the Yoga Sutras. It may not render supernatural vision immediately. A yogi may have to practice for many weeks, months or years to remain in mental silence with no operation of the imagination. Then in time the supernatural perception will manifest.

Sometimes however during meditation, for a split second or for some short duration, the supernatural vision may be available. This gives encouragement to the student yogi.

The disciplinary or controlling effort of yoga practice, culminates in stopping the imagination orb from any conventional expression, whereby it does not produce mental images, sounds or ideas based on memory and sensual data of the physical or lower astral realities.

Initially a student may not understand the purpose of yoga, just as an explorer may not know what he will discover and how that discovery may be useful.

I discovered that the sense of identity when pacified does not point into the imagination orb. Instead it remains neutral and unexcited to anything which the imagination conceives or it may appear as a two armed grasper

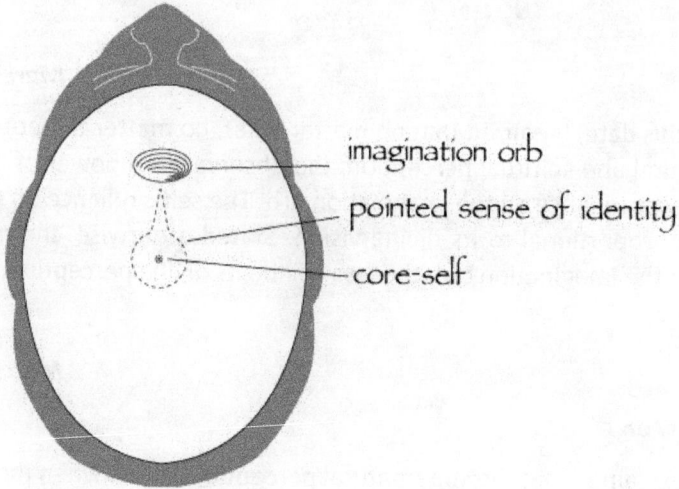

imagination orb
pointed sense of identity
core-self

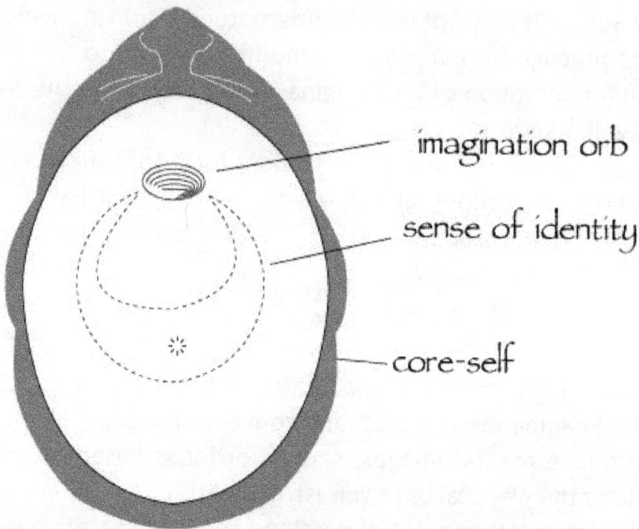

imagination orb
sense of identity
core-self

March 7, 2006

Acharya Mun

He explained that the attention energy should be trained to desist from identifying or wrapping around the imagination orb. It should lose interest in whatever the imagination illustrates. Even attempts to illustrate by the orb should be not invoke a curiosity in the attention. Instead of grasping the imagination, the interest should express an interest gathering focus away from the orb.

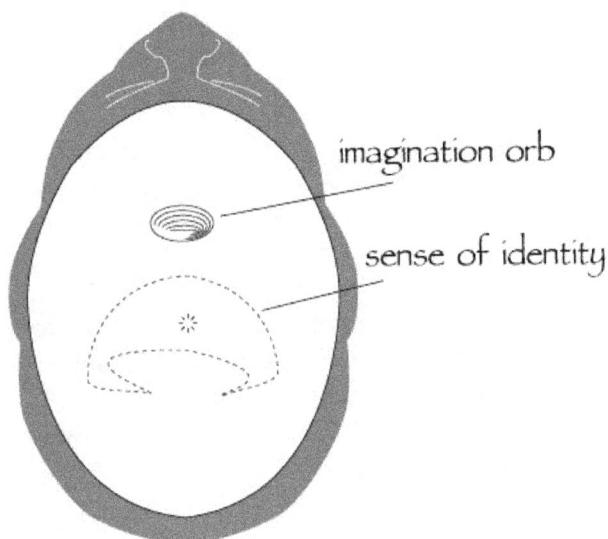

imagination orb

sense of identity

March 8, 2006

I realized that the sense of identity is resistant to naad. It is not enough to desire to reorder the psyche. The yogi must gage the relationship between the coreSelf and the adjuncts. He should take a close look at how the adjuncts interact, particularly how they do so involuntarily. This causes a readjustment in the way one views the psyche.

The sense of identity is reliant on and favors the intellect. It spontaneously goes to the intellect by projecting a ray of its energy which makes contact. The core interprets this as a curiosity about the display produced by the intellect.

Acharya Mun

He mentioned that stomach flexes are useful even in advanced states, even for those who do brahma yoga. In the subtle body, the stomach flexes causes encrusted heavy astral energy to crumble which makes it easy for the system to eliminate this. The removal of such energy causes sluggishness and stupor to vanish. Brahma yoga is more than what happens in the head of the subtle body. It concerns the entire form for removal of retardative influences.

A yogi should target the sense of identity for purification and upgrade. Ideally the sense of identity should be a neutral power but somehow it has a bias towards the intellect. The yogi has the task to restore its neutrality

March 10, 2006

Lahiri

He said that focusing on seeing light, or developing clairvoyance or telepathic clarity is not the objective. One should find a process to remove the darkness which surrounds the intellect.

Acharya Mun

His presence caused the sense of identity to slip away from the coreSelf and stand apart. The default configuration of the sense of identity is spherically as it surrounds the coreSelf. Rarely does it part away from the core but the core may experience a segregation from the sense of identity even when that sense surrounds the core.

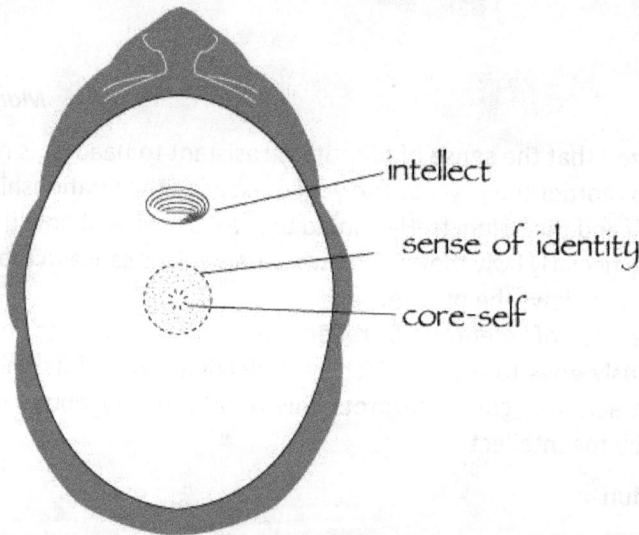

intellect

sense of identity

core-self

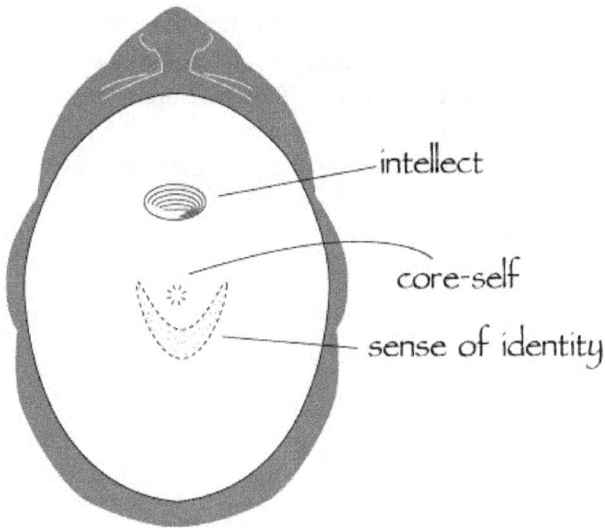

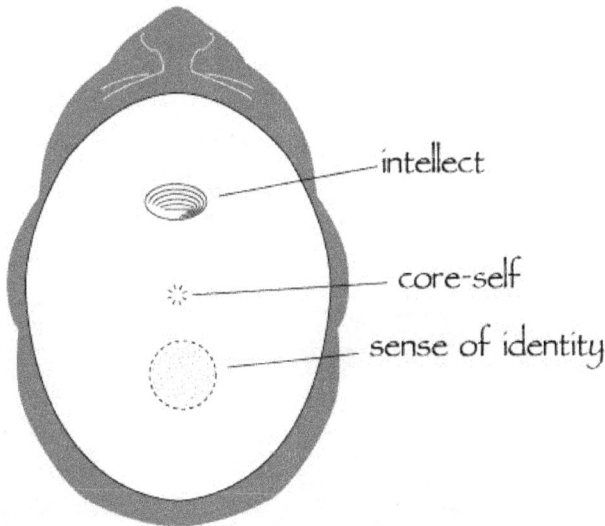

March 11, 2006

Yogi Bhajan

This yogi gets credit for introducing breath infusion with postures. This is bhastrika pranayama with asana postures. The elementary stage of bhastrika is termed as kapalabhati. I established the term breath infusion for pranayama. Bhastrika is a rapid breathing procedure in which certain muscular and focusing actions are applied. It causes the surcharge of kundalini at the base chakra muladhar. This arouses kundalini causing it to move through the spine into the head. This practice should be maintained as an assistant and preparatory action for meditation, which should follow immediately after the subtle body is sufficiently surcharged with fresh breath energy. During the infusion of fresh energy, the used energy which is in the blood stream should be extracted during each exhale.

Breath infusion can be used to segregate the coreSelf from the intellect and also from the sense of identity. The arousal of kundalini into the subtle head may cause the coreSelf to move into higher dimensions where it will have experience of bliss energy and supernatural perception.

aroused kundalini targets segregated sense of identity

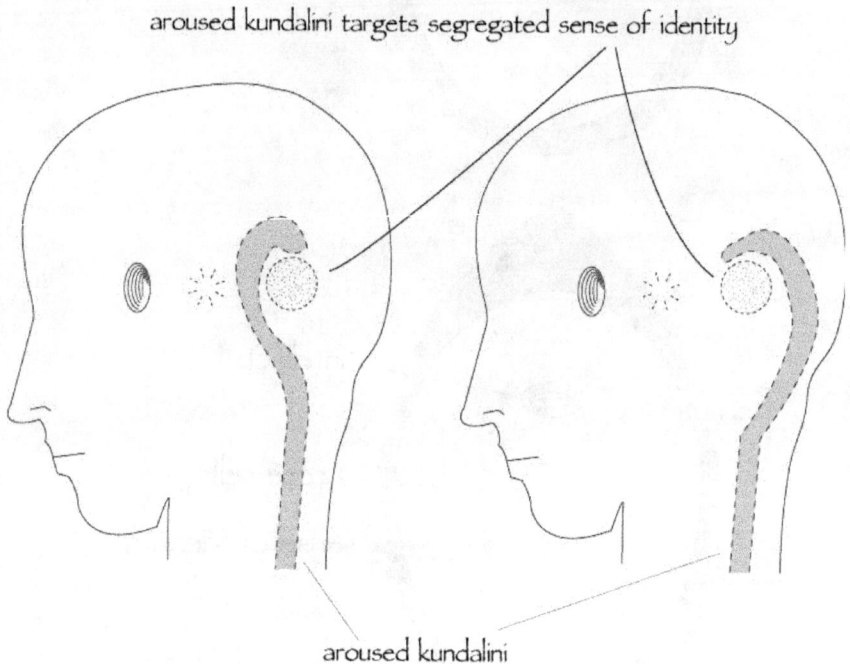

aroused kundalini

The sense of identity must be reformed so that its tendency to align itself with the intellect is changed and it develops instead an attachment to the naad sound resonance and to its innate state of neutrality. Instead of spontaneously reaching to appropriate whatever thoughts, memories, thought responses and imagined ideas are drummed up by the intellect, the identity should cling to naad sound resonance and should instinctively ignore whatever is presented in the mind space by the intellect. This will cause the intellect to assume a silent invisible mode.

The sense of identity should not desire to get supernatural visions or lights through the use of the intellect. Instead it should cling to naad and wait patiently for the supernatural perception to manifest. There are two incidences of supernatural perception:

- pierced from the inside of the psyche
- pierced from the outside of the psyche

That which is from the inside of the psyche, arises because of the increased purity of energy which was generated in the psyche through breath infusion and divine influence.

That which is from outside of the psyche comes from the supernatural and spiritual levels of existence which are beyond the physical and astral planes. This energy may find thin layers of astral force which it can penetrate through and be seen by the coreSelf which is in a cloud of lower astral energy.

In the quest for access to the spiritual sky, the sense of identity is the control lever. This sense has a tendency for witnessing whatever is presented by the intellect. That feature has to change to where the sense of identity become obsessed about naad sound resonance and divine light.

Acharya Mun

He explained that the naad sound resonance cannot be handled by the intellect. Naad remains as it is, as a transcendence level of consciousness. If the sense of identity remains focused on and in naad, the identity will develop a resistance to the intellect, which will free the identity from obsession with the trivial ideas which the intellect generates.

The sense of identity when it is not under the influence of the intellect is discovered to be a neutral energy. The coreSelf is also found to be neutral. Their absorption with the intellect causes obsession with prejudices based on the conclusions of the intellect which they are induced to adopt. Adherence to naad gives the sense of identity and the core the power to abandon those prejudiced notions. It frees the self from being dominated by the intellect which in turn is obsessed with the sensual intake and memories.

March 12, 2006

Acharya Mun

He explained that the intellect comparing faculty uses information from the memory and recent sensual intake plus information from other intellects. This results in a complex mix of ideas from which conclusions are drawn. Patanjali advised that one should deactivate this intellect in both of its accurate and inaccurate calculations.

The sense of identity is neutral but it is tainted because it is impulsively influenced by the intellect which is not a neutral factor. This means that it is important for the sense of identity to be segregated from the intellect. The coreSelf for its part is attached to the sense of identity. Unless it is relocated into the sky of consciousness, the core cannot rid itself of the sense of identity. Hence it is urgent that the sense of identity be free from dominance from the intellect. The identity can be freed if it relies on naad sound resonance.

March 14, 2006

Acharya Mun

He instructed that the intellect must be trained for hours to not absorb impressions. This is similar to the shunya principle in Buddhism. If the intellect remain for long periods in a state of neutrality it could develop supernatural perception. Otherwise it will remain in its lower operation with impressions from the physical and lower astral dimensions.

The intellect creates mental impressions and indulges the self in fantasies which the self is enthralled by. A yogi should know the process of imagination in detail so that he can intercept the activities of the intellect and know how it produces images, ideas and video in the mind chamber.

Impressions are stored in the chest of the subtle body. These move into the head where they assault the intellect which lacks resistance to the bombardment. Memories act like missiles. They target the intellect. When a memory arrives at the edge of the intellect, it penetrates. The intellect becomes affected and according to the energy generated, the intellect is forced to illustrate whatever the memory is capable of displaying. For its part the sense of identity is enthralled by the intellect. This causes the coreSelf to be drawn into whatever the intellect constructs as a mental or emotional focus.

The intellect is affected by telepathic communication which comes from the minds of other persons. It does not matter as to whether one is aware that a thought was native to one's mind or constructed and then transmitted from the mind of someone else. The intellect is affected by its own imaginations and also by the imaginations which broadcast from the minds of others.

The coreSelf must be hostile to self-generated ideas as well as to those which come from others. If the yogi develops resistance to the mind's creations, he will automatically have immunity.

March 15, 2006

I realized that some vices come from supernatural beings who are more powerful than the average yogi. One is influenced by such persons to act in ways which contravene yoga.

There are many contrary influences. Some of these can be banished by a yogi. Some he must endure. Apart from inner influences which the yogi is not powerful enough to terminate, there are influences from other persons who are on par with, lower than or greater than a yogi. Some of these influences cannot be thwarted. What the yogi should have, however, is insight so that he can recognize the influences and their sources. Regardless of whether the yogi can resist an influence or not, he should recognize it and its source.

This is insight perception. It does not mean that in every case, a yogi can thwart a destructive influence but it means that he can recognize the influence and its course.

March 16, 2006

The fifth (5th) stage of yoga is listed as pratyahar by Patanjali. This is the reversal (prati) of consumption (ahara). To achieve this the yogi must revert the sensual outreach back through the senses into the mind. If he is extrovert, he must work to be introverted.

Initially this means to retract the sensual energies into the psyche by pulling in the outward going energy which the psyche emits for sensing and appropriating sense objects. There is an energy which pursues odors, flavors, colors, surfaces and sounds. This is a singular energy but it differentiates according to the particular sense object it pursues.

When one begins sensual energy withdrawal practice, it does not matter which energy one retracts. One should make an effort to retract any energy which courses out of the psyche. However as one advanced it becomes important to sort each sensual outreach, trace its origin in the psyche and return it to its source.

March 18, 2006

During an astral projection, I entered a *living in the past* world. This is on a subterranean astral world which runs parallel to this physical existence but which is subtler. Some persons there had resentment energies towards me. This caused a hostile predisposition. One person there whom I knew, who was a student yogi on the physical side, wanted to hurl a concrete wall at me. I had the mental force to stop him but he threatened to retaliate.

In that astral world gross actions are not executed because subtle actions are perceived concretely.

A woman there had a desire for sexual intercourse. She got her desire fulfilled even without physical contact. She became reclined about two feet from me. She closed her eyes and concentrated to achieve the sexual interaction.

One boy moved his subtle body into the air. He wanted to fly overhead with me at about sixty (60) feet above the ground. Some others who saw what he did, did not have the ability to fly. Some jumped a long distance but could not fly. I asked the boy who flew with me about how he learnt to fly. He did not reply.

Soon after we were at the place where the student wanted to hurl a concrete wall at me but then the flying boy disappeared.

Atmananda

He listed what he considered to be the three most important statements in the Yoga Sutras of Patanjali:

योगश्चित्तवृत्तिनिरोधः ॥२॥

yogaḥcittavṛtti nirodhaḥ

yogaḥ – the skill of yoga; cittavṛtti = citta – mento-emotional energy + vṛtti – vibrational mode; nirodhaḥ – cessation, restraint, non-operation.

The skill of yoga is demonstrated by the conscious non-operation of the vibrational modes of the mento-emotional energy. (Yoga Sutras 1.2)

तदभावात्संयोगाभावो हानं तद्दृशेः कैवल्यम् ॥२५॥

tad abhāvāt saṁyogā abhāvaḥ
hānaṁ taddṛśeḥ kaivalyam

tad = tat – that spiritual ignorance; abhāvāt – resulting from the elimination; saṁyogā – conjunction; abhāvaḥ – disappearance, elimination; hānaṁ – withdrawal, escape; tad = tat – that; dṛśeḥ – of the perceiver; kaivalyam – total separation from the mundane psychology.

The elimination of the conjunction which results from the elimination of that spiritual ignorance is the withdrawal that is the total separation of the perceiver from the mundane psychology. (Yoga Sutras 2.25)

सत्त्वपुरुषयोः शुद्धिसाम्ये कैवल्यमिति ॥ ५६ ॥

sattva puruṣayoḥ śuddhi sāmye kaivalyam iti

sattva – intelligence energy of material nature; puruṣayoḥ – of the spirit; śuddhi – purity; sāmye – on being equal; kaivalyam – total separation from the mundane psychology; iti – thus.

When there is equal purity between the intelligence energy of material nature and the spirit, then there is total separation from the mundane psychology. (Yoga Sutras 3.56)

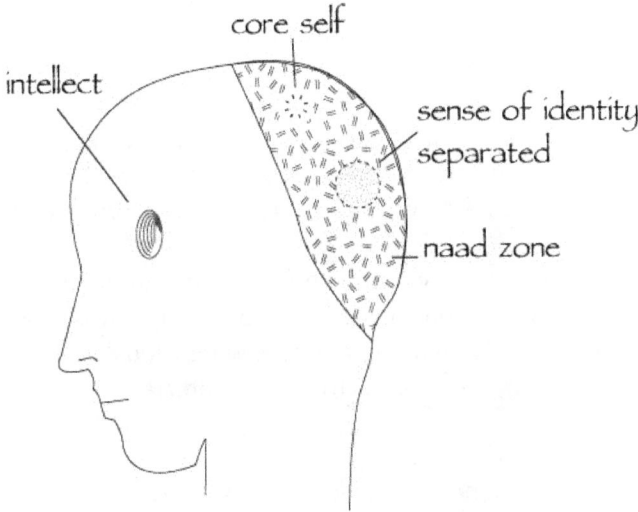

core self

intellect

sense of identity
separated

naad zone

March 20, 2006

Acharya Mun

If someone's focal existence is outside or extrovert in reference to the coreSelf, one has to go outside to relate fully to that person. This is because that person cannot be contacted on the inner levels because of a lack of focus there. Any association with such a person would require that the yogi be extrovert. Hence the need to keep such association to a minimum.

March 22, 2006

Acharya Mun

Under his influence, I located an astral realm where Sanskrit sounds move energy. At a certain point in the earth's history, Sanskrit sounds caused physical actions to occur but the earth is no longer in the vibrational range for this. Hence Sanskrit is not incapable of causing physical actions directly. Just as an electronic signal from a small device may open a car door or cause an engine to start, so formerly Sanskrit sound completed action but it is unable to do this now.

March 23, 2006

Acharya Mun observed that the wife of a student did not have an open sushumna passage. In most humans the sushumna central spinal passage is blocked. This causes lack of insight.

I taught a student the method of introducing the breath infusion practice to his wife. He did as told but his wife had little interest. Her diet was one of oily and spicy foods. Because her sushumna central passage was blocked the energy generated in her form from food remained in the pubic area to sponsor reproduction. As it was she could not raise kundalini through the spine.

Anyone in a similar condition can raise kundalini if sufficient effort is made doing breath infusion under the proper supervision. However the student has to be determined and must show individual interest. Merely to be pushed to do this by a spouse or friend is insufficient.

Acharya Mun

He said that the mind is attached to its stimulations. Objects are seen only as their stimuli in the mind. Patanjali instructed that yogis should cease the stimuli which is generated in the mind. He used the term vritti for such mental activity. Pravritti means accelerated stimuli which compels the interest of the coreSelf to be engaged in a video in the mind. This may or may not be accompanied with corresponding physical acts.

The mind lives in this stimuli and relies on that as an interest. Somehow a yogi must change this habit of the mind. He should replace the mind's natural preoccupation with naad sound resonance absorption.

March 24, 2006

Yogeshwarananda

He stated that kundalini is different to the intellect, which is in the front of the subtle head. Kundalini is resident at the muladhar base chakra. When it is aroused, it moves up the spine into the brain. It may be experienced moving up the front of side of the trunk of the body. One may pull kundalini or push it or attract it into the head of the subtle body. This may be done by doing pranayama breath infusion or by mood adjustment. It may also be achieve by using hallucinogenic substances.

For the purpose of inSelf Yoga the recommendation is breath infusion which is immediately followed by meditation, where one observes the effects of the surcharge energy generated during infusion.

March 25, 2006

Success in meditation hinges on the force of concentration of the yogi. The willpower is relatively weak compared to the natural forces in the psyche. The intellect repeatedly comes under sensual influence and memory. It cannot be relied on to help the coreSelf to achieve vacation of the mind. The core must hold itself in reserve and silently pursue whatever focus it should practice for advanced meditation.

Yogeshwarananda

He said, "If it cannot be done now, it certainly cannot be done then."

He spoke of pulling kundalini from base chakra to brahmrandra crown chakra. If the yogi cannot achieve that during the life of the body, he will not do it at the time of death of the body. Death gives one no advantage one did not earn before death.

March 29, 2006

Consequences supervisor

There are supervisors of consequence. These are supernatural people. We know that physically we have law courts where consequences of actions of both law-abiding and criminal people are enforced. On the supernatural level, there are similar controllers.

A yogi may communicate with one of these controllers and be informed about the enforcement of consequences which affect the yogi or affect those who are socially close to the yogi.

Acharya Mun

He said that one must accept whatever is there as divine light and sound. A yogi should not waste energy being despondent because he is not successful in achieving full divine vision. Whatever little he has he should focus on and cultivate.

Atmananda

He showed an escape route to Satyaloka which is the supernatural place where Brahma, the local creator god resides. This place is sometimes called brahmaloka. This practice can be used only by persons who mastered kundalini and have fully developed brahmrandra crown chakra.

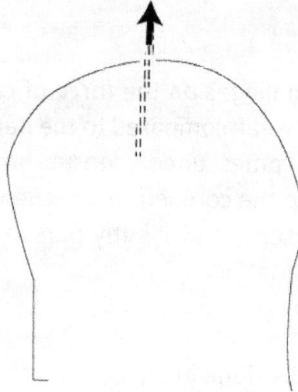

Naad brahma as real mantra

Naad sound resonance is there. It is not created by a limited being. It is not said by a mouth. It cannot be pronounced in an incorrect way. It is not part of an alphabet. It is not to be uttered like a mantra aphorism or prayer.

However the ordinary mind has no interest in naad. When a non-yogi hears naad, he may consider it to be a nuisance. Sometimes even a yogi gets this feeling that naad is undesirable. That happens when the yogi becomes more and more extrovert, when he loses grip on introspective practice.

The memory is hostile to the yogi's absorption in naad. Hence when a yogi is focused on or in naad, the memory projects imprints to the intellect which distracts the yogi. This is so regular that a yogi who is in naad may discover that he was extracted from it long after he was removed from naad and placed for viewing illustrated memories.

The memory goads the intellect to produce picture and sound illustrations in the mind chamber. These carry with them an inducing power which captures the attention of the coreSelf.

A yogi must study the operations within the mind. This will cause insight, resulting in more and more control over the allurements which hamper deep meditation.

Death produced no change in behavior

Most religions operate on the premise that at the time of death, there will be a dramatic change such that the faithful person will go to a heavenly place, leaving aside any sordid habits which are ungodly.

This is a false belief. The evidence is there in the fact that people who take surgery do lose objective consciousness when there are given anesthesia. However when a drug is exhausted in the body, the person awakens physically, reclaims the social identity and continues with the same habits as before.

One's behavior does not change at death if one did not successful endeavor to alter it during the lifespan.

April 1, 2006

Nature awarded some haphazard psychic mechanisms which are inclined to cultural development of material bodies. These adjuncts must be reformed if the ascetic will change the direction of accomplishment. Much effort is required.

April 10, 2006

Acharya Mun

He stated that the intellect and kundalini have such strong attraction to each other, that it makes it near impossible to completely curb the intellect from being influenced by the kundalini. The intellect is a rational organ. The kundalini is an emotional operation. When these adjuncts interact, the kundalini, more frequently, predominates. The kundalini can influence the intellect to use its rationality to promote the urges of the kundalini. This leaves the coreSelf in jeopardy.

Yogeshwarananda

He deposited an energy which was left by his guru, Atmananda. This was an energy which was to free me from wanting sensation and vision in the front of the subtle head. Atmananda instructed that I should give up focus in the front but should focus instead of directing kundalini to the brahmrandra crown chakra.

As the kundalini is lifted, it may be arrested by the intellect. That may cause thoughts, sounds images and ideas, which deprive the self of higher perceptions. If the kundalini avoids the intellect and targets the crown chakra, there will be no mental operations which attract the self to lower pursuits.

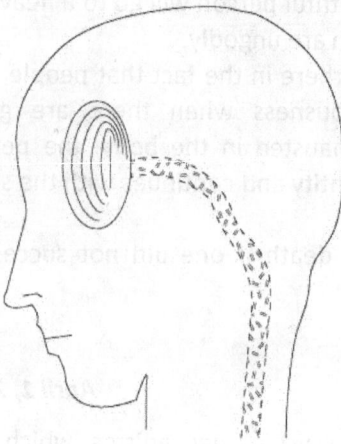

kundalini to intellect   kundalini avoids intellect

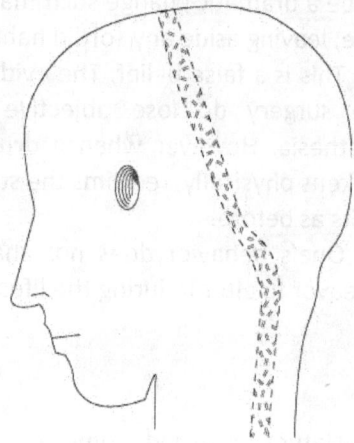

April 12, 2006

Yogeshwarananda / Muktananda

We had a discussion. The conclusion was:

The intellect must be brought to the naad sound resonance so that the intellect can be influenced to be satisfied with higher vibrations. First however the intellect must be made submissive to the coreSelf. As it was designed the intellect is submissive to the kundalini lifeForce. It is resistant to the core. It has the power to ignore the core and to force the core to endorse plans of the lifeForce. This ability of the intellect must be thwarted.

To make the intellect submissive the core must follow the instruction of Patanjali which is to separate from the intellect. When it is separated from the core the intellect becomes powerless. The core can then control the core.

The core for its part must study the enjoyment it gets from the intellect and make a decision to forgo that pleasure.

Once the core gets the intellect into a submissive position, the core can take the intellect to the naad sound resonance, where the intellect will be conditioned to exist without being enthralled by the kundalini sensuousness and the memory imprints which carry a seductive charge.

There is a technicality in this method which is that the attention of the core should go to naad and when doing so, pull the intellect into naad. If the attention tries to arrest the intellect, it may find that it becomes captured by the intellect which would be a failure. To avoid being captured by the idea image constructions of the intellect, the attention should go to naad. When it is situated there, it should pull the intellect into naad. It is too risky for the coreSelf to make contact with the intellect before the core is embedded in naad.

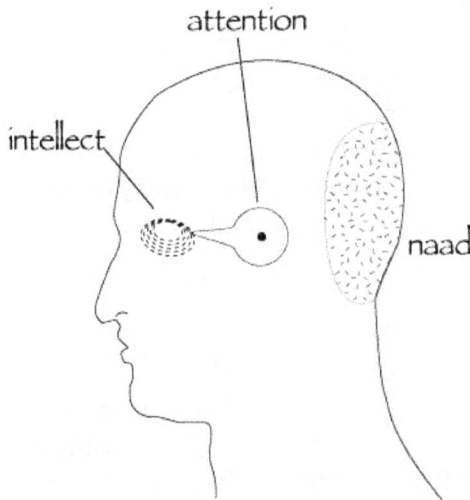

attention

intellect

naad

attention captured
by the intellect

attention embedded in naad
while pulling intellect to naad

intellect

naad

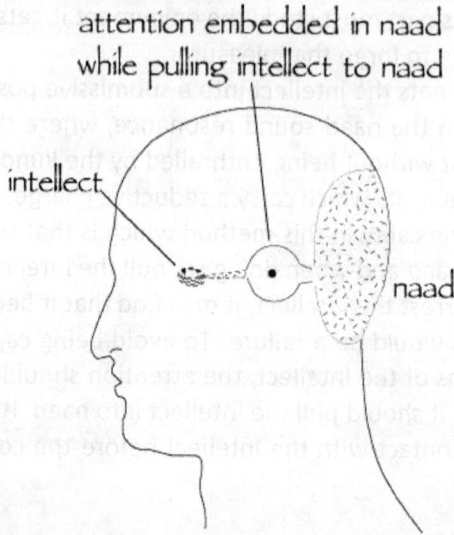

Detaching the attention from the intellect and attaching it to naad is done in meditation, not otherwise.

During meditation when this was realized, I saw a bright moon but only for four seconds. That is a supernatural moon. The duration of these perceptions increases as one meditates and gains proficiency at keeping the attention attached to naad and detached from the intellect and its machinations.

April 15, 2006

The attention turns away from naad to follow the intellect's presentations. It does this spontaneously and without being observed by the coreSelf even. This is the main hurdle in attaining supernatural and spiritual perception. So long as the attention is attached to the intellect, full success in yoga cannot be achieved.

The attention beam is emitted by the sense of identity. That beam is the culprit. Its addiction and reliance on the intellect is the cause of the coreSelf's lack of supernatural and spiritual perception. The key is to orient the attention to the naad sound resonance as a substitute for the attention's love of the intellect.

April 18, 2006

Every effort should be made to keep the intellect controlled even when one is not meditating. One should curtail its interaction urges for reasoning, justifying or criticizing.

April 22, 2006

The regular experience of sensing the intellect when one is absorbed in naad is that the intellect will seem to be non-existent or invisible. On occasion however it will be seen in one shape or another. During a meditation, it felt like a grey-brown subtle golf ball with grey-brown energy. I held it but I did not lose track of naad sound resonance.

If while in naad, one releases focus from naad and attaches focus to the intellect, one will find that the self becomes enthralled with the mental constructions which the intellect instantly produces. In fact one may be hypnotizes by the theatrics without realizing it except after some time passed and one found the core to be gazing at the constructions.

The ascetic should be anchored in naad and not become attached to the intellect. The greed for sensation is the problem. It is a tendency that cannot be eliminated. The secret is to transfer the interest to higher dimensions where the sense objects are not detrimental to the coreSelf. However this presents another problem which is that there is a gap where there are no sensations. This gap is a blank place. One must remain in that gap for a time before one develops the supernatural and spiritual perception. Patience is required during meditation to remain in the blank place until the higher perception develops.

April 25, 2006

Naad intellect thrust force

This practice shown in the diagram below is a situation in which the naad energy has a thrusting power which goes in the direction of the intellect. Simultaneously the intellect has a thrusting power which goes in the direction of naad force. These two energies are experienced as an interspaced zone.

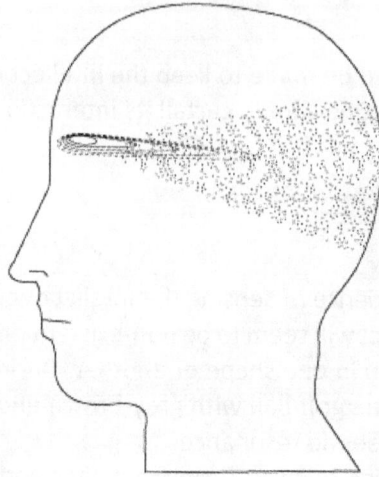

May 1, 2006

Animal body

These human bodies are part of the animal kingdom. There is no sense of divinity in them. The individuality is mistaken for something divine but that social unit is actually part of the material nature mock up with a spiritual core which serves only as a power supply and not as a directive agent.

I travelled on this day and was on the island of Trinidad. Due to that travelling my excretion system shut down. I realized that even if one does asana postures and pranayama breath infusion, still this physical form is an animal mechanism. It will regress into animal behavior at the slightest opportunity. My body became constipated due to the travelling because the kundalini lifeForce shut down the transit of waste through the colon. I endeavored to stimulate the rectum and the transit of waste resumed.

May 10, 2006

Location is important in meditation, to know where the various adjuncts are located as default positions. Direction is also important for knowing the details about how energy travels and how influences spread from one adjunct to another. Environment is also important to understand that an adjunct behaves in a demeaning way when it is in a low energy environment and then the same adjunct supplements the objectives of yoga when it is in a high energy dimension.

May 15, 2006

Dharma

Dharma is the supernatural being who is the patron deity of righteous conduct. His advice is productive because he has supernatural insight to see past lives of all concerned. Righteous conduct which is composed on the basis of the current life, without respect to past lives, may be faulty. Hence one should have insight into past lives or one should be advised by someone who does.

This deity spoke about my getting released from the obligations of righteous lifestyle within the framework of the present body. If a yogi only adheres to righteous conduct which is supportive of his current body and its ancestry, he will lose touch with his progress in yoga in many past lives. That is detrimental. For others, it is constructive to be engaged in acts to support the present status quo in the ancestry of one's body but a yogi should not be limited to that. In fact a yogi should break free from that so that he can be open to insight regarding obligations from many past lives. He should also establish a lifestyle which facilitates life with yoga teachers hereafter and in any mandatory future lives.

This deity, the personification of righteous conduct may advice one for limited success based on this one life or for spiritual progress based on many past and projected future lives. He took from my psyche some ancestral energy which comprised obligations for someone to pursuit a materialistic course for upgrade of the family in terms of wealth and status. He transferred that energy into other relatives, persons who have no interest in yoga but who were livid about the materialistic progress.

May 19, 2006

I realized that while developing an embryo, one, even a yogi, invests one's confidence energy into the would-be parents. That is the way of rebirth. The difference for a yogi is that he should recall most of this confidence energy once the body reaches adulthood.

The convention is that one keeps close to one's parents throughout their lives but a yogi should by all means curtail, if not eliminate, this affection because otherwise, energy from the ancestors will commandeer the life of the yogi which means that his spiritual progress will be nil. He will make social progress but his spiritual acceleration will not happen.

Confidence, which is also known as faith, is based on attachment which is a spontaneous impulsive principle. It is a constant in a living being. However a yogi should focus it on the yoga teacher and practice.

Confidence energy should be inspected in meditation. A yogi should know how much of it is invested to this or that interest. He should redirect it for increasing yoga practice. Whatever was established at birth, should be reconfigured once the body reaches adulthood. One should not assume that nature will change the faith investments in one's interest, because nature will not do so. One should gain insight in meditation and reconfigure the energy.

Energy inspection

During some meditations, a yogi should inspect the various energies which abound in the psyche. Anything which is resistant to yoga should be collected and be hurled out of the psyche. When one finds that one does not have the power to handle a yogic-resistant energy, one should cordon it while doing breath infusion. By directing the infused energy into the area or zone of the resistance that unwanted energy will explode into subtle fragments which can easily be thrown out of the psyche and be exchanged for constructive fresh energy.

Sexual energy may be lodged in various parts of the psyche from various sources, from past lives even. This energy may be activated when one least expects. It may cause sexual arousals in the physical presence of the persons concerned or in their astral proximity. A yogi must develop the psychic sensitivity to trace this to its particular cause. Someone does not have to be physically present to create a sexual arousal in the form of a yogi. The person may be present astrally or may be distance physically and astrally, and still cause sexual energy to flare in the psyche.

Curiosity is the enemy of the self but it is an eternal energy in the psyche. One must learn when to encourage it and when to squelch it. In some experiences one cannot stop the development of a curiosity because one simply does not have the power to do so. On occasion however one can dismiss it so that it ceases development and subsides into nothingness.

A yogi may gather the already manifested arousal energies. But then he has to decide what he will do with it. When collecting it he may realize that he cannot rid the psyche of it and must procure sexual access to exhaust its energy.

One dangerous source of sexual arousal energy is the memory. This is easy to control if the yogi has the ability to trace impressions which come from the memory and strike the intellect. Whatever is in the memory has to travel to the intellect because these two adjuncts have different default locations. The intellect is in the frontal part of the subtle head. The memory is in the chest of the subtle body. Even though memory transits instantly, it still takes time to travel to the intellect. A yogi must develop speed perception by detaching the sense of identity attention probe from the intellect. If he can keep the attention probe out of reach of the intellect he will have the ability to speed-see when memories leave or are about to leave the memory. He can stop these from transiting which will prevent his having to see exploded views of previous sexual activity from this or previous lives.

May 28, 2006

Confidence energy details

Confidence energy is usually applied before there is deliberation about the application. This is because the energy has a magnetic draw to some other aspect of nature.

The confidence energy, as soon as it is activated pursues a psychic object, even a thought, image or feeling. It penetrates that object and becomes a belief in the psyche. A yogi should observe this behavior. During meditation, it is best that the yogi move the confidence energy into naad sound resonance.

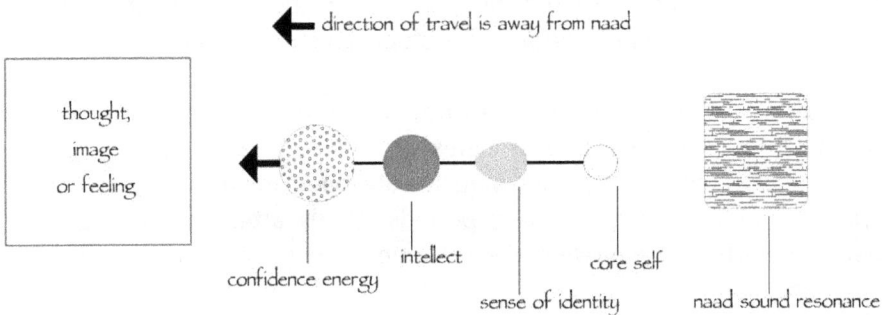

direction of travel is away from naad

thought, image or feeling

confidence energy

intellect

sense of identity

core self

naad sound resonance

May 29, 2006

Chit akash sky of consciousness

I was near the Misawa US Air Force Base in Japan. A daughter of my body produced a son of her body on this day.

I had the first steady experience of the chit akash sky of consciousness. Usually these experiences occur during meditation haphazardly without rhyme or reason. They are distinct but they last for seconds only.

During this, at first there was an experience of clouds, thin ones assembling in the sky. This seemed dream like. I thought it was a dream experience in the astral world. Then there was a blank no memory state. Then there was a wide horizontal opening. This vision was not shifty. It was steady. It was not a glimpse. The vision was wide across and steady.

Meditation progression goes in bits and starts, sometimes up sometime down, sometimes there are significant and sensation perception. Sometimes there is barely any advancement and it is incremental. At this time I was detailing the confidence energy. In the Bhagavad Gita, Krishna spoke of the hazard of contemplating the objects of the senses. The application of one's attention when doing that is an exhibition of confidence in the senses. One has to cease this investment of attachment or confidence in the senses and put the confidence in naad sound resonance absorption.

The supernatural sky and clouds I experienced in the subtle head had such clarity as to be amazing. It was more substantial than the sky and clouds of the physical environment. During that experience, suddenly, there was a bright light that hit me. A ray of it hit me. I did not turn to peer at it. Before I would have pursued that light but repeated experience of this nature, where the light disappears if one turns to pursue, caused me to develop an instinct not to pursue it.

The clouds were moving to the right. Some clouds seem to have the shape of a lion's head. Then cows were seen floating like clouds. One was brown. One was white. The animals stood amidst the clouds. No human figures were seen.

For meditation, one should learn to sit for long periods, if possible for hours. Of course one has to have a lifestyle that is agreeable to this. It cannot be done effectively without a conducive lifestyle. One must also focus into naad sound resonance for long periods. One's attention must develop detachment from the intellect and become attached instead to naad sound resonance.

The convention is that the attention is attached to the intellect which in turn is attached to the sensory impulse and memories. This natural way must be altered in meditation.

Later after having the experience with the clouds, I verified by checking with Lahiri, that this was an experience of the sky of consciousness, the chit akash. The experience occurred because of the presence of Lahiri but at the time, I did not realize this.

A student may progress without knowing that he is being assisted or graced by a teacher. However if one is not intrinsically dishonest, one will realize which teacher was responsible for rendering the progression.

May 30, 2006

Lahiri

He explained that the process of third eye meditation which was introduced by Yogananda, lacked the breath infusion precondition. Western students of Yogananda may lack this breath infusion practice. Their meditation will not be productive because of this. They will not be absorbed in naad sound resonance because their minds would not be as introspective as it should be.

Before each session of meditation one should complete pratyahar sensual energy withdrawal and introspection. Meditation is listed as the three highest stages of ashtanga yoga. This is how it was expounded by Patanjali. The stage before that is pratyahar. Hence if the student did not complete pratyahar, the meditation will be an attempt at meditation only. Patanjali gave meditation as samyama which are the three highest stages of ashtanga yoga as one sequential event, beginning with dharana, then dhyana, then samadhi as a progressive process of mind internalization.

With naad sound resonance as a background for focus and reliance, the yogi from within the subtle head, can focus forward into the surcharged space where the intellect is stationed. The intellect should be silent. If it has images, sounds and ideas which concern physical and lower astral existence, it will upset the attempt at meditation by producing a video show which will take the self out of naad focus.

When the intellect is quiet there is the likelihood that one may see a tiny star ahead instead of the intellect's theatrical shenanigans.

Part 3

One should curb many habits of the intellect which are non-productive and harmful to meditation. The intellect has a habit of invoking memories and mixes these with sensual inputs to create new mento-emotional events. This is horrible for yoga practice. It should be stopped. One must study how the mind drums up ideas, images and sounds. From that insight one can develop methods of suppressing these operations and eventually ceasing them.

In meditation, there is naad sound resonance but the mind may instead point the attention to imagined images and sounds. This is how the self becomes enthralled. Whenever the attention strays away from naad, one should capture the attention and turn it to naad. Do this repeatedly until the attention becomes attached to naad and it instinctively abandons the media displays.

Naad has all the value in the world to an advanced yogin. However a student may not be attracted to naad and may find listening to it as being a boring chore. Still because I advised you to listen you should confidently do so. In time, you will develop an affinity for naad. It will serve as spiritual nourishment and shelter.

May 2, 2006

Lahiri

He explained that *Om* as a sound which is uttered in the human mouth should lead to focus on the unuttered *Om* which is naad. Naad he said is the real *Om*. It is not uttered by anyone. It is in the universe and is heard as well in the human psyche. The requirement is not to say it but rather to apply the self in listening to it.

June 6, 2006

Lahiri

He advised that I should curtail the various concern energies, and refer the concern tendency to naad sound resonance. Once naad focus is steady in meditation, one may focus forward but that is provided that the intellect has voluntarily ceased it meditation-hostile activities.

June 7, 2006

In this meditation, I turned up the attention orb. It usually points forward to link with the intellect which supplies it with subjects of interest which satisfies its curiosity. It points upward or backward when the core commands it to focus on naad or to be of a blank interest and content.

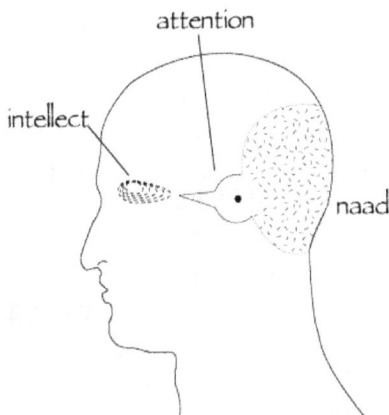

attention attached to intellect

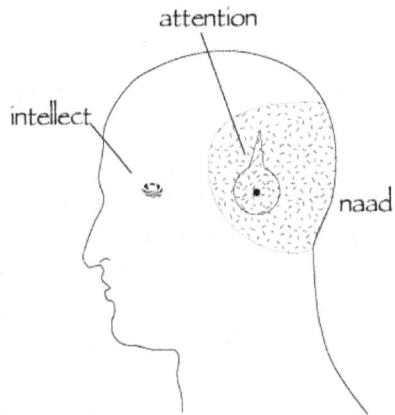

attention detached from intellect
due to being absorbed in naad

June 8, 2006

Yogeshwarananda

He explained that physical existence is important. Being an observer means a certain perspective. Meditation in the back of the subtle head is important because it allows the yogi to understand the frontal part as being the stage of disturbances. Merely by moving about in the subtle head, a yogi can understand the functions of each part and come to position the coreSelf for resistance to random thinking and imaging.

June 9, 2006

Lahiri

He clarified that all care and concern energy must be brought under control. The tendency for this energy is random application and impulsive distribution on the basis of body relationships. For acute renunciation, paravairagya, this concern energy must be restricted. Its random application and its social distribution causes unwanted rebirth. A yogi must curb it.

June 11, 2006

Lahiri

On this day there was a steady flow of energy from the cosmic intellect. This lasted for about 15 minutes. Usually one make contact with the cosmic intellect for a few seconds only. In meditation, one should sit properly so that the spine is braced properly. If one fails to do this, the spine will collapse forward or backward or there will be strain in the muscles which will disturb the session and prevent a deep state of consciousness.

The flow of energy from the cosmic intellect entered the subtle head through the third eye brow chakra. I applied a continuous effort to keep this energy flowing. When effort is required it is termed as a dharana practice as compared to a dhyana or samadhi practice which is effortless.

This flow through the brow chakra was streaks of light passing through darkness. It came from high up outside the subtle body and entered at an angle through the brow chakra.

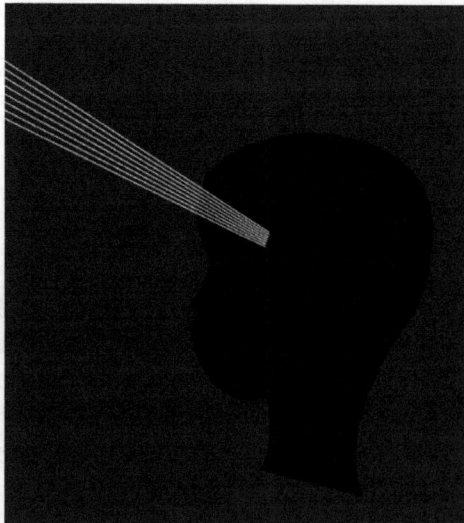

June 13, 2006

I realized that there should be transfer of the interest energy to naad sound resonance even when one is not meditating. A steady endeavor is required to achieve this. If one does meditation techniques only during the session, the progress will be much slower than if one does so at other times when it is possible. Constant application will be productive and will yield faster progress.

June 18, 2006

Krishna

On this day I proofread my translation and commentary of the *Uddhava Gita*. In chapter 18 there is an instruction to Uddhava about the intellect leaving aside the sense objects:

तस्मात् सर्वात्मना तात
निगृहाण मनो धिया ।
मय्य् आवेशितया युक्त
एतावान् योग-सङ्ग्रहः ॥१८ ६१॥

tasmāt sarvātmanā tāta
nigṛhāṇa mano dhiyā
mayy āveśitayā yukta
etāvān yoga-saṅgrahaḥ (18 61)

tasmāt — therefore; sarvātmanā — by all your soul; tāta — dear friend; nigrhāna — restraining; mano = manaḥ — mind; dhiyā — by the intellect; mayy = mayi — in me; āveśitayā — being absorbed; yukta = yuktaḥ — connected; etāvān — thus; yoga – yoga practice; saṅgrahaḥ — the gist.

Therefore my dear friend, with all your soul, restrain the mind by the intellect and be connected by being absorbed in Me. This much is the gist of yoga practice. (Uddhava Gita 18.61)

The inability to keep the intellect from hashing over the information gathered by the senses is the main cause for failure to grasp the position and importance of the coreSelf and the Supreme Person who is Krishna.

In this life we can see how people are so involved in the constructions of the intellect that they cannot objectify the coreSelf from it. Their view is that the core is the intellect. This happens because of the influence of the senses which have the intellect under full control. The self is required to break this combination, to segregate the core from its adjuncts.

If one does not have the strength to challenge the authority of the intellect and the senses, then one should take help from an advanced teacher or from the deity, from Krishna, Shiva or Brahma directly. Somehow one must break the spell.

The meditation where one becomes absorbed in naad sound resonance is vital because it serves as the fitting substitute for being hypnotized by the intellect's mental construction. One must take help from naad in meditation so as to break the hold which the intellect has on the self. This in turn, indirectly will cause the intellect to resist the sensual information which hypnotizes it. Thus overall the psyche would make progress.

One must take help from higher authorities, from the greater selves and from the Supreme self. It is not possible to do this without getting assistance. There must be a transmission of psychic strength from the authorities. A yogi must open his mind to this so that he can make progress rapidly. He cannot figure this by himself. It is not that one must have a guru who has a physical body. That is not it. But there must be a guru either astrally or physically. Somehow one must get assistance. It is sheer tomfoolery for one to think that one can become liberated by oneself. That is nonsensical. It may satisfy the sense of pride but otherwise it is ludicrous.

July 19, 2006

Determination and willpower are weak forces. These must be reinforced with confidence energy. When it is unified, one may act vibrantly but one may think that it is only willpower while it is that in combined with confidence. When the willpower operates on its own without being supplemented by the confidence energy, one experiences failure in effectiveness.

June 20, 2006

Naad spread

Naad sound resonance occurs in a particular part of the psyche, mostly in the subtle head. One should become emerged in it. When the coreSelf is habituated to naad focus, attempts should be made to induce naad to spread through the entire subtle head and then into the rest of the subtle body.

The core may pull or push naad or even call naad to places in the psyche where naad has no presence. The aim is to make naad saturate the subtle body.

June 27, 2006

Imagination orb and naad

The imagination orb is part of the intellect. It is difficult to resist the mental and emotional constructions of this orb. It allures the sense of identity which in turn hypnotizes the core. There are many ways of hammering the imagination orb into submission. One method is to bombard it with the naad sound resonance energy.

When the core finds that it is preoccupied with the imagination, the core should immediately refocus itself on itself. Then it should be aware of naad by focusing the listening sense.

Once naad is in focus, the core should pull naad to the imagination orb. If the orb is invisible, that does not matter, the core should focus the naad energy into the place where the last operation of the imagination occurred.

Renunciation absolute

Paravairagya is absolute renunciation but without reactionary energy. Whimsical renunciation carries with it a reactionary energy which undermines its effectiveness. The renunciation should be with insight and coolly done with no excitement.

The technique concerns the coreSelf and its adjuncts. It is not a social disinterest. It is not a renunciation of people or things. It is the breaking of reliance of the coreSelf on its adjuncts and the disconnection of one adjunct from another which is reliant on it. It is an inSelf series of actions, not a social activity.

June 28, 2006

Naad magic

Naad sound resonance is a magic vibration. It has a seeing aspect which opens after much absorption. Naad cannot be overestimated. It is effective but one has to derive confidence from a great yogin who speaks of the glories of naad. Naad is known as the ghosa subtle sound which supports the astral existences. It is supernatural. Its influence is wholesome for a yogin.

By focusing in naad one reforms many bad habits of the subtle body. It also changes the shape of the subtle body and replaces bad astral energy with wholesome vibrations.

Nityananda

His subtle body is filled with naad sound. He said that in his last physical body, there were problems. That form was bloated on occasion. It all happened under the influence of ancestors and followers whose desires he absorbed. But he said that his subtle form remained proper because of absorption with naad.

One who is not enriched with naad is a fake yogi. That is the opinion of Nityananda. He stated that it has nothing to do with how charismatic the teacher is or how many followers he has.

He explained that a yogi must by any means reach the stage of non-appropriation. This is used on two levels. One is in reference to sense objects where the senses reach out to appropriate what they desire. The other is the meaningful type, which is when the interest of the coreSelf reaches out to the intellect for its presentations which act as a lure to confiscate energy from the core.

A yogi must develop the non-appropriation tendency on the internal level so that his interest is contained and does not issue commands for the intellect to develop plans to appropriate sense objects.

Nityananda made a remark about Muktananda. The opinion was that before Muktananda presented himself as a guru he was not sufficiently attached to naad. Muktananda could not resist expressing charismatic powers. That ruined the mission.

July 1, 2006

Nityananda

He explained that hatha yoga practice should continue till the end of the physical body. That secures that if the ascetic must take another embryo, the subtle body will influence that physical structure to practice early on. One cannot rely on anything but one's acquired tendencies. These will seep into the next birth as instincts.

July 3, 2006

I entered a parallel world. There were humans there, mostly Chinese looking bodies. Someone there showed me the written language. Each bar on a stroke was a syllable of a word. A set of such bars was the word. The person who directed me made four books. These had a red cover.

The books explained kriya yoga in the language of those people.

July 4, 2006

In time a yogi should learn how to transmit social involvement outcome energies to the cosmic intellect. The individual intellect is limited. It becomes overpowered by the outcome energies of social involvement. To free it, one should release the outcome energies on a daily basis or from time to time.

All social roles can be assumed by other entities. No person is indispensable. One should understand this, act as commissioned by providence but with the understanding that one is not necessary. Fate could find another agent. It frequently does.

Once when Krishna's foster mother, Yashoda, challenged the toddler Krishna about eating dirt, Krishna opened his mouth at her request for an inspection. When he did this, Yashoda perceived the universe in the mouth of Krishna and felt that she would be sucked into his abdomen. After this Yashoda began to question her identity as the mother of Krishna. She concluded that it was an illusion where somehow she became convinced of herself as such even though that was not the case.

July 10, 2006

Inner ears

When listening to naad sound resonance, a yogi may discover that this is done with one inner ear but there is yet another which may be focused on other sounds. There is an interest in sounds which are counterproductive to yoga. That is yet another ear. For instance if there is a physical sound, an energy of inquiry may leave the psyche of the yogi to find that noise. If there is a thought sound, then another inner interest of the yogi will pursue that.

The question arises as to if any of these ears are one and the same or are they different orifices or different pursuits originating in the same orifice.

Clarity about this is essential in higher yoga so that the yogi can operate one of these as desired without any other one functioning.

When listening to naad sound, the yogi should close the other orifices so that full concentration can be applied. If however he fails to do that, he should have sufficient clarity to know the source of the other sounds and the reason for their impulsiveness.

Center gap kundalini

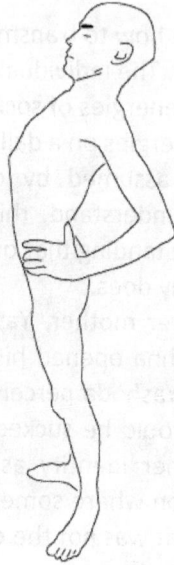

This was in Misawa, Japan.

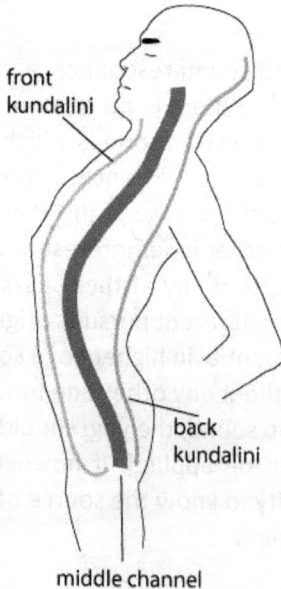

front
kundalini

back
kundalini

middle channel

Nityananda

He listed two gates. In one there are outlets such as memory, imagination faculty, sleep, reasoning and stupidity. In the other there is naad sound resonance which develops into jnana chakshu supernatural vision.

Thigh stretch notation

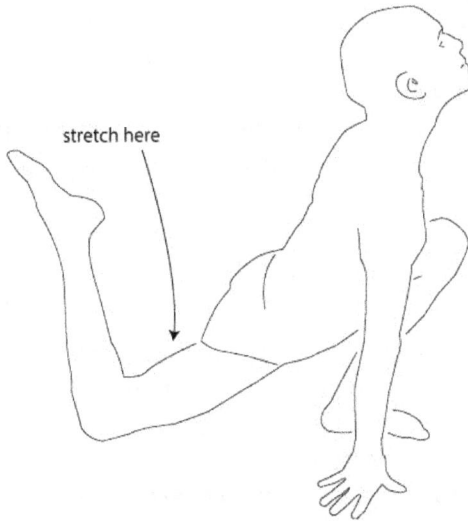

stretch here

The thigh muscles creates and hoards energy which supplements the sex function of the body. This assistance undermines higher yoga because while the yogi strives for reforming the sex energy, the thighs hold back some of that energy and contributes those reserves to sexual influences which bear down on the yogi from all sides. For the purpose of reproduction, these reserves of energy are necessary but for one who desires to exit these realms, they are an impediment.

A yogi may reform the thigh area by doing asana postures which target the thighs. Stretching, relaxing, infusing fresh breath energy and extracting polluted energy from the thighs will eventually result in a different purpose where the thighs will no longer hold reserves of its energy for sexual purposes. It will relinquish its energy upwards into the chest area.

Higher achievements sporadic?

The higher achievements in meditation occur sporadically at first. If however the yogi persists, these will be consistent daily developments which will anchor the yogi to higher states even when he is not meditating. One action that should be taken is the thought check and termination activity. This is done in the mind of the yogi either during a session or otherwise.

As soon as the mind begins an unwanted thought sequence the yogi should stop the mind. Alternately if the yogi did not realize that a thought began, he should once he realizes that it is in progression terminate it promptly.

The shelter of the yogi in the mind should be the naad sound resonance. As much as he can a yogi should resort to hearing naad. Whenever he realizes that his mind is involved with the conventional mental supports, he should abandon those and shift to naad

Remarks and investigation which are impulsively created or done in the mind by the mind, should be terminated by having a lack of interest and a blocking of the curiosity urge.

July 19, 2006

I realized that the present mental and emotion system is counterproductive to the yogic objective. There must be constant effort to redesign the system because it did not come with a natural restraint for what is contributory to higher perception.

The mind will always revert back to the convention which is that it seeks impressions from objects in the physical and lower astral dimensions. It regurgitates these in imaginative ways. These activities stifle the possibility for higher perception.

The source energy of the physical existence and lower astral planes is the causal zone. All the energy which is used here was a development of a tiny bit of energy from the causal plane. A yogi should become absorbed in naad and not remain under dominance of the imaginations faculty of the mind. This naad reliance will in time cause one to develop resistance to lower realities. If one becomes anchored in naad, supernatural vision will emerge.

July 21, 2006

Third eye vision

There are various types of vision which occur at the brow chakra. These are called third eye perceptions. During meditation any of these perceptions may occur. They are located at the center of the eyebrows or may be a little higher in the middle of the forehead.

Some of these perceptions are clear like looking through a transparent window. Some are hazy like seeing through fog in the day time. It may be wide angle or through a narrow slit. The opening may be round, oval, square or rectangular.

The yogi may be at a distance from the opening such that it seems that he is several feet or several hundred feet away from it. In that case he may not perceive what is beyond the opening but may perceive that there is an environment there even though he is too far from the opening to see it. It may be perception of a sky environment, like looking through a sky which has no objects and no visible terrain.

He may see faces of persons who are in those other dimensions. He may see other lifeforms which exist there. A yogi may also see the past, present or future history of some other dimension or of this earthly realm.

In some perceptions the persons and objects seen may be seen as only silhouettes or semi-transparencies. A person may be seen who uses a transparent body or a semitransparent form.

Cosmic Intellect

The cosmic intellect is actually a cosmic pool of unused intellects which were not assigned to any individual coreSelves. There is a supreme intellect which is used by the primal creator god but that is not the same as the cosmic pool of limited intellects.

The intellect which I use, or the one which you use, came from the cosmic pool of unused intellects, except that now my individual intellect is segregated from the cosmic reservoir. The universe has a potential but only a small part of this is in manifestation. The main potency is held in reserves and is not expressed during the creation except in tiny releases here and there. These tiny releases are sufficient to produce what we observe and experience.

Under the influence of the intellect, I act as an agent of the cosmic pool of intellects in terms of fulfilling urges which were in the individual intellect which I was assigned at the beginning of my time. At this stage of the creation, when I realize that being an agent of this power is not in my interest, I may take steps to sidestep that influence, to move from being its target. Meditation on naad is the way to begin developing resistance to the influence of the intellect. This allows the yogi to go with the siddhas and to develop another interest.

August 1, 2006

A limited being cannot be doing anything in this creation for himself or herself because that is not allowed. There is no way to initiate anything afresh. One cannot do anything novel here because everything is circumspect according to the causal energies which produced this. One cannot begin anything now. Everything is a continuation of the potential energy which comprised causal energies at the onset of the time which produced this.

A yogi should slide out from under these energies. He should allow others to take his place participating in the development of this. If this must go on, then a yogi should be exempt from it and should realize that his absence will never cause this to cease.

August 2, 2006

Supernatural supervision

There are gods and there is a supreme God. Everything personal and natural is supervised. The interaction of the persons and the environment is supervised.

The difficulty with proving this is that the supervisory agencies are usually in a higher dimension. That prohibits visibility. Their actions affect us but we cannot trace their movements and effects. If however someone develops the perception into higher dimension, it would be possible to trace some of the supernatural actions to physical history.

For a yogi concern for this world is a mistake because this situation is controlled by supernatural forces which are immune to the willpower or desire needs of a limited person here. We may take advantage of opportunities which are afforded to us here but invariably we will discover that some circumstances are for our displeasure. Since we cannot control this in a territorial way, it is best to figure how to shift from here into an environment which lacks fatiguing trauma.

Nityananda advised that a yogi should aim for full application of renunciation but in such a way that others do not know of his action. He may be with others but they should not be given the opportunity to become hostile because of his renunciation. Hence he may participate when it is necessary, when he is in a certain circumstance but deep within there should be no attachment and no interest in the affairs.

This creation will continue as it is indefinitely. A yogi cannot alter it substantially. He should understand this and apply his detachment energies within the psyche so that his intellect and lifeForce becomes neutral to the excitements which are generated in this creation.

A yogi must understand that he is not needed. If he were to vanish from this place, nature would go on without him. In fact it may do better in absence.

August 3, 2006

Thinking alarm

A yogi should see thinking as evidence of contact between the intellect and the sensual energy and/or memory. During meditation this contact should cease. However because the psyche was designed to think, a yogi must make the effort to change this tendency, so that the mind becomes attached to either a blank state, being absorbed in naad sound resonance or using an access to the chit akash sky of consciousness. During meditation, any thinking should be regarded as an alarm or notice that the mind is out of control and deviated from what is intended.

August 18, 2006

Buddha Shakyamuni (Xian Da Ci En temple, Xian China)

I was in China on this day in the city of Xian. I visited a Buddhist temple where a form of Buddha Shakyamuni had twenty (20) other Buddhas to his right and left. The first one said this, "You need more silence."

The Buddha in the center said, "Each ascetic must attain enlightenment individually."

The third Buddha said, "You attain what you honestly work for. You attain nothing else."

August 20, 2006

Taoist deity

I visited a Taoist temple in Xian China. The deity said this, "The way one emerged is the way one will return. No one can adjust that. One should be harmonious with what is or what occurs. One is no more than part of the flowing flux of energy."

August 22, 2006

Taoist temple, Beijing China

I was on a plane from Xian to Beijing. A departed swami came astrally. He was with one of his disciples who was also deceased. They were in astral forms which had a shadow energy. This swami proposed that *Hare Krishna* (not the entire *Hare Krishna* mantra) could be used to reach naad sound resonance. He did not like the *Om namo Shivaya* mantra which is traditionally used to aid in meditation. His idea was that since Krishna explained about naad in the conversation with Uddhava, Krishna's name is affiliated with naad and should be used.

Later that day, Yogeshwarananda came and said that the Swami was out of his mind. Yogeshwarananda said this, "They do not want to follow what Krishna said. They are introducing other methods as per authorities in their sect after Krishna made statements. Why not honestly say that Krishna did not say such and such but this other person, Krishna's devotee, said this and we prefer what this other person said."

He remarked further, "It is clear in the Bhagavad Gita that Krishna said to use Om. These people are not sincere even to their deity. Krishna also directed them in brow chakra focus. Check the verse about *bruvoh*. Whatever mantra one uses, one will still be left with the struggle for mind control because the memory will be the problem. There is a verse where Krishna speaks about yogis who only pretend to meditate because while sitting as yogis, these persons continue under mental dominance with the mind showing them thoughts, images and ideas, which they are hypnotized by.

"Once a mantra takes the yogi to naad, then what? He will have to leave that mantra. It will not help him then. He will be haunted by memories and will continue the addiction to mental images. This is the issue. That is a struggle on the psychological plane between the coreSelf and the imagination faculty."

August 27, 2006

China Location

Meditation and psychic communication is not dependent on the physical location. One can reach anyone else psychically from any physical location. This gives the yogi the freedom to practice and get instructions no matter where he is physically. On this date, I was in Beijing, China.

In some meditation session, the intellect is discovered to be overactive, such that even if the yogi uses an intended focus, still a part of the attention is used by the intellect to pursue distractions. When this happens a yogi can do breath infusion to increase the frequency and purity of the subtle body. Then he may attempt meditation again. Or he can gather the portion of the attention energy which is attracted to the distraction and command that energy to focus instead on naad sound resonance. The yogi should instruct the intellect to be attentive to naad so that memories of naad are imprinted in the subconscious.

Naad has a visual aspect but it is not realized until one become proficient in naad absorption. Since initially there is the inner hearing aspect and no other sensual register of naad, the intellect may have a neutral attitude to it which will result in no memory record in the subconscious.

The intellect likes to have at least two sensual registers before it forms a memory impression. If there is just one, like the hearing aspect for naad listening, then it is likely that even if the yogi hears naad for extended periods of time in many sessions, still the intellect will retain no memory of it. Hence the necessarily to make the intellect record naad resonance.

Pranayama breath infusion before meditation, helps to shift the intellect to a higher plane, where visions, apparitions and higher perceptions occur, where higher concentration forces exist. These experiences forcibly attract the intellect causing it to abandon its tendency to pursue lower realities.

August 28, 2006

Yogeshwarananda

On this day I left Beijing, China to travel to Misawa, Japan. From an astral dimension, Yogesh instructed that I should work harder to remove the gap between infused fresh air and polluted energy which is in the psyche. When doing breath infusion, one has to do it rapidly so that the fresh energy is accumulated and compacted. This will travel down and around the body into the central spinal passage. It will push pollution out of the system. There will be a gap area which has a mixture of fresh energy and polluted energy. One should push fresh energy against this pollution, forcing the physical portion of it to go to the lungs where it would be expelled from the body. This occurs on both the physical and astral levels.

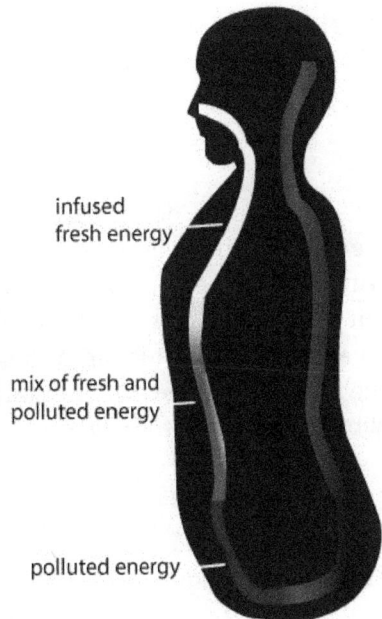

infused
fresh energy

mix of fresh and
polluted energy

polluted energy

There is a practice of opening the memory to naad. The memory is resistant to naad just as the pleasure seeking sense is resistant to neutral bliss energy. The pleasure seeking sense craves sexually charged energies but it is reluctant to take note of neutral bliss energy which pervades higher levels of existence.

The yogi should train the mind so that naad is noted as a memory impression. This will allow the intellect to become attached to naad. However since naad is subtle in comparison to physical or lower astral sounds and since naad is heard by the inner hearing sense and not by the outer one, the intellect will note naad sublimely and not as a sensation. This means that it will remember naad in a non-sensational way which the yogi must become conversant with.

August 29, 2006

I was at Misawa Air Base in Japan. Yogeshwarananda came there psychically. He said that a thorough bhastrika breath infusion practice is absolutely necessary to light up the frontal part of the subtle head, otherwise it is an endless struggle to clear this area of physically related ideas and lower astral energy. The kundalini must be aroused consistently otherwise if it is on a lower plane, it will obstruct advanced meditation attempts.

September 1, 2006

One should do a thorough bhastrika breath infusion session before meditation. This will cause the psyche to be introverted and to be saturated with fresh subtle energy. An unenergized psyche is incapable of higher focus but it efficiently taps into and exploits the lower realities. It is not a matter of what one desires. It is rather the capability of the subtle body according to the level of energy which saturates it. If it has a higher grade of energy, the subtle form will automatically give access to higher perceptions.

September 3, 2006

Yogeshwarananda

He said that the quality of thoughts related directly to the condition of the kundalini lifeForce. A yogi should remove the lower astral energy from the psyche. He should displace it with a higher grade of subtle energy. The reliable way of doing this is to do breath infusion just before meditation.

September 6, 2006

Yogeshwarananda

He said that a yogi's ability to lift the frontal lobe is directly related to the energy which saturates the lower belly. If that energy is high grade the frontal lobe contents will lift easily. It will be submissive to the yogi. Otherwise it will be resistant and will conduct ideas which are hostile to meditation.

September 7, 2006

Yogeshwarananda

He said that there is a right method and a wrong way in the practice of yoga at each stage. Doing the practice in the incorrect way is okay, provided the yogi has the temperament of one who is willing to learn and adapt. It is unavoidable that one may use a wrong method. Even if one is shown the correct way, one may misunderstand or one may stubbornly feel one has a better method. This is okay provided one learns and recognizes when a method is nonproductive.

A teacher may give the wrong method but teachers who give methods they practice will give practical methods except that those methods may not work for some students. This is due to differences in psyche design.

Yogesh showed how to infuse breath energy into the lower abdomen so as to stimulate muladhar base chakra. One should keep one's attention within the psyche during breath infusion practice. The mind should not be allowed to wonder. One should mentally direct the infused energy according to how one was instructed by the teacher. This may be a physical or astral instructor.

While doing breath infusion, it may happen that the infused energy accumulates a high charge. Then it may move towards certain pollutions. When it enters these areas it may ignite subtly and then move again to other pollutions or to block passages. A yogi should do this and direct the energy so that it can complete the eradication of polluted lumps of energies and blocked nadi passages. One does not have to be instructed in this. It is self-evident when one practices. There is no need to get instructions from the teacher about this because some of this is self-evident.

September 8, 2006

Yogeshwarananda

Naad sound is clearer, more precise, more reliable, less blurry, and not vague when the psyche is energized with breath infusion prior to meditation.

September 19, 2006

Lu Kuan Yu

He gave diagrams showing how the aroused kundalini would revert downward to the navel. I got in touch with this Taoist yogi after going to China and visiting three Taoist temples. I was unable to contact any proficient teachers there. At one temple in Xian, a student said that the teacher was not present. The student said he was not qualified to discuss advanced practice. We had some difficulty with translating English to Chinese and Chinese to English. Due to the sweeping changes in China made by the Cultural Revolution, the Taoist temples which survived do so in a sort of *frozen in time* state, where when one visits one gets the feeling that the hands of the clock stopped.

When I returned to the USA from the visit to China, I found a used book called *Taoist Yoga* in State College, Pennsylvania. It was by Lu Kuan Yu. Soon after this I got into mystic contact with this Taoist yogi.

He gave these diagrams.

kundalini to crown chakra

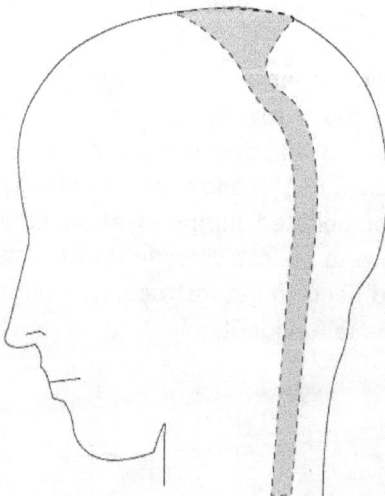

kundalini influenced to frontal part of head

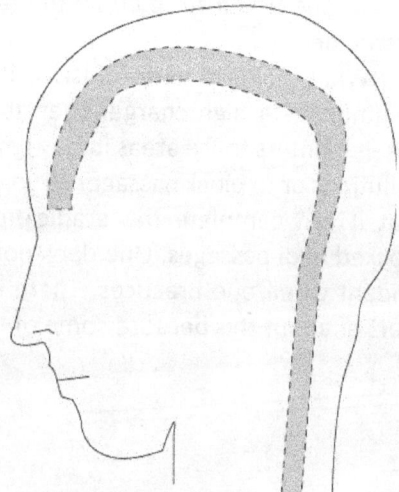

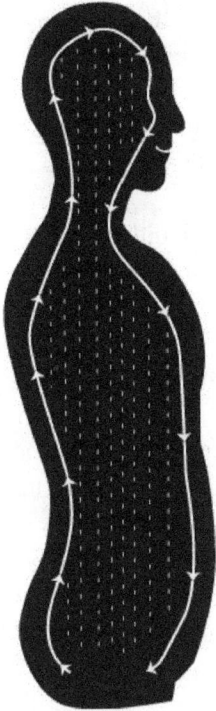

kundalini aroused
through central back nadi
loops around head
travels down front
expresses spray of
energy influence in center

A yogi must advance beyond merely raising kundalini through the central sushumna nadi channel. Eventually kundalini must be aroused through every part of the body, including the feet and hands. When kundalini is aroused in the conventional way through the central sushumna channel, it barges into the head of the subtle body and attacksk the intellect, the brow chakra and the crown chakra. However this does not mean that it affects all parts of the subtle body which are below the neck. A yogi must attack these parts by directing kundalini to move into other areas.

First one should become proficient in spinal arousal. Then one should direct infused breath energy into other parts of the subtle body, so that every part is bombarded by infused breath energy and kundalini comes alive in every part. This includes the extremities which are the fingers and toes.

September 24, 2006

Lu Kuan Yu

He suggested that when kundalini is aroused the intellect should be combed back from the frontal lobe to the back part of the subtle head. A yogi may do this if he is proficient in elevating kundalini through the central spinal column. He has to remain objectively aware while this happens, otherwise if he loses consciousness control, he will not be in a position to direct the intellect.

Those who are not proficient in arousing kundalini through the spine, should practice more and more until the expertise is gained. Then they can do this practice.

The intellect is attracted to the kundalini either in its aroused or unaroused state, either when it is in a lower vibration or when it is infused with breath energy and is elevated in energy. The intellect moves to meet the kundalini either for lower or higher objectives. However when kundalini is aroused through the spine, it does that in a haste and the intellect is usually caught off-guard where before it could move to the kundalini when the kundalini emerges through the neck, the intellect is struck by the kundalini,

Kundalini is attracted to the intellect but the kundalini influences the intellect. Therefore if the kundalini is in a lower vibration its influence will result in the intellect sponsoring and developing a lower objective. This is why it is necessary to elevate the kundalini so that it pursues and has interest in higher objectives which are consistent with the aims of yoga practice.

September 25, 2006

I made a notation about the allegiance of the intellect. It is a serious mistake for a yogi to continue thinking that the intellect is attached to the coreSelf. It is not. The quicker one realizes this, the better one will be. The intellect is attached foremost to the kundalini psychic lifeForce. It is partial towards that and is oriented primarily to that. This dependence of the intellect can change but as soon as the tension for that change is removed, the intellect will resume allegiance to the kundalini.

The coreSelf should not assume that it will convince the intellect to abandon the kundalini. That can only happen by advanced meditation and only for as long as the core maintains that. The intellect will always resume the attachment and reliance on the kundalini. This must be accepted.

September 26, 2006

The intellect's reliance on the kundalini sensual apparatus is one problem. The attention's attachment to the intellect is yet another. The attention is the focus of the sense of identity which always surrounds the coreSelf. This attention is helplessly attached to the intellect. It is so attached that it frequently focuses on the intellect and does not realize that it did so until sometime after the connection was made. This makes it difficult for it to retract itself and disconnect from the intellect's influence.

Because the attention is hypnotized by the intellect that attention cannot exert its full power to detach from the intellect. Its detachment power is attenuated when it connects to the intellect. The longer it takes for the attention to realize that it is hypnotized by the intellect, the less and less the attention can disconnect itself. This perplexity can only be solved in deep abstract meditation where the coreSelf minutely studies its situations and partitions the psyche, the collective so called self.

The fact is that the observing self, the *I am* central power, is part of the psyche. It is part of the self when the word self means the composite unit which consist of an I core, a sense of identity, an intellect, memories and a sensual kundalini lifeForce held together in a psyche and functioning as one being who could be targeted for sensual energy transfers.

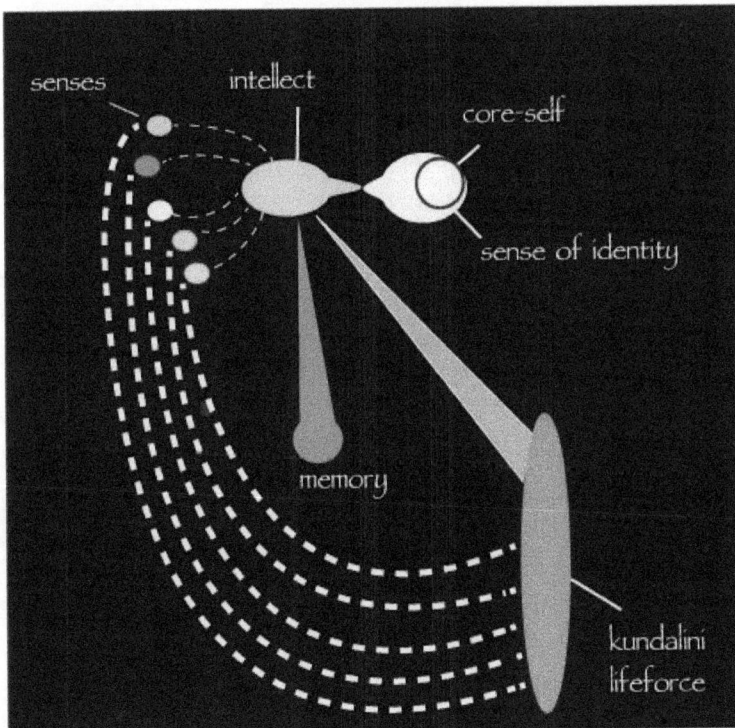

core-self with its adjuncts

Lu Kuan Yu

He stated that the kundalini lifeForce has a stiff demeanor. It takes some practice to make it submissive. When it is aroused through the sushumna central passage into the head of the subtle body, it attacks the intellect which is its natural target. Then it may go through the brahmrandra crown chakra.

However the kundalini energy will eventually be altered so that it spreads equally through the psyche. Initially the target is to get it to go the top chakra but when this happens frequently, a yogi should train kundalini to remain in the psyche and not puncture the crown chakra to go outside the psyche.

All dark zones in the psyche must be shattered by using the kundalini energy to light these areas. Once the head of the subtle body is bombarded sufficiently with the energy from the aroused kundalini, the yogi should direct kundalini energy to other parts and get those areas to become translucent and highly energized as well.

Yogeshwarananda

Frontal nadis

I saw some back of the head nadis. Since Yogesh was present, I question him about it. He said that when he did the related practice while his physical body lived, he did not notice those nadis. He surmised that Atmananda, his primary yoga teacher influenced me to see those nadis.

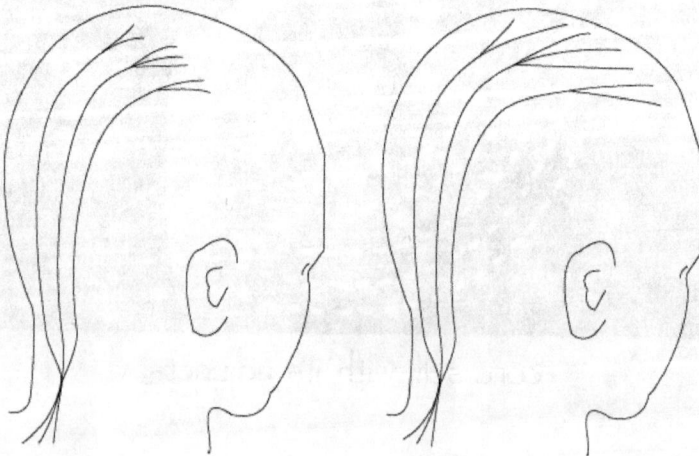

Ku Luan Yu

This Taoist master was of the opinion that the kundalini should be divested through the entire psyche and not through the head only. That is the aim in the Taoist system of kundalini yoga as contrasted to the Indian methods which stress sushumna nadi clearance as the ultimate effort.

Naad sound resonance should be used to pull the attention energy away from the intellect. The addiction of the attention energy is to give itself to the intellect. The yogi has the task of changing this so that the attention becomes attached to the naad sound resonance instead.

October 4, 2006

Neck clearance

After sushumna nadi is sufficiently cleared where no heavy astral energy or subtle pollutants are present in it, the yogi should focus on clearing the neck itself. The clearance of the spine in the neck should be extended to the entire neck

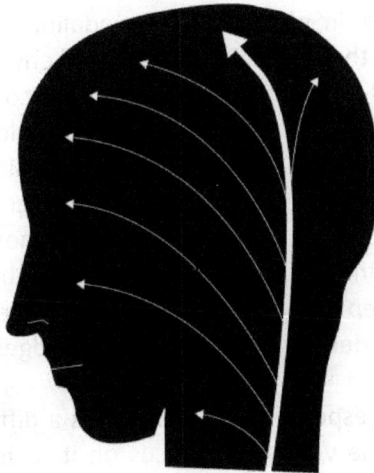

sushumna nadi

head clearance

sushumna nadi
central spine clearance

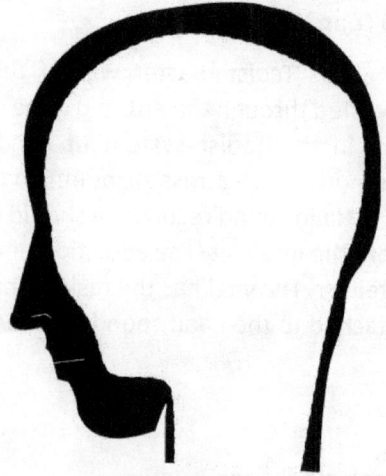

whole neck
complete clearance

October 7, 2006

For the purpose of inSelf Yoga™ the kundalini needs to be used in the psyche only and not in the physical or lower astral environments. It should be used in the psyche for attaining inner vision of the components. Kundalini's interest in whatever exist outside the psyche should be to peer into the higher supernatural environment and the full spiritual existence.

Self-psyche research is everything to an advanced yogi, for clarity into what comprises the psyche and how to govern it most efficiently and with insight clarity. Kundalini must help in this venture by getting its energies upgraded. It should keep the sushumna central passage clear at all times, and clear away any subtle debris and energy which lodges here or there in the psyche.

The navel area is especially important. It is a difficult to reach area. It evades purification. The yogi should focus on it. Using breath infusion he should bombard it daily until it yields and the mass of it is shattered into small fragments of kundalini energy which give a bliss energy which gives a neutral or semi-neutral happiness

As the convention states, there are five (5) main chakras on the spine. These with two other primary chakras in the head are regarded as the seven (7) chakras which govern the flow of subtle energy. A yogi should get control of the five spinal chakras so that he can direct that the entire neck and trunk of the subtle body be cleared of subtle pollutions. It is not satisfactory to clear the sushumna nadi central passage while the rest of the psyche harbors pollutants.

Low energy in the trunk of the body, in the arm and legs contribute to undermining the progress made with kundalini. To eliminate this, the yogi must clear all parts of the subtle body.

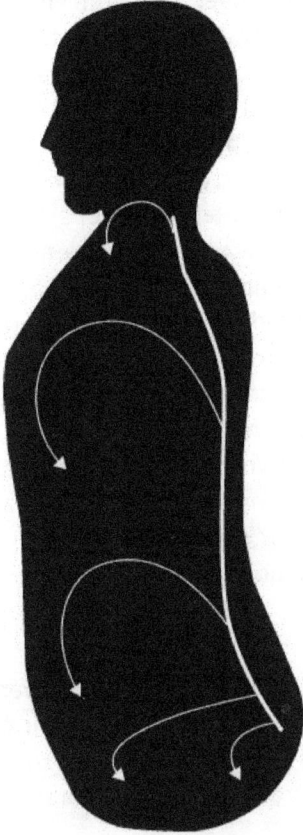

kundalini spread
from spinal passage
through trunk and neck

October 10, 2006

When the frontal part of the subtle head is cleared of mental chatter and heavy astral energy, the naad sound is clearer and louder. One may also develop visual naad perception at this time, where when one opens the inner vision one sees a glow of light in all directions. If one remains in this glow while hearing naad resonance, there will be opening to the chit akash sky of consciousness.

The intellect appears to be one viewing instrument where one sees reconstructed memories and imagines new ideas or see ideas which are currently being displayed based on sensual input. However within the intellect there are small orbs which a yogi may discover. Just as an engine can be regarded as a unit, so the mind itself may be regarded as a unit, and the intellect which is a psychic object in the mind can also be regarded as a unit. The fact is however that these units have composite parts.

During meditation, I noticed that a small orb in the intellect acts to support and protect distractions. It reserves a portion of the attention energy for itself. It deprives one of full focus on transcendental objects or states. The grip on focus which the coreSelf has applies to a portion of the attention energy. Hence when focus is applied some of the attention energy evades the grasp of the core. The remnant portion is reserved for use by the imagination orb. The small orb which I saw is the part of the intellect which supports and protects distractions. Hence when the core becomes absorbed, its full application of interest does not use all of the attention.

Yogesh sent a message through the crown chakra stating that the distraction support orb is part of the intellect complex. He stated that a yogi who abandons practice as the primary activity and who becomes dedicated to teachings others does not realize this distraction orb.

Front kundalini effects

Front, middle and sides kundalini rises are different to the convention which is sushumna nadi central spinal arousals. After becoming proficient in sushumna nadi clearance, a yogi will graduate to front and cell kundalini releases. These are vital for removing heavy astral energy and pollutants from hard to reach parts of the subtle body.

In the trunk of the subtle body, there is an *up force* resistance. This powerful energy prohibits beginners from pulling up hormonal energy and other types of charged force through the trunk of the subtle body. This is based on the reproductive function which is built into an adult body.

As soon as the yogi becomes proficient in sushumna clearance, he instinctively switches to front kundalini rises. The idea is to pull up the hormonal energy so that it no longer travels down to the genitals. At the genitals hormonal energy acquires a lust charge which either is attracted to the kundalini or attracts the kundalini. If it attracts the kundalini, the result is sexual climax experience. If it is attracted to the kundalini, the result is the ascension of the combined energy through sushumna nadi into the subtle head.

The preferred experience is for the yogi to use the hormonal energy without a lust charge. This will cause the yogi to be attracted to the highest of the astral locations, places where siddhas and their superiors abound.

There is a resistance in the psyche, which prohibits charged energies from going upwards, where this energy falls down through the body. If a yogi wants to go to the highest of the astral zones, he would have to change the subtle body, so that its energy gravitates upwards. This is done by developing front, middle, sides and cell kundalini.

October 18, 2006

The impurities in the navel region as well as the chest area must be dealt with using bhastrika breath infusion. Those sectors should be directly targeted. The intestinal mass and the stomach should be targeted. So long as the subtle body mimics the physical system, there will be no chance for the yogi to go to the highest astral regions which are named as Maharloka, Janaloka, Tapoloka and Satyaloka.

A yogi can do breath infusion after finally being evicted from the physical body. He can make further progress then. However one should do as much as one can before losing the physical form because in the hereafter, there is the likelihood that one will become an embryo and will not remain as an astral being practicing yoga.

Below the higher astral places, there is siddhaloka which is a great attainment for a yogi. If he can do sufficient austerities to qualify to be in that place, he can complete the practice to go higher from that place, making it unnecessary to take another embryo which is risky.

A yogi should do the practice of elimination of the astral stomach so that there is no urge in the subtle body to eat, digest and evacuate as in a physical form. This is called agnisara, or using fire energy to burn and demolish the abdominal digestive organs. This is done using breath infusion particularly rapid bellows breathing or bhastrika.

When the yogi targets the gut system, the breath energy which reaches that area is absorbed into it. Then as more and more breath energy is infused, the digestive organs shrink. They implode inwards on themselves. This causes them to explode outwards in fragments. Eventually by doing this day after day, once or twice per day the yogi eliminates the organs in the subtle form and is prepared to transit to siddhaloka with a subtle form that will not mimic the last physical body in terms of eating, digesting and excreting as before.

When the gut system is reformed, it appears to be a hard ball located slightly below the navel. In some yogis it is experienced as a clump of hard energy like a granite brick. Eventually this ball moves up and as it does so it shrinks in size. It may reach the throat where it will again shrink in size.

Then it will seem to disappear after several intense breath infusions using bhastrika rapid breath absorption. Then again it will appear as a subtle shriveled misshaped leather bag. And at last that will disappear after enough breath energy is infused into it during several sessions.

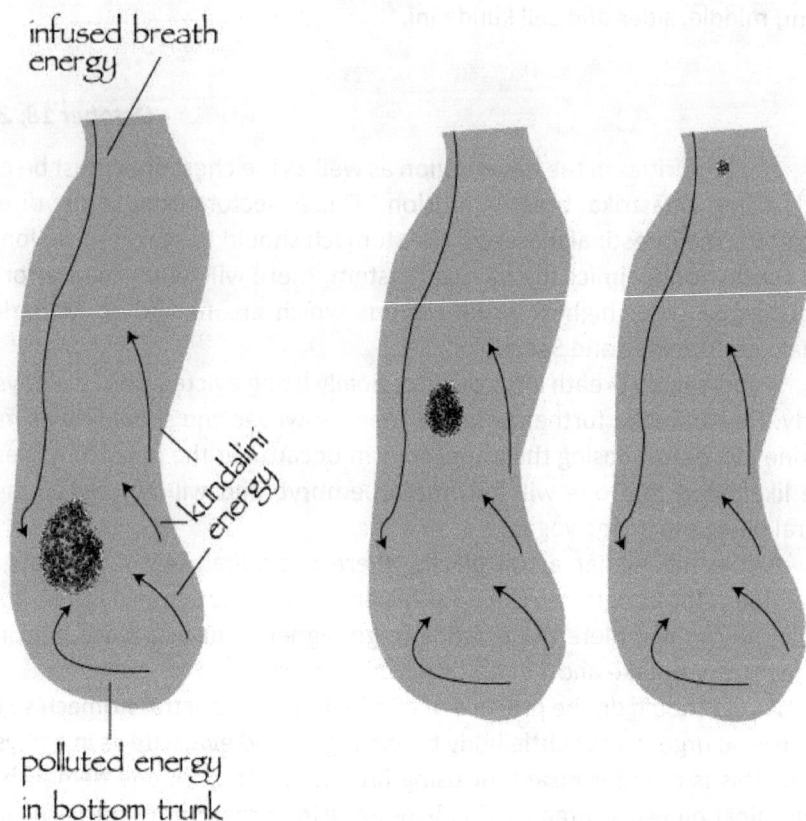

infused breath energy

kundalini energy

polluted energy in bottom trunk

September 29, 2006

Spiritual focus missing

In most humans the spiritual focus is missing. Instead there is an interest for pleasure seeking in tangible ways through smelling, tasting, seeing, touching and hearing with focus on physical substance and emotional trauma. These experiences are pleasant, neutral or unpleasant. The pleasurable experiences max out in sexual climax which nature designed for facilitating reproduction of new bodies by cell replication.

If one is observant, if one becomes objective to sex pleasure experience, one will realize it as a battery power which is expressed through pleasure circuits. This is interpreted as pleasure but it is a bio-electric discharge in the physical body and a psycho-electronic discharge in the subtle form.

November 2, 2006

During breath infusion, a fan spray of kundalini manifested. I stretched the spine upward and curved it backward while standing. This caused kundalini to rush up the front of the body.

November 17, 2006

Front kundalini arousal is important for elimination of thought producing impulsions. There is a thought receptor bulb in the front of the head which is receptive to the thoughts and demands of others. This bulb is silenced by the aroused front kundalini.

A yogi must be socially isolated but he must also get instructions from superior souls. No limited person is totally immune from lower influence. Thus a yogi must take precautions to limit his association with persons who have no interest in the hereafter and those who have such interest but are disinclined to researching it here and now.

Krishna

I got a communication from Krishna. There is a prayer which is.
Sri Krishna sharanam mama
This means:
Lord Krishna, you are for me, the only reliance.
Actually it may not be possible to live merely on the association of Lord Krishna. Unless one is existentially directly connected to Krishna, that is not possible. However Krishna explained in Bhagavad Gita that everyone is connected to him in one way or the other, directly or indirectly. In that sense everyone relies on Krishna. It is assuring to know that. One should have confidence in what Krishna explained in the Bhagavad Gita and should allow that energy to support one's spiritual practices.

In the communication Krishna said that it took him six months as instructed by Upamanyu Rishi, for him to switch over to the required insight perception to see Shiva. It was six months of meditative silence with special mantras and with naad sound resonance being the basic focus.

November 18, 2006

Forceful thoughts

During meditation one may have forceful thoughts which are so impulsive that even if one tries to stop them, they continue and hold one's attention. These powerful impulsions should be studied to determine the source of the strength of the energy. Why is it that a particular thought stands its ground against the willpower effectively, while another thought ceases development and fizzes out as soon as one expresses a lack of desire to view it?

Meditation attempts may become attempts only because of the strength of certain thoughts where these impressions successfully challenge one's willpower. A yogi must examine those incidences where he is forced to give up his focus in meditation and he is maneuvered into a position in the head of the subtle body where he is subjected to the development of a sequences of thoughts which the intellect displays.

The power in these thoughts was developed in them when particular incidences occurred and were observed through a sensual orifice. The kundalini gives a high or lower value to any sensual input. If one is marked with a high value, that one will compel the self to observe it when it is displayed as a memory construction in the intellect.

This means that the solution to the problem of compulsive thinking during meditation attempts is not to stop the thinking or to attempt to do so, but it is to control the value system which the kundalini uses in dealing with incoming impulses from sense objects observed.

A yogi should still resist these powerful image displays in the mind but he must train his kundalini energy and the senses which are offshoots of the kundalini, not to award high values to memories which pertain to the physical existence and to the lower astral realms. Some experiences impress upon the yogi in a forceful way so that no matter what, the yogi should turn away from accepting impressions from these sense objects.

One must admit if one is not strong enough to resist certain sensual delights or horrors. A yogi should not think that he can resist every reality. The truth is that some realities are irresistible because the limited self is infinitesimal not infinite. That is just fine. It is not a cause for embarrassment or negativity. The solution is to realize that there are objects which would supersede one's willpower. One should avoid these if they would have a negative impact on self-realization.

November 25, 2006

Reduction of use of intellect

Patanjali in the *Yoga Sutras* gave precise information about the intellect. He instructed that it should not be used. In the Bhagavad Gita the most of chapter two is about buddhi yoga which is the technique for bringing the intellect under control. Patanjali indicated that initially for kaivalyam or the understanding of what the observing self is, there must be a separation between that self and the intellect.

The intellect can provide supernatural and spiritual perception but it is unable to do so when it is attracted to the physical and lower astral realms.

The solution is to cease the reliance on the intellect. One has to meditate and habituate the self to not being entertained by it.

December 7, 2006

Dhyana compared to dharana

Dharana concerns making efforts to initiate and maintain a specific focus which is transcendental or which will lead to a transcendental dimension or location. It has effort as its method. As soon as the effort is eased, the focus slackens and the attention moves to something which is deviant from the objective.

Dhyana concerns a spontaneous contact with something or someone who is transcendental. It entails no effort. Instead it happens on its own and the yogi does not have to exert himself. In dhyana the focus continues and does not deviate to anything else. Dhyana may last for moments, minutes or more.

Dhyana or spontaneous contact does not occur when resistant energies are in the psyche. These energies suppress any affinity the person may have for transcendental realities, either as energies, environments or deities. Naad sound resonance absorption changes the texture of the psyche so its resistance to transcendental focus is reduced, making the psyche more capable of spontaneously reaching transcendence.

Part 4

Breath infusion value

Breath infusion should be directed to all parts of the psyche but in a systematic way and over a long period of daily kundalini yoga practice. First one should clear the sushumna central passage which is the middle of the spinal column.

That achievement is the stepping stone to expressing kundalini elsewhere in the psyche. It is not sufficient to clear the spinal column. All parts of the psyche should be infused with fresh energy. All pollutants should be attacked with fresh energy which comes into the psyche when doing pranayama breath infusion.

December 18, 2006

Yogi Bhajan + another kundalini yoga teacher

Yogi Bhajan said that after spinal kundalini is awakened consistently, one should do front kundalini. One should direct the energy through the front of the chest of the subtle body and not be concerned as before with getting it through the center of the spine into the head.

He said that this will eventually purify the memory chamber and cause the yogi to tap into the causal form.

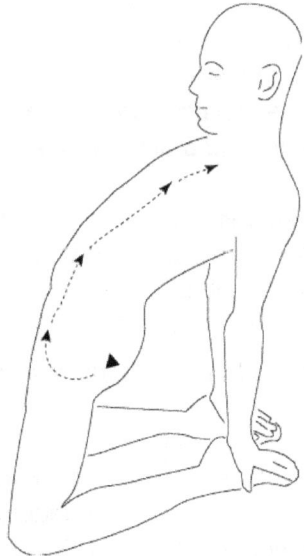

December 31, 2006

There may be a lack of success due to having an interest in others. This happens to student yogis who are trigger happy about helping others. Some persons are like this from day one, even from before they begin an ardent yoga practice under a capable teacher. Others develop a need to help others soon after practicing sincerely and getting desired results.

The student gets the feeling that he or she should share the teaching and method to others or that others should be introduced to the capable teacher. In either case if one switched to an interest in others and became reduced in self-development, one's practice will suffer. Spiritual progress will be incremental or nil.

Hearing and seeing channels

Once the student masters pratyahar sensual energy withdrawal, it becomes necessary to catalog the terrain of the mind. Initially the mind may seem to be one respondent energy with no parts as if it was one sensitive something which is the self. However after one turns inwards fully, one discovers that there are psychic adjuncts and an observing self in the mind. There is one essential self. Sometimes there may be more than one self in the mind. For instance a deity or a yoga guru may appear in the mind along with the one essential observing self.

The actions of the intellect are observed in the mind. These are not physical motions. These are psychic movements. The two primal senses in this observation are the hearing and seeing channels. These use many routes through psychic switching which is almost invisible. A yogi must sort these perception tools for clarity in knowing which adjunct operates in the production of mental architecture and emotional conjecture.

In meditation, the yogi must stand guard so that the intellect does not operate in its conventional way to construct mental images and sounds based on memory impressions and sensual input.

The energy which is used to help others should be back-traced to its latent form in the psyche so that it can be stopped before its spreads its influence through the mind. Many energies manifest as impulsive tendencies after they develop in the mind. Before they are developed they can be controlled. However perceiving them before they expand into ideas and images is difficult because of their abstraction in the mind.

The energy which one uses to help others is a small orb of energy in the psyche. It should be controlled in its minute form when it first arises. It cannot be controlled once it expands and expresses a forceful influence which becomes the desire of the self.

January 2, 2007

Naad influence

Naad is a necessary influence in higher meditation. A yogin must take help from naad instead of hanging out in a voidal state without a sense of direction. One may spend millions of year in a voidal state, going nowhere and doing absolutely nothing. At the end of that period one will find the self in a realm which demands social participation.

I recommend that one stick with naad, become absorbed in it because that will develop into chit akash penetration which will give one access to a spiritual dimension or to the highest astral existences.

Physical social involvement carries with it traumatic returns which are scary and which cause one to think that it is best to be in a personless place without traumatic engagements. However one should accept my advice and take to naad sound resonance where one can wait for access to the chit akash sky of consciousness, a place where adverse traumas do not and cannot occur.

At first naad is found in a zone which penetrates into the self, into the psyche. The observing self should enter into that zone and become absorbed in it. As this develops naad will spread through the psyche so that no part of the psyche is without the influence of naad sound resonance. This will lead to sky of consciousness access.

January 15, 2007

Attention identification

It is necessary to sort between the coreSelf, the sense of identity, the attention energy and the intellect. This should be researched in meditation. There will be difficulty separating the coreSelf from the sense of identity and the sense of identity from the attention energy and that from the intellect, but it can be done.

First of all one should integrate the information I divulge so that one has a theoretical understanding of the coreSelf and the adjuncts which it relates to in the head of the subtle body.

First of all the coreSelf is perpetually surrounded on all sides by the sense of identity. This means that there will never be a time while one is in this cosmos when one will remove the sense of identity so that it is no longer spherically covering the core. It will continue to do so until the end of time. Only if one leaves this physio-astral cosmos will that separation occur in an ultimate sense. Still the core can transcend the sense of identity from time to time, even though that sense will be present in any case.

The sense of identity is a problem only when it is influenced by the intellect. Then it carries a prejudiced notion which the core is circumstantially forced to accept. Hence if a yogi can make the sense of identity be neutral in reference to the intellect, the identity will not hinder the core.

The attention is merely an offshoot, a ray that comes out of the sense of identity. It shoots in the direction of the intellect. It is the arm of the sense of identity which touches the intellect. This means that the attention is part of the sense of identity, which means that if the sense of identity is curbed, the attention is curbed as well.

The intellect is completely separate from the core. It does not surround the core on all sides like the sense of identity. It cannot directly relate to the core but it may do so by influencing the sense of identity.

The sense of identity is completely transparent. It is colorless. It is so translucent that it cannot hardly be seen. It can only be perceived in very advanced meditations. The intellect however is visible as its operations. When the intellect is out of commission it becomes invisible and is not seen. It should be accepted that the intellect is the first eye of the observing self. This is so because whatever is detected by any of the senses, is made known to the self by the intellect which uses sensual information to illustrate what was contacted.

To discover the attention, one should sit in a dark room, close the eyes, focus forward in the subtle head, and begin a sweeping action of interest in the mind from right to left. As soon as one begins this action cease doing it. Then begin another sweeping action from left to right. As soon as one begins this converse sweeping action cease it.

Do this repeatedly until one has a firm idea of the energy used to initiate the sweep? This energy is the attention energy.

Notice that it stars at about the existential middle of the head and its beam of energy continues from there to the front of the face sweeping right and then left.

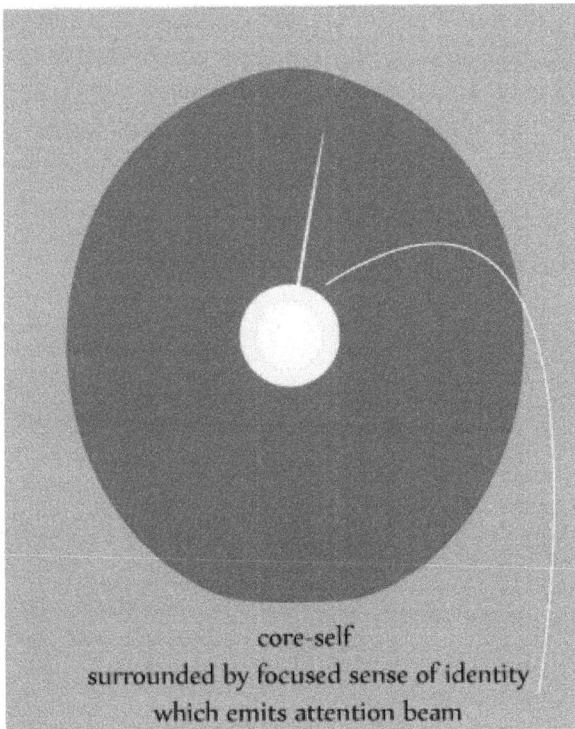

core-self
surrounded by focused sense of identity
which emits attention beam

January 16, 2007

Kundalini clearance

One cannot have consistent progress and full success in yoga unless one does kundalini yoga and clears the lifeForce of pollution. There will always be distractions and obstructions to progress if the kundalini has impurity in any part of its diverse system of energy distribution.

The intellect is so linked to the kundalini, and so reliant on its energy that if the kundalini has pollution the intellect just cannot function with full clarity. For this pranayama breath infusion is necessary because that is the efficient way to get the kundalini to release pollutants and absorb clean fresh astral energy to fuel its operations.

January 17, 2007

Toe tapping

One method for stimulating muladhar base chakra is to aggressively tap the toes on the ground while doing breath infusion. The toes and feet should be flat down in one session and the toes and feet should be up in the following series of breaths. The nerves and muscles in the toes have electrical routing to the base chakra. This practice is done on all fours.

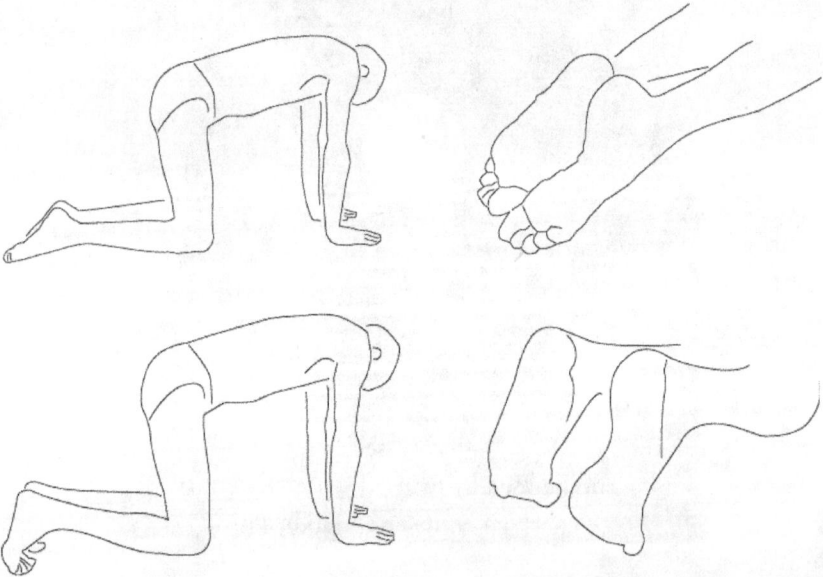

January 20, 2007

Reorientation of or conquest of the reproductive functions in the body is done by breath infusion with focus on the sexual organs hormone production and sexual intercourse urge, along with thigh subjugation. Even if a yogi gets the hormonal system in order, there will be a challenge to change the method of energy release of the thighs.

The thighs support the reproductive system. They are design by nature to assist in conveying plasma to embryos. This is good for continuing a species but it is a handicap for a yogi because the energy used by the thighs is part of the psyche. If that energy is not invested in giving attention to the spiritual objectives, it will contravene the aims of yoga.

Breath infusion into the thighs is the way to change the intention of the thighs. Breath infusion there surcharges the thighs with a non-lusty energy and causes release of energy instead of storage and transfer to the sex organs.

January 22, 2007

I entered a bliss yielding dimension where the negative traumas which are native to this material world are absent. There I saw a religious man who is in the Vaishnava society. These people do not do ashtanga yoga with postures and breath infusion. This particular person is involved in conniving to get money from rich people who are affiliated with their sect. There were many complaints about his attitude and methods.

However in that bliss yielding dimension, I notice that his subtle body had no vicious tendencies. He was amiable to everyone and did not consider anyone as a victim for his criminal methods which on earth he perpetrates under the guise of religion. Such people misuse the name of the deity by convincing the public that they need money to build, establish and maintain temples in various ways. The truth is that it has nothing to do with the temple or the deity. It has everything to do with their need to exploit others.

Still we should consider how it is possible for this person who is a vicious religious person on earth, to be in a higher dimension where his vicious nature is completely absent. How is that possible?

Obviously it means that the subtle body which he uses while he is in the physical form has the vicious system as its potential. In combination of his coreSelf and that vicious system, he displays a criminal mentality which is disguised as religious service. Why does he not resist or leave aside the vicious potential of the lower phases of the subtle body?

That is a question which is worth pondering.

To establish the self as a righteous person on earth, the core has to resist the potential of the lower subtle and physical systems. What the core lacks is the resistance whereby it would not contribute itself to the vicious actions or at least reduce its contribution to an absolute minimum.

If one does not have the resistance, if one cannot generate that, then one should take help from deities and from yoga gurus. By all means because of the danger of lower transmigrations in predatory species of life, one must somehow or the other move away from the vicious lifestyle, even the disguised criminal behavior which passes as religious acts.

Since we have the potential for being criminal, it is important that we rely on those physical and psychic associations which encourage and promote righteous conduct.

January 28, 2007

Sleep

Sleep is one of the involuntary psychic operations which must be regulated and minimized. It is not possible to rid the self of it altogether but its stupefying aspect must be curtained by the yogi.

Patanjali listed sleep as one of the hindrances to deep meditation. Since it cannot be eliminated, one must supervise it. It should not be expressed from the psyche during meditation sessions.

A yogi should regard sleep as a set of dimensions in which the coreSelf loses objectivity on the physical side and gains or does not gain objectify on the astral level. Breath infusion is the method for decreasing the amount of sleep energy in the psyche. The more pollution there is in the subtle body, the more tendency for sleeping increases and the more stupefied the coreSelf becomes when it is under the influence of the intellect.

January 27, 2007

Domain entry

Before the coreSelf can enter or be cognizant of certain dimensions or domains it must have certain accessories with it. In fact it must have access to certain sensory equipment for perceptions of physical or psychic objects in various environments.

If it enters a domain and does not have the appropriate sensing connections, it may develop what is necessary by remaining in the domain and being subjected to the means of developing the required senses. We experienced this while developing the embryo in the mother's passage. To perceive physical objects, one has to have a physical body with suitable senses. The same process is required in subtle existence, in the astral world and beyond.

January 29, 2007

Dissipating chambers

I discovered three dissipating chambers. These hang like cauldrons. The subtle hormonal energy in these can be dissipated by doing breath infusion and directing the energy to compress, implode and explode.

The reproduction reservoir is the first to tackle. This one takes support from gravity and from the thighs and buttocks. By the grace of gravity, this reservoir gets energy from the digestive system. It concentrates this energy to produce reproductive fluids which are used to create sperm, ovary and embryo. In the process of its use, one may enjoy its electric fluctuations as sexual pleasure. These are electric movements which the mind may interpret as pleasure or as acute sensations which are overwhelming.

thought energy reservoir

digestive reservoir

reproduction reservoir

When doing kundalini yoga using kapalabhati/bhastrika pranayama breath infusion, a yogi will tackle these reservoirs in the effort to ignite them in the subtle plane. The infused compressed energy uses them as targets where they implode and explode alternately. They are reconstructed again and again until after much practice they are eliminated one by one in the subtle body. First the reproduction reservoir is eliminated, then the digestive one and then at last the thought energy zone. Usually it takes years of practice to achieve this.

Advice for others

Especially in social matters, a yogi should not be eager to advise others. He should be confident that no matter what this social situation can go on just fine without him. Students who are gung ho about advising others and who hawk themselves and the teacher about it, are under a pressure of the

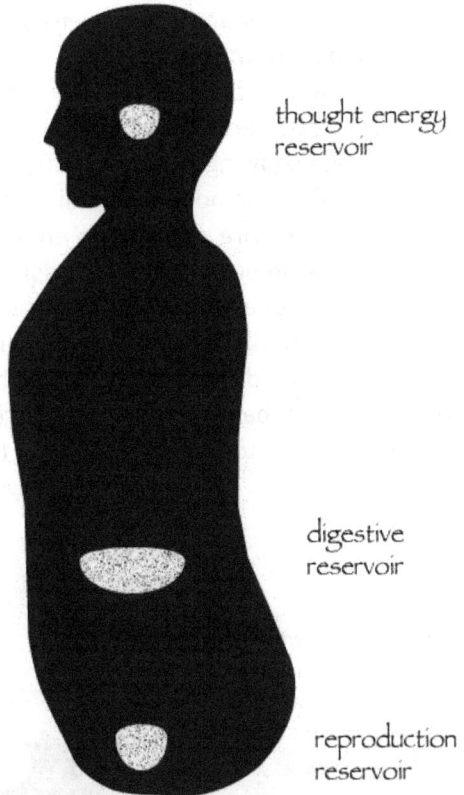

passionate energy of nature. They feel that they initiated the urge to help others but they are hypnotized by the passion energy and have no idea that they are impulsively driven. They lack the insight to understand how nature grabs the coreSelf and used its energy to sponsors nature's concerns which are of no benefit to the core.

Entertainers do hasty performances or quick dances on a stage. The audience for its part, do not participate except by looking. Because the actors on the stage show agile movements, the audience identify with the displays even though their bodies sit still and get no exercise while sitting there. Similarly those core selves who endorse passionate energy movements in their minds gain nothing from the actions. In fact instead of getting a benefit they lose vital energy but with no insight into how that occurs, they derive a false confidence in thinking that they are beneficiaries.

A yogi should stand apart and not be engaged in passionate movements. He should step back and look at nature's operations so that he understand how it functions to motivate the core to contribute its energies for nature's operations.

Feb 11, 2007

Savituh gayatri mantra

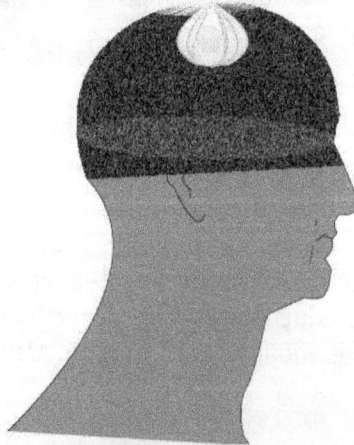

Yogeshwarananda suggested using the Savituh gayatri mantra at the brahmrandra crown chakra globe, while avoiding the frontal part of the subtle head. He said that constant repetition of this mantra at that place is beneficial and would accelerate efforts to gain chit akash access. He said that the actor part of the intellect should be engaged in mentally saying the mantra there. This actor part interferes with meditation but if it is engaged it can be made to help the objective.

Yogesh said that a horse in a paddock must be taken on walks, trots and runs for a certain minimum exercise. When the mind apparatus is disciplined, the ascetic must study its real needs and provide some minimum guided fulfillments.

The mind has a passivity and an activity feature. During some meditation if one recognizes that both features operate, one should direct them to assist the meditation. If on the other hand, one engages the passive side or the active side and does not engage its converse, that other feature may interrupt the meditation.

February 13, 2007

Boredom with naad

If one becomes bored listening to naad or if naad seems to be a nuisance sound, that is an indication that one is not seasoned in advanced meditation and one's mind is habituated to thinking and imaging excitements from the physical and lower astral environments.

Naad is nourishment for advanced yogis. Their access to it occurs on a higher level where it is enriching to the psyche. If possible one should do breath infusion before meditating because that process will upgrade the energy of the subtle body and cause one to enter meditation from a higher plane of consciousness and one which is resistant to lower vibrations and which does not crave lower excitements.

The intellect which hungers for lower excitements cannot appreciation naad. It may dislike naad or feel depressed or bored because naad offers nothing like the excitement it gets from sensual intake and memory stimulation. And yet, if a yogi forcibly indulges the intellect in naad, over time naad will become pleasant and desirable.

Nandi

Nandi is the bull which carries Shiva. He is a great devotee of Shiva and gives instruction to submissive yogis who regard him as a deity. He told me not to worry about my upkeep, that he would arrange everything. No matter the circumstances, he suggested that I should continue the practice in a quiet way.

He said this:

"Do not try to force time and circumstance. Do not tamper with the onward progress of this situation. Everything will occur according to the needs of the material nature. There will be opportunities now and again. The focus for you would be to leave aside or take the risks involved."

Elementals who obstruct yogis

A yogi will suffer setbacks from time to time. A yogi may see elemental beings who life in subterranean astral dimensions and who emit energies which cause social complications or cause the mind to assume a low level of energy which deters meditation.

Much must be tolerated by a yogin but he should persists and not hold grudges against anyone, not even against persons who blatantly do things which upset or degrade the practice.

Yogeshwarananda

He showed this meditation:

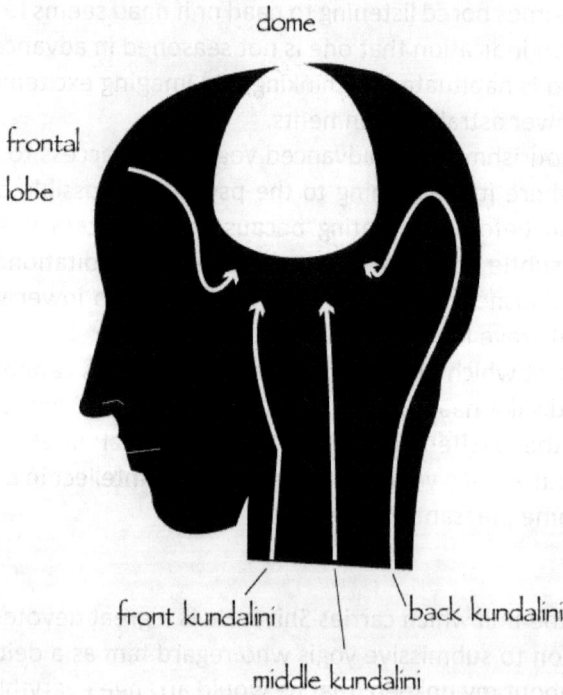

dome

frontal
lobe

front kundalini   middle kundalini   back kundalini

February 14, 2007

Yogeshwarananda

In his view, the memory is curbed by the clarified upgraded kundalini which was treated with breath infusion energy.

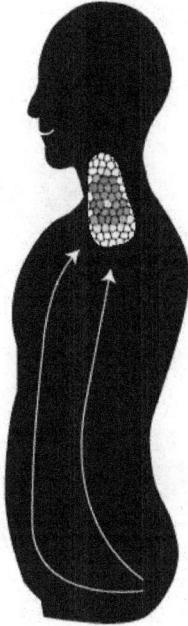

Patanjali earmarked the memory as one of the five upsets in the mind of a yogi. It releases charged impressions which penetrate and infest the intellect, which in turns attracts the attention of the coreSelf. During meditation a yogi may be fatigued making several attempts to do assigned focuses but the intellect as it is assaulted by memory impressions, does not cooperate and instead sabotages the efforts.

The yogi must find a way of reducing the intercourse between the memory and the intellect. If he fails to do so, he will never be absorbed deeply as required for advanced practice.

February 15, 2007

Yogeshwarananda

In his presence I experienced a bright white torchlight, which entered the psyche from the left temple. This light which was intense lasted only for ten seconds. However these experiences though fleeting have significance as they permit entry into the chit akash sky of consciousness and renders transcendence experience of supernormal atmospheres.

This was an overwhelming blast of transcendental energy which had a sustaining life-giving perpetual feeling.

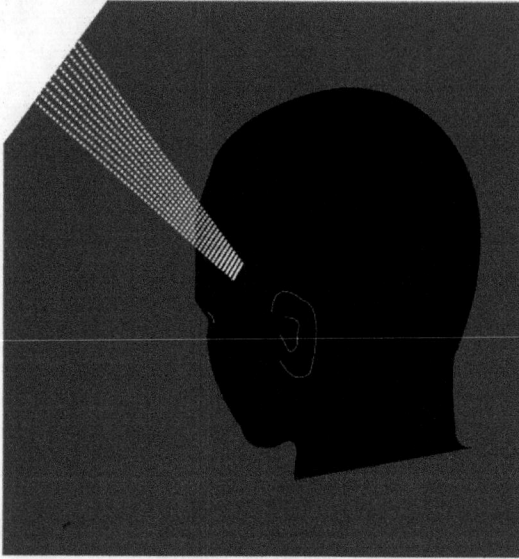

February 16, 2007

Whole Body Kundalini

Whole body kundalini movements are hard to attain but it can be done after one mastered spinal kundalini rises into the head consistently over a period of years. The creation of an embryo means yielding to the style of the kundalini in terms of what it does for the creation of a new lifeform. Hence a yogi must retrain the system so that the primal urges and methods are disabled.

This requires the use of breath infusion because the kundalini's mainstay for energy is breath. In a material body, breath is subsidized by diet. Nevertheless even though food is necessary, breath has priority. Feelings as emotions or as sensations is the main current produced by the actions of kundalini. In a way, the kundalini may be controlled by controlling the feelings and emotions, except that is more theoretical than practical. Kundalini produces feelings which the mind interprets to be pleasant, unpleasant or neutral sensations. To create feelings the coreSelf must use the intellect but since the intellect is partial towards the kundalini, it will only cooperate if it senses that the interest of the kundalini is being promoted. Hence feelings is not a reliable way to control the kundalini.

Breath infusion is the method. During such action when the charged energy targets kundalini successfully, there will arise feelings of a higher grade which the core can control by using special muscular contractions and mental pressures.

See the diagram below where the kundalini functions for the entire trunk of the subtle body. That energy as one complex spread of bliss feelings rises through the trunk. It rises through the neck and goes into the brahmrandra crown chakra.

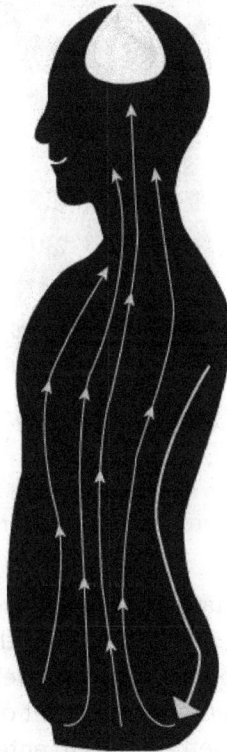

February 18, 2007

Kundalini in trunk of body

This diagram below shows a spread of kundalini which instead of originating at the base muladhar chakra at the base of the spine, comes from the sexual energy reservoir. The reproductive energy is accumulated in the body. Then it is discharged in sexual intercourse or masturbation. This same energy may be used to fire kundalini through the trunk of the body. Using breath infusion a yogi can arouse this energy so that it does not go to the spinal passage but instead ascends through the trunk of the subtle body.

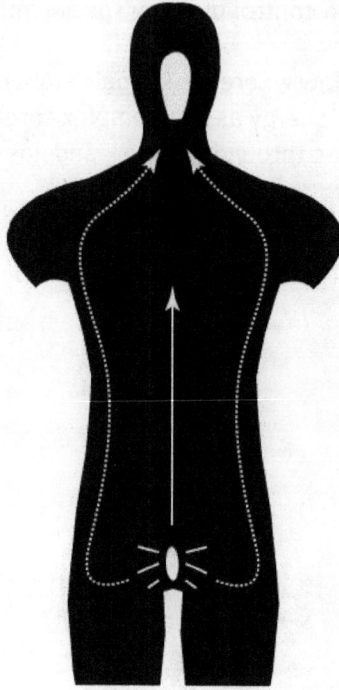

kundalini from
reproductive reservoir

In the diagram below, kundalini energy rises through the trunk of the body from the sex reservoir in the center of the body and from the base chakra muladhar. From the base chakra it travels through the center of the spine and also through the center of the front of the body. When it reaches into the head it goes up and then ascends to enter the crown chakra complex from its bottom.

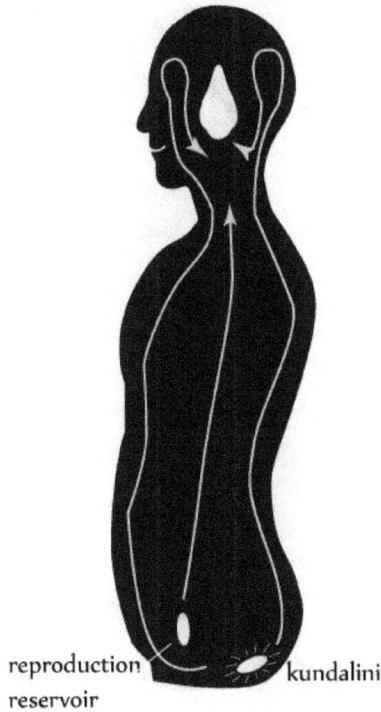

reproduction   kundalini
reservoir

February 19, 2007

Diverting kundalini

There are many methods for diverting kundalini from the central spinal column. Below is a diagram with a method used for dealing wIth internal chaos in the trunk of the subtle body. One can divert the kundalini by giving it mental commands and emotional pulls during breath infusion, so that it travels in other parts of the body, targeting organs or muscle bunches or zones which have compact polluted subtle energy which should be removed from the psyche.

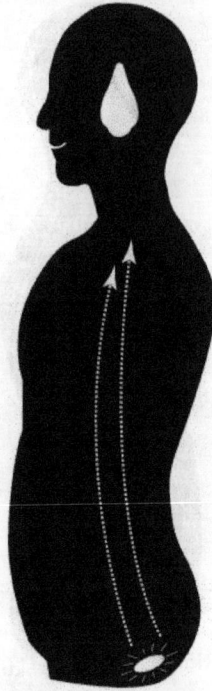

diverting kundalini
from sushumna nadi
central spinal passage

February 27, 2007

Sleep impulse reduction

Of the mental processes which should be eliminated during meditation, the sleep impulsive is the most subtle and most difficult one to bring to term. While other negative processes of the mind and emotions may be dealt with head on, the sleep impulse approaches the coreSelf from behind, which makes it difficult to perceive much less reform.

The four other impediments of emotional and mental process are right analysis, wrong analysis, imagination and memory. These four are illustrated by the intellect only. That means that by studying their intellectual operations one may restrict them, either to reduce or eliminate them, at least during the time set for meditation.

The sleep impulse is different. It is not illustrated by the intellect except as a demonstration of drowsiness and stupor, states which rob the self of objectivity. Since the sleep impulse applies itself to the intellect by dumbing down insight and perception, it is not easy to bring this impulse under control.

A yogi should use breath infusion to target the sleep collector location which is near to the muladhar base chakra on the inside of the body. This infusement would draw out some of the dulling energy and cause the sleep impulse to be relieved of dark astral force, replacing that with fresh subtle energy.

The yogi should adjust his or her lifestyle so that the sleep impulse is kept to a minimum. Eating habits should be upgraded. The time of eating should be meticulously monitored and enforced. Prompt evacuation should be done. The physical body should get sufficient rest and at the right time of day and night.

The sleep impulse cannot be eliminated but it can be fine-tuned for more efficient operation. It should be absent during the meditation practice. If one finds that it asserts itself during meditation, one should check to be sure that the physical system is getting sufficient rest, that the time of eating and evacuating are conducive for yoga and that breath infusion is complete during each session.

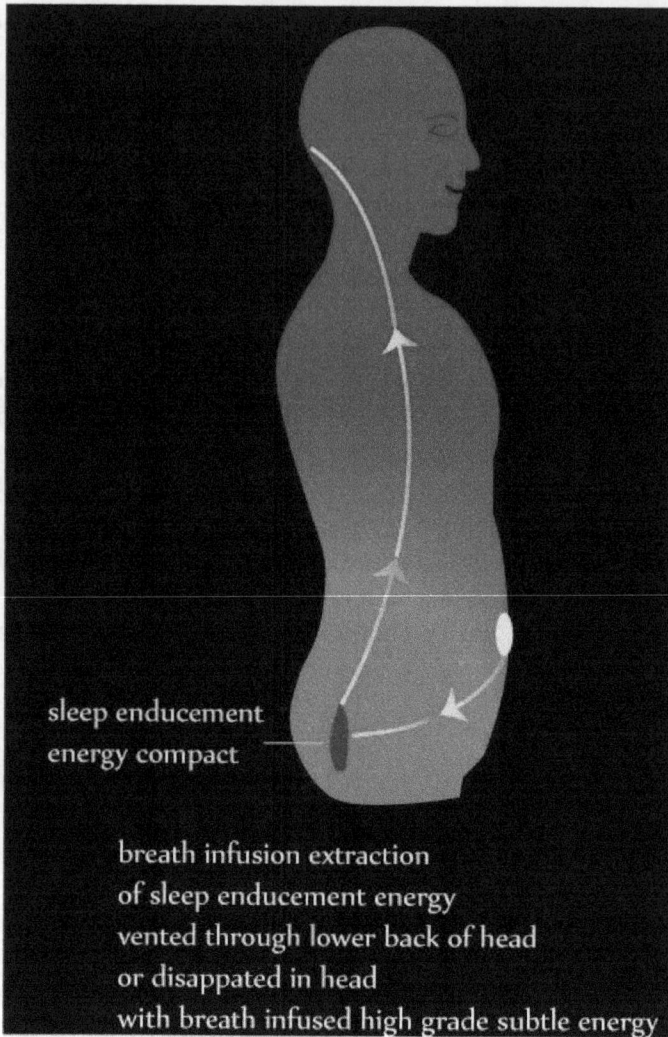

sleep enducement
energy compact

breath infusion extraction
of sleep enducement energy
vented through lower back of head
or disappated in head
with breath infused high grade subtle energy

Gender body

Each yogi has a gender body which may be confused with the sex-reproduction body. The gender body yields a neutral bliss energy and is not charged with a lust polarity force. The sex body is highly charged with bio-electric energy which is polarized as a lust force and which is not a neutral bliss energy.

The yogi should shift attention from the sex-reproduction form to the gender body, so that the interest in sexual linking and expression becomes foregone. A tremendous amount of energy is used in sexual linkage. This energy should be invested in meditative focus on naad sound resonance and supernatural light. A lack of increased focus on transcendence will inevitably mean that the yogi will again take an embryo and be subjected to reproductive needs.

March 8, 2007

LifeForce redirection

The lifeForce has its own interest. It controls most of the emotional and mental operations in the average person. A yogi by doing kundalini yoga day after day gains proficiency in diverting the lifeForce from its habits which are counterproductive to yoga and which causes the ascetic to act in ways which cause failure in practice.

The highlight of the lifeForce is sexual pleasure experience. A yogi should change this so that the main interest is kundalini arousal up through the spine into the head of the subtle body, or up through the trunk into the neck and head of the subtle body.

By all means the lifeForce should be lifted and motivated to move away from the muladhar base chakra but it should move upwards. It should be subjected to naad influence. It should abandon lower sound pursuits.

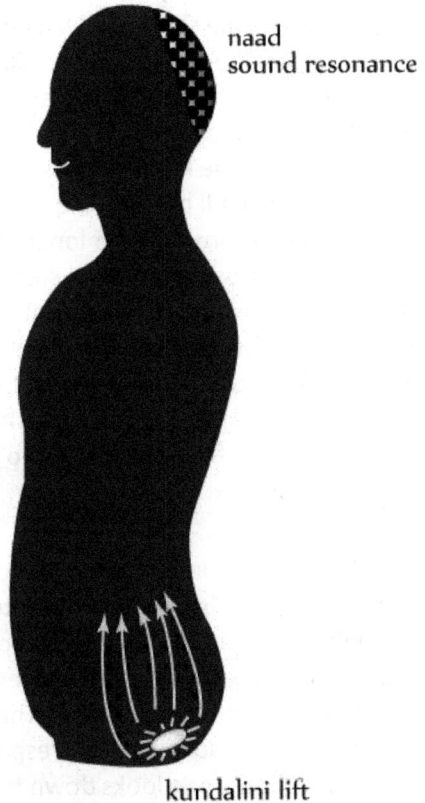

naad
sound resonance

kundalini lift

March 9, 2007

Kundalini reconfiguration

Kundalini must be reconfigured in various ways. As one proceeds and masters kundalini lifeForce so that it has free passage through the sushumna nadi central spinal passage, one will be inspired to cause kundalini to become elevated in every part of the subtle body. The clearance of the spinal passage may be considered to be the beginning of the process of elevating every part of the subtle body.

The necessity of clearing the subtle body is understood by a yogi who understands that so long as he or she transmigrates in various physical bodies and in various subtle dimensions, he or she will use the same subtle body either in an upgraded, mediocre or degraded state. It is in the interest of the yogi to elevate the subtle body. If he becomes liberated from the physical and psychic mundane existence, he will have no concern about the subtle form but if he fails in that bid, he has every concern to be sure that the subtle body is in the highest possible configuration.

As soon as the kundalini has consistent access so that it can flow through the sushumna nadi passage the shape of the subtle body changes into that of a bubble body format. It no longer has the spinal configuration. It no longer has a need to be in creature survival physical bodies which are produced though a form of sexual or asexual reproduction. It is not easy to abandon the reproduction orientation but it can be done by those who master kundalini yoga and keep practicing ardently. In the bubble body the kundalini is present as the bottom node. It along with the brahmrandra crown chakra illuminates the bubble body from the inside. No part of that form has heavy astral energy.

Kundalini divert

More and more, as one practices kundalini arousal and is successful in routing out the sushumna nadi central spinal passage and the crown chakra, one will be inspired in higher processes which include other parts of the subtle body besides its spinal route and head. There is a bubble body which has no limbs extending from it. This is a super-subtle form which is higher than the subtle body which corresponds to the physical form.

In that body, one looks down from the top of it and perceives sheer light energy which shines down from the coreSelf and shines up from where the muladhar base chakra was.

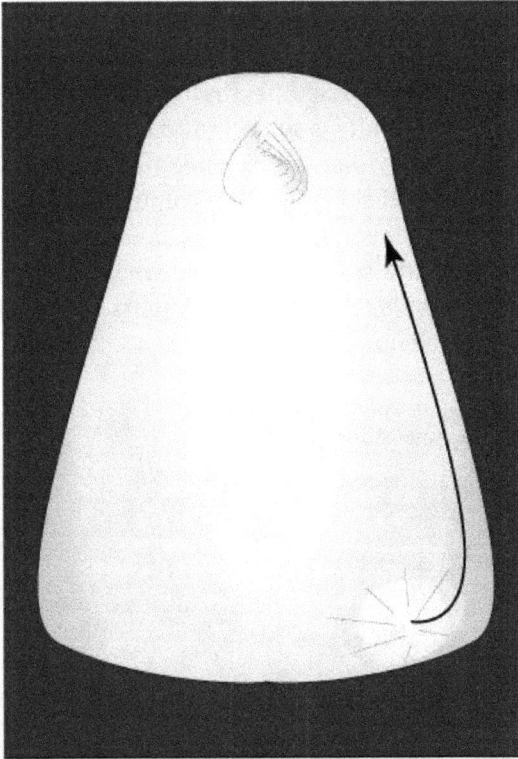

bubble body with core-self at top
and muladhar light at bottom

black arrow is previous path
through sushumna nadi central passage

March 10, 2007

I researched and can confirm by meditation that there are two primary operations in the psyche. These are:

- intellect communication to the senses
- kundalini direction to the senses

The kundalini is involved in directing the senses. The kundalini manufactured the senses. Hence the senses are loyal to the kundalini more than they are to anything else.

The senses are involved in supplying information to the intellect. The senses do this as prompted by the kundalini. The value of the intellect to the kundalini is that the intellect influences the sense of identity which in turn prompts the coreSelf to permit the release of energy for the operations of the intellect.

The mistake of the coreSelf is that it assumes responsibility for everything the sense of identity is subjected to by the intellect. The coreSelf needs to break away from the sense of identity so that it can be more objective and can check the intellect's recommendations rather than be induced to endorse whatever the intellect presents. The core needs to increase its perception rate so that it can see what the adjuncts do in slow motion, otherwise the rapidity of their movements will cause the core to be ill-informed and to be hypnotized.

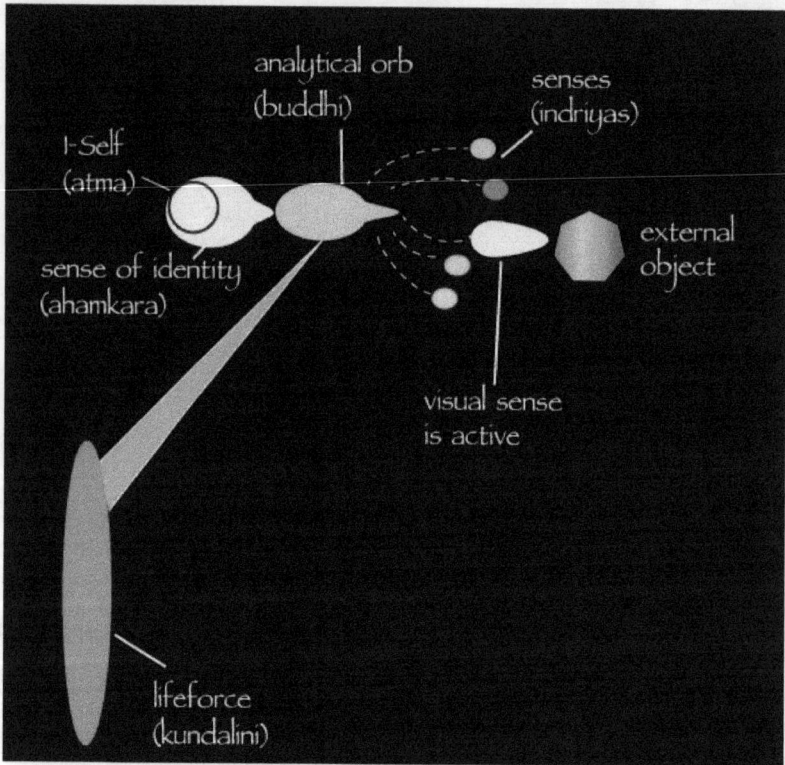

The lifeForce is individualized such that there are variations in behavior however slight between one person and another. Initially a lifeForce attached itself to a certain I-self, sense of identity and intellect. It remains with that I-self as if it were permanently glued to it, the way barnacles remain attached to the hull of a ship. As the vessel cannot remove the barnacles so the I-self has difficulty perceiving, what to speak of removing, the lifeForce. However by meditation, it becomes possible to break the adhesive which causes the lifeForce to be attached to the intellect.

A yogi must understand that the adhesion occurs between the lifeForce and the intellect. There is no direct connection between the lifeForce and the coreSelf. For that matter even the intellect is not directly connected to the coreSelf. The intellect is connected to the sense of identity which surrounds the core. These clarifications need be made in meditation. The insight derived from this gives the yogi the power to organize the psyche in a way which is conducive to advanced meditation.

Sushumna nadi

Sushumna nadi is essential so long as one has a subtle body with limbs and senses. Beyond such a form there is the bubble body which is filled with the highest type of subtle energy and which is resplendent. The bubble body has no limbs. It has no chakra configuration like that of the subtle form. It is a bliss body but the energy is neutral and transcendental. It expresses no desire. It does not endeavor for anything.

March 13, 2007

Yogeshwarananda

I recalled living with a young woman when I was in the Philippines during 1971. The memory emerged from a memory chamber without being requested. Yogesh realized the memory as well because he was in my psyche when it arose. Since I had a feeling to review it, he criticized that action saying that such memories should be ignored because otherwise any interest causes reinforcement which strengthens their power and sets the stage for link completion in a future life.

Once one has a memory and one reviews it, the material nature regards that as reinforcement. It creates a basis for future circumstances where one can further develop the relationship which concerns the memory. Yogesh felt that this is suicidal for a yogin.

Part 5

Lahiri

From another dimension, he repeated this date, March 10, 1929. He said this thrice as a date either of the death of a previous body or a levitation experience in a previous body. The body rose from the ground and went upward while I had an imagination orb focus.

Lahiri wanted to remove doubts which I had about the physical body levitating. It is possible to levitate the physical body but currently yogis do not do enough practice to make this happen. In past lives I did this. I experienced my physical form from a past life doing this.

Realization about wealth

Becoming wealthy by good or criminal methods does not solve cultural complications. It does not absolve one from having to do menial services. For instance a wealthy man who has a consequential energy where he should do menial service for someone else should not pay another person to do that service. If he does so, it does not absolve him from that service. In fact he compounds the obligation so that in the future fate will put in him in a position where regardless of having money or lacking it, he will have to complete the menial work plus a penalty for assigning someone to do it previously.

A yogi should never think that if he got more money, his problems will be solved. Here on earth it is service to another person which removes obligations not wealth. One cannot buy out one's debt to someone where one owed that person menial service. It cannot be done.

Naad assistance

Naad sound resonance is the great inner assistant to a yogi. It is free of charge and does not require any more endeavor but to locate and be absorbed in it. As soon as the intellect attempts to form an opinion, illustrate a memory or appropriate some sense information, the yogi should turn to naad, listen and be absorbed in it. This is an effective method of curbing the intellect so that the intellect can no longer continue distracting the yogi and putting a damper on deep meditation.

Chin lock

Chin lock should be with an erect neck with the chin pulled back to compress the throat. Chin lock should not be with a bent-forward neck or a hunched back and forward curved neck. The inverse lock is a neck lock with chin all the way up and head curved back as far as possible. This is an effective neck lock.

When moving from the inverse neck lock to the chin lock a yogi should be attentive in the mind so that the kundalini does not express itself haphazardly. There should be no relaxation of the muscles when moving from the inverse neck lock to the chin lock.

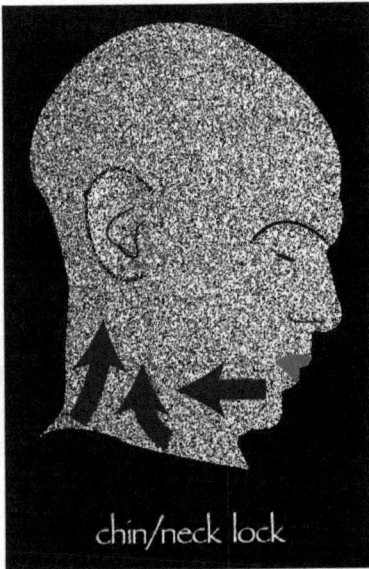

chin/neck lock

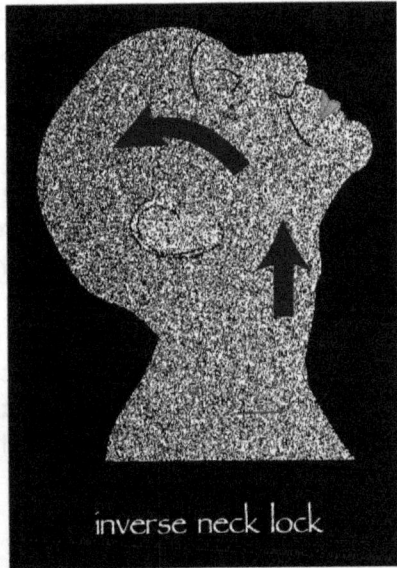

inverse neck lock

Chin lock is important when doing kapalabhati/bhastrika pranayama. It allows the yogi to control how kundalini ascends through the neck into the brain. The aroused kundalini should be forced to use the central sushumna passage as it ascends into the brain. It should not take a haphazard route. The coreSelf should be vigilant to be sure that it does not lose sight of the surcharged energy and that the energy is suppressed or channeled as intended.

Kundalini/naad hit

Kundalini could be retrained to target naad in the back of the subtle head. Usually kundalini avoids the back of head. Its convention is to influence the intellect. Kundalini takes help from the intellect to better influence the coreSelf for endorsing the creature survival actions which kundalini deems to be necessary in the struggle for existence.

When a yogi diverts kundalini from expressing itself through the chakras on the spinal column, the kundalini refrains from the chakras on the spine. Instead it moves through the spine, while ignoring the chakras. It moves through the neck into the brain. There is a moment or a few moments of hesitation when kundalini first enters the brain. This happens for a split second which even the coreSelf may not perceive. In that time, the kundalini determines where the intellect is located in the head of the subtle body. It then moves in a flash to strike the intellect. Sometimes it strikes the coreSelf in its attack on the intellect. This may happen if the core is located before the intellect where the kundalini finds that it cannot reach the intellect except by moving through the coreSelf.

When this happens the core finds itself to be by itself in a bright translucent light which is transparent. This may be crystal colored or gold colored. It has a bliss feeling either intensely sensual or neutral in pleasure yield.

After arousing kundalini day after day for a time, a yogi can learn how to direct it to the naad sound resonance instead of allowing it to hit the intellect. It is important that the yogi causes the aroused kundalini to travel through all parts of the subtle body. This is achieved after months or years of practice, day after day painstakingly.

core-self

intellect

naad sound

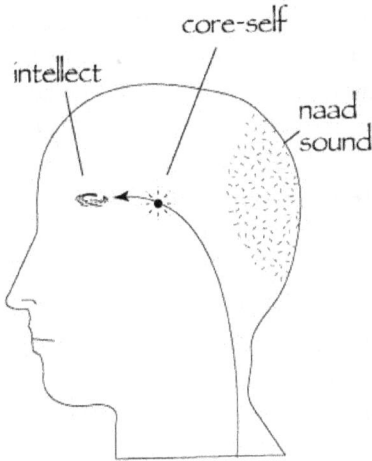

kundalini hits core-self
as it targets intellect

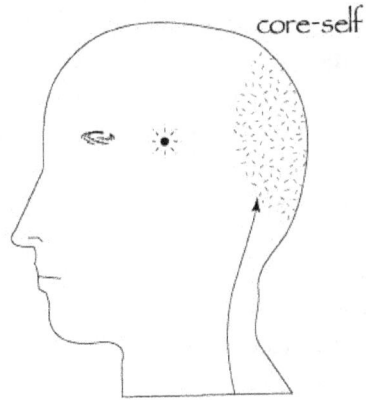

core-self

kundalini piloted to naad,
showing no interest in intellect

March 24, 2007

Limit of intellect display power

The intellect is involved in four functions which contravene higher yoga. These are:

- correct analysis
- erroneous analysis
- imagination
- processing of memory

For each of these to be enacted, the intellect must take help from the kundalini. It also needs help from the sense of identity which has access to a constant supply of energy from the coreSelf. There is a miniscule amount of energy flowing between the coreSelf and the adjuncts which include the intellect, memory and kundalini but that small amount of energy is insufficient for completion of intellect operations. The intellect can begin an operation but it cannot complete one unless it gets attentive energy from the coreSelf.

Because the intellect requires special input of energy from the core to develop and complete operations, the core is in a position to reform the intellect. It can bring the intellect under control.

The operations of correct and erroneous analysis once started by the intellect subside into nothing unless the intellect can procure energy from the core for further development. To encourage the core in making the donation, the intellect exposes the sense of identity to a flash of information. The sense of identity has the flaw of curiosity. Because it needs to satisfy the sense of curiosity, it uses its energy to finance the development of the idea. This causes the full blown display in the mind.

The coreSelf cannot directly give energy to the intellect. It can only do so indirectly by working through the sense of identity. Hence the core has to control its relationship to the sense of identity. Any effort the core makes to directly handle the intellect may be misplaced and will result in failure. However if the core notices that the sense of identity is eager to satisfy its curiosity about an idea of the intellect, the core can stop the flow of energy from itself to the identity. This will cause the intellect to immediately cease the operation.

A yogi must be willing to do this over and over in meditation. Eventually this will occur effortlessly and higher meditation will be a constant possibility for that ascetic.

Imagination occurs with or without memory input, where the intellect begins a construction of something novel. It uses energy from previous memories or from recent or current sensual information. As soon as it begins an operation, it sends for contributory energy from the sense of identity. Again because of the curiosity flaw in the sense of identity, that adjunct is likely to induce the core to contribute energy based on a promise or hope for fulfillment. The core for its part may be duped by this operation but when a yogi meditates, he eventually realizes that this procedure of mind is repeated again and again and that he should indulge the psyche in this no longer. He should as soon as there is a request or even as soon as the core detects that there will be a request, not give permission to the identity to continue a contribution.

The process of memory is done by the intellect. The memories are either current ones which are recently formed, past ones from this life which are stored in the subconscious energy or long past ones from previous lives which are lodged deep in the subconscious as predispositions and instincts. When these move into the intellect they trigger operations for full development but the intellect cannot complete this without getting contributory energy from the sense of identity. Here again the core may stop the identity from trying to fulfill its curiosity.

The intellect is directly fueled by the kundalini. It has an ongoing involuntary relationship with the kundalini, such that from behind it is motivated to meet the needs of the kundalini and to produce justifications for the kundalini's decisions.

The coreSelf should study this relationship between the kundalini and the intellect. It is necessary to understand in slow motion how these adjuncts interact. Their love affair, their water-tight relationship must be understood by the core through internal observation and detailed study.

The senses are offshoots of the kundalini but their sensibility is funded by the intellect. Hence one should not make the mistake into thinking that the senses are offshoots of the intellect. They are offshoot or developments which bud out from the kundalini but their precision and inspection abilities come from the intellect which transmits to them those abilities.

Because the senses are offshoots of the kundalini, the way flowers are offshoots of a plant, the control of the senses concerns the kundalini and not the intellect. Some yogis teach that the control of the intellect will give sense control but this is untrue. It is a fact however that the control of the intellect greatly limits the functionality and spread of the sensual influences. They continue but their position is weakened if the intellect is restricted.

To really control the senses one has to treat the kundalini lifeForce. Because the lifeForce cannot be wished away, the solution for its control is not termination but elevation. As soon as the yogi elevates the energy which the kundalini uses, that adjunct behaves in a way which facilities the yogic aims of the self. Then the senses do likewise because they are outcrops from the kundalini. Mastery of kundalini is mastery of the senses just as control of the soil which feeds a plant is a sure way of controlling the vegetation.

Pranayama breath infusion is a definite method for upgrading the energy of the kundalini. Once this is done, the kundalini will influence the intellect in a way which facilities yoga. For that matter it will cause the intellect to manifest supernatural and spiritual perception, insights which will help the coreSelf to better define itself as a spiritual being.

April 4, 2007

Intellect weight

The impure low energy intellect is heavy in mental weight. It becomes lighter and lighter, with more insightful energy when the kundalini is surcharged with fresh breath energy. It becomes light-weight and can be lifted easily. Or it seems to disappear and does not generate images or ideas based on sensual input and memory. During meditation it ceases activity and does not be a nuisance to the yogi.

On occasion in its purified state, the intellect converts into a supernatural/spiritual vision tool which allows perception into the supernatural or spiritual environments.

When a yogi arouses kundalini day after day for some months or years, his sushumna nadi central spinal passage remains cleared of heavy astral energy. This causes clairvoyance and clairaudience to be continuous for the yogi. However he does not reveal this to others. He remains silent and uses the higher information to promote advancement. The insight gained is useful for mapping the dimensions, treating the psyche for elevation to higher realms, reaching deities and better complying with the instruction of yoga teachers.

The yogi gets the insight that other parts of the psyche must be cleared of subtle pollutions. He realizes that he has no time to engage in teaching others. He needs the energy to assist himself, to qualify for higher association and to reach superior beings in higher dimensions.

April 20, 2007

Naad clarity

Naad sound resonance has various frequencies according to the condition of energy in the mind. When the mind is filled with higher subtle energy, naad is more pleasing and its absorption results in higher states of awareness. When the kundalini is aroused and consist of a high subtle energy charge, naad is clearer, more definite, more pleasant, and is encouraging of higher meditation.

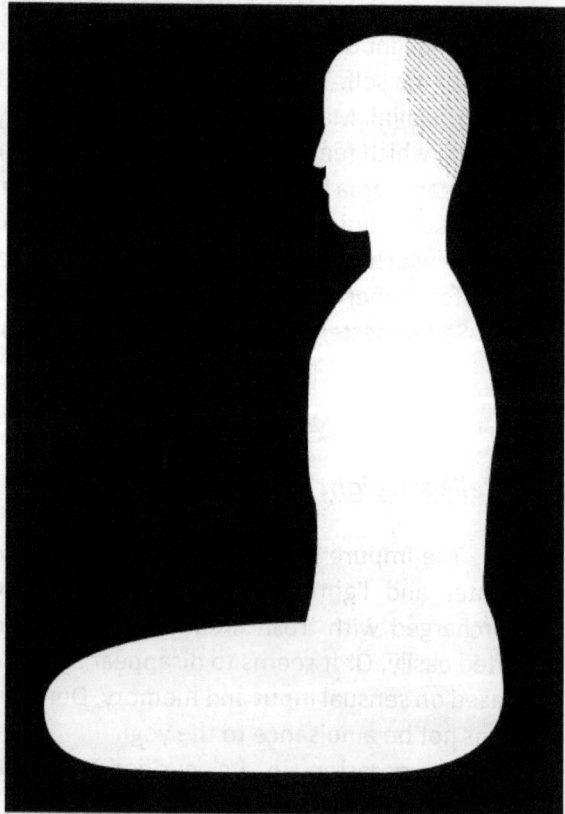

naad sound resonance in back of subtle head

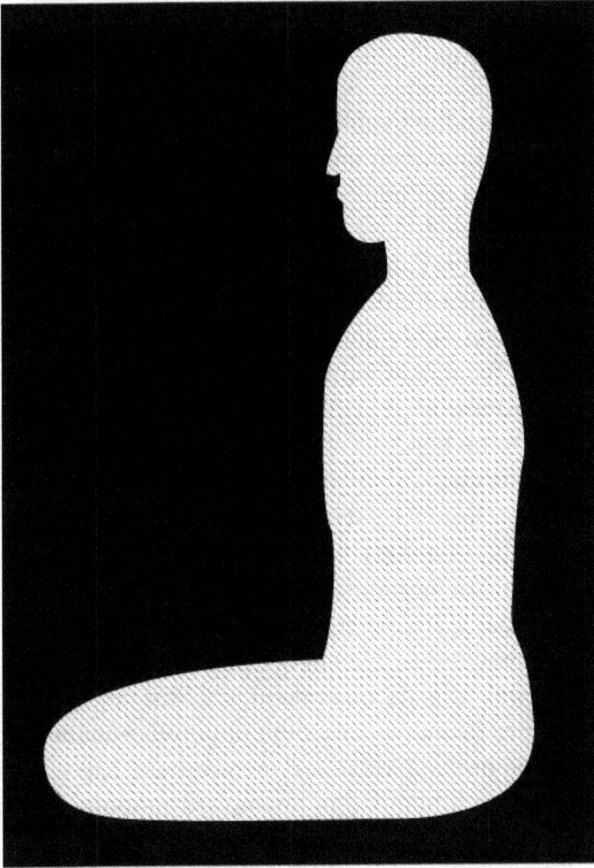

naad sound resonance in entire subtle body

Intellect addiction

The intellect is by nature addicted to receiving promptings from the kundalini. These are transmitted to it through feelings or sensual imaging. In either case emotions are the electricity which convey the information. A yogi should take the time in meditation to study this transmission system. Then he can take steps to terminate some of it and to orient the intellect to being obedient to the coreSelf and regularly unresponsive to the kundalini lifeForce.

The intellect is intimidated by the emotions. It is deadly afraid of traumatic energies. It should be trained to deal with these powers head on, abandoning its fear of these.

May 27, 2007

Nityananda

This yogi developed the bubble body which is a supernatural neutral bliss energy form which has no limbs and senses like the subtle form. The bubble body unlike the astral one, has no limbs and sense and does not have an interest in developing and using physical species. When kundalini yoga is proficiently done, the yogi eliminates the need for the spinal chakra system. After relocating kundalini from muladhar base chakra into the head of the subtle body, the chakras on the spine disappear. Then the yogi can look down through the neck of the subtle form and see through the trunk of that form. By arousal of cell kundalini in organs and zones, he eventually causes the entire subtle body to be kundalini aroused. Gradually over time, the bubble form becomes manifested.

A yogi must have lost interest in sexual pleasure before the bubble body is manifested. This is an energy concern not a moral one. He should use breath infusion to lift the hormonal energy which is used by and treated by the reproductive organs. This energy naturally goes downward through the genitals. The yogi should pull this energy through the trunk of the body. In time this energy will lose its downward impetus and will flow upwards through the neck into the head. This is the required celibate action. It is not a matter of continuing or stopping sexual involvement. Mere physical celibacy cannot accomplish the lifting of the downward tendency of the hormonal energy.

Yogeshwarananda

He gave a notation about keeping the naad sound resonance focus during visions while meditating. One should not pursue the visions which occur in meditation. One should not develop anxiety when the visions occur. Pursuit and anxiety may cause the visions to terminate. One should be unexcited and should not clamber after an apparition or vision.

A yogi may see a moon during meditation. This would be in the mind itself without using physical or subtle eyes. He may see a light which is so brilliant as to be blinding. He should note these but do so without getting excited. If one gets excited, it may result in lowering one's vibration which will result in immediate termination of the experience.

The yogi must be alert to cancel thoughts which arise during meditation. Even when in higher states of consciousness, there is the likelihood that the mind will revert to a lower level which is its default condition. A yogi must have an effective method of preventing the mind from doing so.

June 14, 2007

Yogeshwarananda

He explained that the idea of focusing on a point in the mind, either between the eyebrows or elsewhere from within the mindscape, is an improper method, unless there is a transcendence object which is point like and which actually exist and is not imagined or visualized. If such an object is in the mind space, focusing on it is beneficial but if one has to imagine or assume such an object even though it is not there in its own right, focusing is not recommended.

Instead one should find or locate naad sound resonance and become absorbed in that medium. By waiting in naad one will cause that eventually there will be access to higher dimensions or the penetration of light from higher dimensions into the mind space.

June 16, 2007

Kundalini arousal / upper chest

Kundalini arousal in the upper chest and fleshy part of the neck is different to its ascent through the sushumna central spinal passage. Kundalini can be aroused in any part of the body, either in a bunch of cells which are adjacent to each other, in an organ, in a mass of muscle, through the skin, in a bone or anywhere else. Kundalini is not limited to spinal ascent.

June 20, 2007

Taoist master

I was with a Taoist master in the astral world. I did not get his name. He showed how to better focus the breath charge which accumulates when doing kapalabhati/bhastrika pranayama breath infusion or any similar method which results in subtle energy accumulating rapidly in the psyche.

He suggested that after a session of breath infusion, one should retreat to the great emptiness, and wait in that state. Otherwise he said if one continues the interactions which pertain to this physical world, one will make endorsements to things of this world.

Such energy is irrelevant to spiritual life and serves to pull the psyche from higher dimensions and from developing the potential for elevation to supernatural association and energy. He said that breath infusion is part of higher nutrition which sponsors higher awareness and frees the psyche from the need for the lower energies.

June 27, 2007

Yogeshwarananda

Naad assistance

Naad sound resonance renders great assistance to the ascetic in the quest to silence the intellect from its upsets during meditation. The coreSelf should be anchored in naad. If when doing this it feels attracted to mental imaging, it should double down in naad resonance, abandoning the intellect's shenanigans.

If while being in naad, the core senses that the frontal part of the subtle head is blank where it does not generate images or is not interested in doing so, the core should look ahead to speckled light in the frontal part of the subtle head. The core should remain anchored in naad while doing this.

Master of attachment

In the astral world, I was with some Vaishnava swamis and their followers. One Swami came to a follower who sat near to me. He said this:

"manesh mukesh."

This meant:

The master of attachment becomes the master of detachment.

This happens in time where a person who is prone to attachment will eventually after many births, practice and become detached. The follower was disappointed because his aspirations to be a swami, to be detached, was continually frustrated because his nature was to be attached. The senior swami alerted him that sometime in the future he will develop the detached nature.

July 1, 2007

Naad wider application

Initially the naad sound resonance focus is done by the coreSelf as it is surrounded by the sense of identity. No other adjunct is involved in the preliminary meditation on naad. After some months of this focus, the yogi should use naad to target the intellect or pull the intellect into the naad zone.

Unless it is encouraged or forced even, the intellect will either remain in a blank condition or be involved in its default operation which is to process sensual input and memories. A yogi should add one more duty to the intellect which is for it to focus into naad, to be oriented to naad, to be friendly with naad, and to accept naad as a preferred influence.

July 16, 2007

The mind is enthused to do psychic displays which are seen mentally by the coreSelf. The mind does this as an encouragement. If the coreSelf does not respond to a prompt, the mind loses impetus and the displays are not perceived.

The coreSelf should realize that it cannot directly sponsor mental displays. It does so in an indirect way by giving energy to the sense of identity which emits an attention beam of energy. It is this beam which endorses and encourages the ideas to develop in the mind.

By reducing its emotional relationship with the sense of identity, the core can gain control of the endorsement procedure. Otherwise, the core will continue to be liable for mental actions which are suicidal.

July 16, 2007

Lift intellect

There is a practice for lifting the intellect. This adjunct is invisible most of the time with its presence being discovered through its mental figuring. As soon as the intellect displays anything it is seen in the mind as the very image or idea which it displays. As soon as the intellect goes blank it is not seen because it only appears visibly when operating to display something.

A yogi can figure the intellect by trying to lift it into the top part of the forehead. One will feel a mental muscle when trying to do so. At the end of the muscles one will find the intellect but it will be invisible even though it is definitely felt.

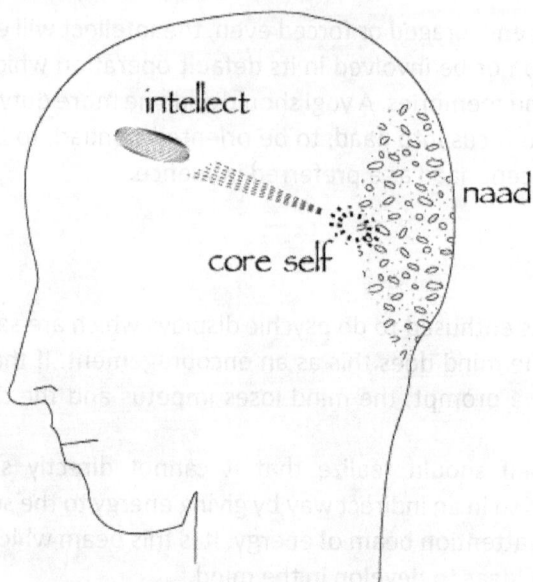

intellect

naad

core self

In some meditation when one tries to lift the intellect, it will feel as if it is a gap, a blank space, as a location which is vacant and which welcomes impressions for development. The coreSelf should remain in contact with naad sound resonance, while lifting the intellect. There may be apparitions and shadows of astral objects which appear where the gap is located.

There may be speckled lights or blended micro spots of light slowly moving in and out. The yogi should remain calm and observe whatever happens. He should remain in the mind and not allow his attention to venture outside the psyche unless a window in time opens to a higher dimension. The quality of energy of a higher dimension will be higher in texture and will be bliss yielding without trauma potential. The bliss may be mild or intense or it may be a neutral translucent energy which is nourishing to the coreSelf.

Front kundalini arousal necessary

The front kundalini should be aroused. In fact the entire subtle body should have the collective of itself aroused so that kundalini is highlighted in each part of it. This should be done part by part using breath infusion. Over time of becoming proficient in this, the yogi will lose fear of haphazard rebirth.

Even if spinal kundalini is aroused, still if the rest of the subtle body has lower quality subtle energy, there is the likelihood that despite the accomplishment and the ability to enter into deep absorption or samadhi, still the yogi may find himself to become an embryo which has to be delivered through a woman's passage. This is likely to happen because ultimately the kundalini must take into account the average energy in the psyche and not just what is happening in the spine or head of the subtle form.

Imagination orb

The imagination orb is a part of the intellect. It is the most important part of it. The best method for controlling it is to either lift it above its default position or saturate it with a high quality of surcharged energy. That means breath infusion practice and taking reliance on naad sound resonance.

The imagination orb may be attacked by the infused breath energy. This can be done directly by focusing in the head of the subtle body, while doing breath infusion sessions.

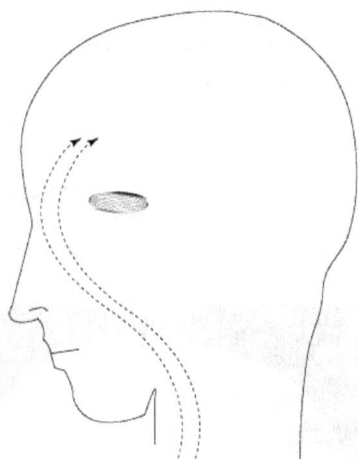

infused breath energy
directed before intellect

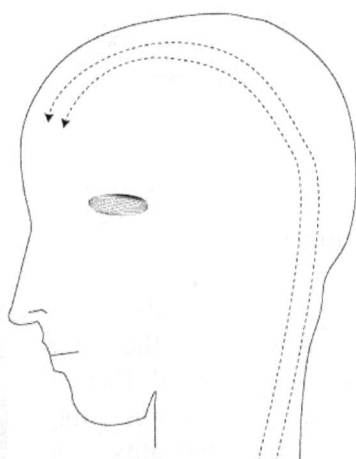

infused breath energy
directed around skull

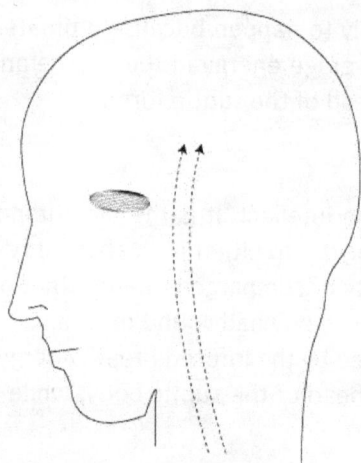

infused breath energy
directed behind intellect

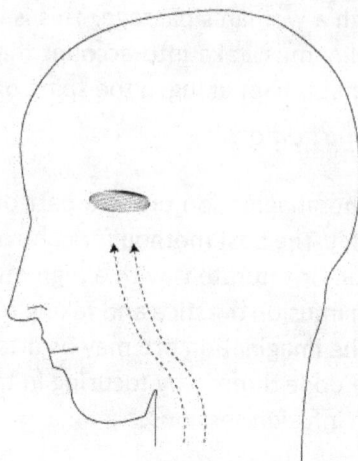

infused breath energy
under intellect

July 27, 2007

Thought receptor

There is a subtle spongy material which is in the frontal part of the subtle head. This area acts as a receptor for foreign thoughts. These thoughts which originate from the minds of others carry a sensing mechanism which locates targets and punctures the minds of the targets. Once a foreign thoughts hits the head of the subtle body, it becomes anchored there. It discharges a simple or complex impression, which is accepted or rejected by the intellect. The intellect illustrates the idea to the coreSelf which either sponsors or makes efforts to squelch it.

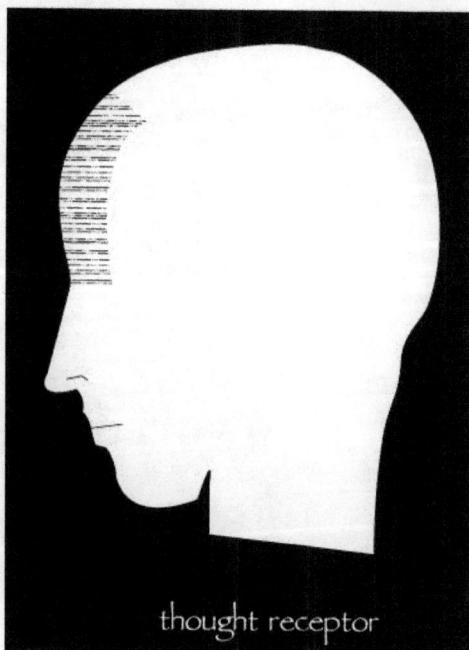

thought receptor

Kundalini relation to intellect

The kundalini lifeForce influences the intellect. To understand this first hand, a yogi should do breath infusion to notice how the attitude of the intellect and its perceptive ability changes according to the quantity of fresh subtle energy the kundalini ingests. The more fresh energy the kundalini digest, the more insightful the intellect is. The more polluted energy the kundalini absorbs, the more stupefying the intellect becomes to the disadvantage of the coreSelf.

A yogi should do whatever he or she can to elevate the energy intake of the kundalini. There are various ways in which the kundalini absorbs energy but the three main routes are:

- food intake
- breath intake
- emotions intake
- mental concept intake

Various senses are used in the collection of these consumptions but ultimately they are processed by the kundalini which influences the intellect to present plans to the coreSelf for approval.

Handling the intellect

Initially a yogi cannot directly command the intellect except when it does something which the coreSelf feels comfortable with and wants to enjoy. Even then however on close analysis we see that the self was induced and did not begin the mental or emotional activity. The coreSelf cannot directly handle the intellect because that adjunct is in a lower dimension where the core cannot directly act to do anything. The realm of the intellect and the one of the coreSelf is supernatural but each is on a different plane which does not interact with the other.

To handle the intellect the core must use the sense of identity which surrounds the core spherically. The effort to handle the intellect, to direct it to do anything, to indulge in its constructions results in a protrusion of the sense of identity which the core experiences as an expression of willpower or as an interest in the form of attention.

However for this communication to occur, some kundalini energy must be utilized because the kundalini energy is there as the environment around the adjuncts. As one must reach through the air to pick up something, the core must express its interest or will power through the kundalini energy to handle the intellect.

This is why it is important to keep the kundalini in its highest possible vibration with the highest possible grade of subtle energy being ingested into it. This causes the kundalini to be more cooperative with the core, where it endorses the higher aspirations of the psyche and does not undermine the meditation practice.

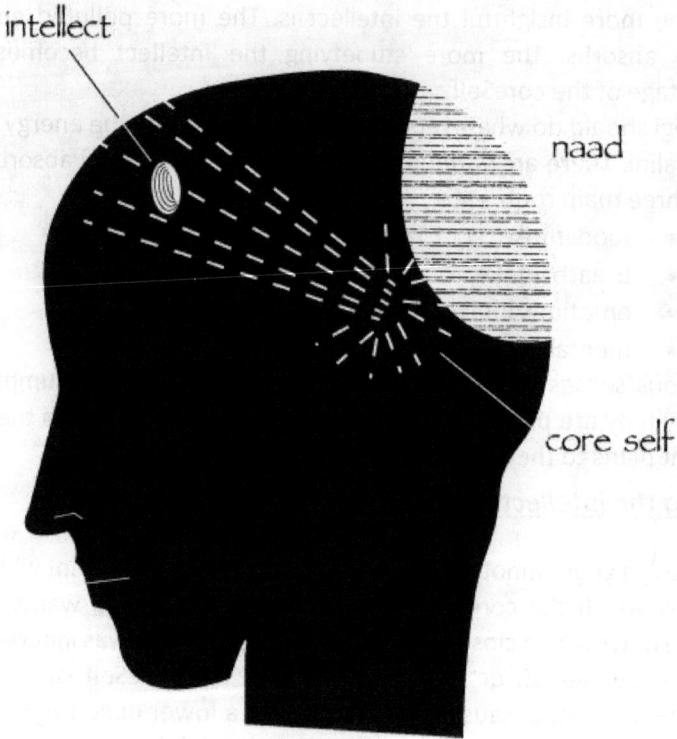

intellect

naad

core self

August 6, 2007

Pranayama breath infusion

Breath infusion is necessary if the subtle body must be purified of polluted subtle energy. If one is uncertain about being able to get rid of the subtle body, then the best course is to upgrade it and keep it on the highest possible level of consciousness, where it consumes and is surrounded by a high grade of bliss energy which is lust free.

Those who feel that clarification of the subtle body is superfluous because the self is the coreSelf and is not the subtle body encasement, should consider that until a particular core is released from the need for a subtle body, it is in the interest of that core to keep the subtle body as elevated as it can be.

The core is not the subtle body but presently it is confined in the subtle body and has to identify with its psychic form. Until the core is liberated from the need of a subtle form, that core should do whatever is necessary to keep the subtle form elevated.

The general energy which is in the subtle body is the kundalini psychic lifeForce energy. As nature would have it, this is a downward moving force with upward spread only on occasion. A yogi should do kundalini yoga to change the kundalini into being an upward moving force. When the kundalini is aroused it could go in any direction, up, down, left or right. It may even scatter from any place in the psyche to any other place, or explode energy or implode upon the aroused zone.

The downward movement of kundalini is the default condition. It sponsor sex indulgence primarily and in that way it supports efforts at begetting progeny. For yogic purposes, the ascetic should train kundalini to be an upward moving force.

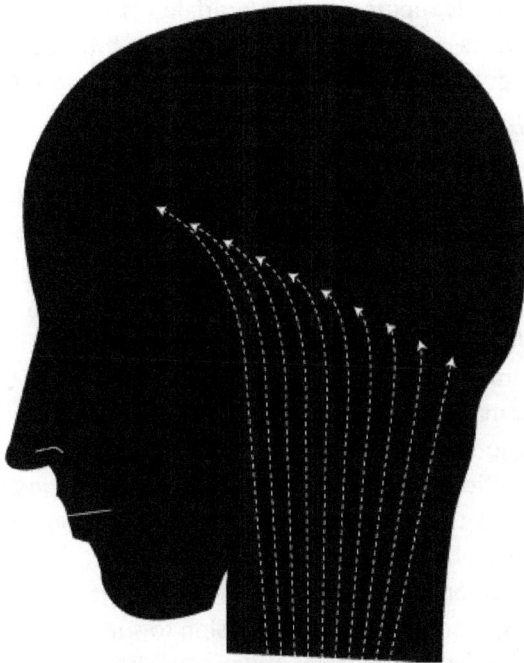

Intellect locator

The kundalini psychic lifeForce directly controls the intellect. Part of the intellect is its imagination faculty which operates as an orb. That imagination orb is vital for supernatural perception. It lowly use is for imagination. It lofty use is for supernatural viewing of higher dimensions and spiritual reality.

The condition of the kundalini energy is directly related to the behavior of the imagination orb. If the kundalini energy is low grade the imagination orb will ingest a low energy and will act on that basis.

The will power is an accessory for giving commands to the intellect which includes the imagination orb. However the will power is effective only if the intellect has the proper grade of energy required for specific operations. If the will power gives a command which the intellect cannot operate because the kundalini provided the intellect with a low grade of energy, the desire of the will power will be ignored by the intellect.

It is important to provide the intellect with an energy which causes it to function in the desired way, otherwise mere will power commands may prove to be ineffective unless by chance a specific command is allowed because the intellect got the proper grade of energy from the kundalini.

Stated differently, upgrading the kundalini is the sure way to upgrade the intellect. That is a direct way to cause the intellect to abandon low pursuits and adopt higher perceptions which are useful to the yogi.

Sense of identity focus

The coreSelf is forever surrounded by the sense of identity which is a neutral energy which becomes prejudiced if it makes contact with the intellect. There are two ways to keep the sense of identity loyal to the core. These are:

- isolate the sense of identity from the intellect
- upgrade the intellect so that its loses interest in lower pursuits and maintains neutrality to the kundalini

The first option is the most difficult one to accomplish. For that matter the complete isolation of the sense of identity is near impossible for the core to achieve because the identity is so close in vibration to the core, as to almost indistinguishable.

The second option is the practical one because the yogi can upgrade the kundalini by doing pranayama breath infusion to surcharge the kundalini and remove from it heavy dense astral energy which keeps it functioning on a lower plane. If the kundalini is upgraded, the intellect is automatically affected positively because the intellect floats in the energy which the kundalini provides as an atmosphere within the psyche. The intellect is directly and immediately affected by the condition of the kundalini.

The sense of identity likes to touch the intellect but in touching, the identity becomes influenced. As soon as there is a desire for the identity to make contact with the intellect, the identity sends out a ray of inquiry energy which is formatted as the attention of the core. This same attention may be formatted as the willpower of the core. When this touches the intellect it becomes influenced by whatever the intellect intended to develop.

Since the intellect is prompted, goaded and controlled by the kundalini, any ideas which the intellect fosters will be developed under the influence of the kundalini. This means that when the identity touches the intellect, that identity will be influenced to support the ideas of the kundalini irrespective of the desire of the core.

August 8, 2007

Yogeshwarananda

In a miniature form he was located in the subtle head. He gave this diagram for isolating the sense of identity from the intellect.

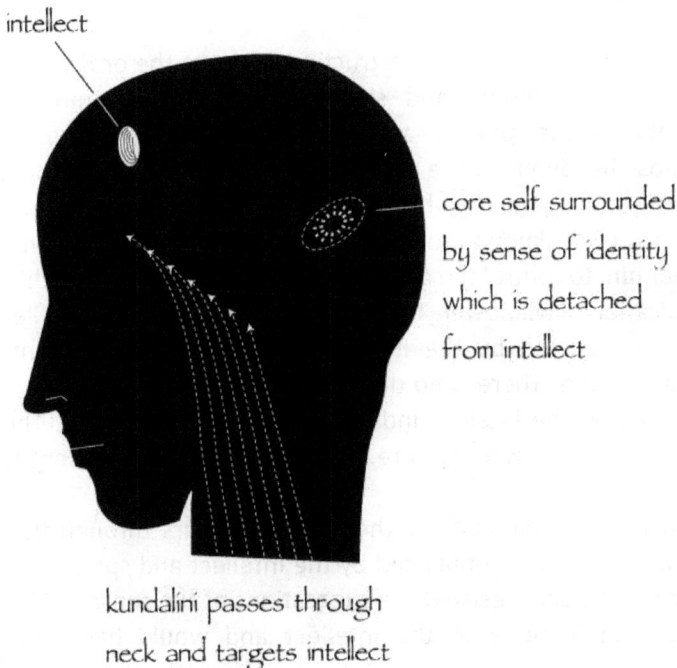

intellect

core self surrounded
by sense of identity
which is detached
from intellect

kundalini passes through
neck and targets intellect

Astral friend

I met a deceased friend in an astral dimension. He left his last physical body some years ago after it was afflicted with the HIV. During that life he exhibited and played out homosexual tendencies. When there was an epidemic of homosexual men infected with HIV, he became a victim. His body deteriorated and he passed on to the astral existence. At first for seven years, his astral body was in a dimension where it floated in association with other gay individuals. The astral form could not move without having pains. Eventually the damage done to it was repaired. This happened after seven years of remaining in a near comatose condition on an astral level which is adjacent to this physical dimension.

This friend's astral form recovered. It looked as if it was about twenty-five years of age. It was vibrant. We were in a canoe which he maneuvered by willpower. He lost the interest in homosexual activities and also had no heterosexual interest. He did want to be in a family and to be a father of a family but without sexual connection with anyone.

August 12, 2007

Strategy for mind control

To comply with Patanjali's instruction to cease the ordinary operations of the intellect, memory and sleep impulse, a yogi must study the components in the psyche and their default interactions. Once he understands the layout of the psyche, he can make attempts to order the components to facilitate the objectives of meditation.

Unless the yogi knows the details of the mind operation, it would not be possible for him to control the mind for meditation merely by wishful thinking or by application of willpower. The relationship between the intellect and the coreSelf is conducted by the intellect and the sense of identity which surrounds the core. There is no direct handling of the intellect by the core. The core handles the intellect indirectly through the identity. The intellect also has no direct access to the core. It too, uses the sense of identity to relate to the core.

Subjugation of the core by the intellect occurs through the sense of identity which becomes influenced by the intellect and spreads that energy to the core. If the core resisted the suggestions of the sense of identity, that core would be immune to the intellect and would have the required autonomy.

As long as the self or psyche is seen as one unit something without differentiating the adjuncts from the coreSelf, the yogi cannot achieve liberation. First he must recognize the various parts, the adjuncts which make up the so called self. He should study how the components interact. With that insight he may get the required clarity which would empower him to control the relationships before the core and the various adjuncts, as well as between one adjunct and another.

The sense of identity is like a transparent fluid around the coreSelf. The core perceives by looking through that transparent supernatural material but it is so transparent that the core does not realize the identity as the medium for all types of contact.

The sense of identity for its part is concerned with making contact with the intellect. That is its obsession. It has an irresistible attraction to the intellect. This causes it to be influenced by the intellect. Because the core relies on the sense of identity for information, that core is influenced by the identity just as the identity is influenced by the intellect.

August 13, 2007

Sense of identity / attachment

The sense of identity has attachment to the intellect. The sense of identity always adheres to the coreSelf but nevertheless it has attachment to the intellect and will act in the interest of the intellect even when the intellect acts in a manner which is contrary to the core.

The unfortunate part of this is that the higher principle is being controlled or influence by the lower principle. This is the natural situation which a yogi endeavors to reverse

Beginning with the kundalini and the memories in the trunk of the subtle body, each adjunct which is lower in vibration dominates the higher adjunct which is attached to it. At the top is located the coreSelf but it dominated by the sense of identity, which in turn is dominated by the intellect which is commanded by kundalini and memories. The senses are offshoots of the kundalini but they appear to be separate and to wield their own powers over the intellect.

To gain control the yogi must sort the adjuncts. He must study how they operate. He should upset their organization.

Willpower

The willpower is an expression which is projected from the sense of identity. It limited in scope and power. For its efficient use, it requires the cooperation of the intellect and the kundalini. It is likely that unless the intellect and kundalini are in agreement the willpower even though it is expressed will be ineffective.

Willpower is also expressed in another format as the attention or interest of the coreSelf. This interest is an expression which is projected from the sense of identity but it is the same power as the willpower except that it has a slightly different approach to how it relates to the intellect.

As will power the sense or identity tries to command the intellect and the kundalini, while as attention of interest, it tries to bargain with the intellect to get more information from it. In either case, the sense of identity takes a bemeaning position in reference to the intellect, even though in fact the sense of identity is a higher frequency energy than the intellect or the kundalini.

There are two verses in the Bhagavad Gita which should be studied:

इन्द्रियाणि पराण्याहुर्
इन्द्रियेभ्यः परं मनः ।
मनसस्तु परा बुद्धिर्
यो बुद्धेः परतस्तु सः ॥३.४२॥

indriyāṇi parāṇyāhur
indriyebhyaḥ paraṁ manaḥ
manasastu parā buddhir
yo buddheḥ paratastu saḥ (3.42)

indriyāṇi — the senses; parāṇyāhur = parāṇi — are energetic; āhur (āhuḥ) — the ancient psychologists say; indriyebhyaḥ — the senses; paraṁ — more energetic; manaḥ — the mind; manasas — in contrast to the mind; tu — but; parā — more sensitive; buddhir = buddhiḥ — the intelligence; yo = yaḥ — which; buddheḥ — in reference to the intelligence; paratas — most sensitive; tu — but; saḥ — he, the spirit

The ancient psychologists say that the senses are energetic, but in comparison to the senses, the mind is more energetic. In contrast to the mind, the intelligence is even more sensitive. But in reference, the spirit is most elevated. (Bhagavad Gita 3.42)

एवं बुद्धेः परं बुद्ध्वा
संस्तभ्यात्मानमात्मना ।
जहि शत्रुं महाबाहो
कामरूपं दुरासदम् ॥३.४३॥

evaṁ buddheḥ paraṁ buddhvā
saṁstabhyātmānamātmanā
jahi śatruṁ mahābāho
kāmarūpaṁ durāsadam (3.43)

evaṁ — thus; *buddheḥ* — than the intelligence; *paraṁ* — higher; *buddhvā* — having understood; *saṁstabhyātmānamātmanā* = *saṁstabhya* — keeping together + *ātmānam* — the personal energies+ *ātmanā* — by the spirit; *jahi* — uproot; *śatruṁ* — enemy; *mahābāho* — O powerful man; *kāmarūpaṁ* — form of passionate desire; *durāsadam* — difficult to grasp

Thus having understood what is higher than intelligence, keeping the personal energies under control of the spirit, uproot, O powerful man, the enemy, the form of passionate desire which is difficult to grasp. (Bhagavad Gita 3.43)

These verses describe the exception. The standard is that the lower controls the higher. It should be that as Krishna indicated the sensual energies or the kundalini is energetic, but in comparison to the kundalini, the intellect or mind is more energetic. In contrast to that, the sense of identity is even more sensitive. In reference, the coreSelf is most elevated.

Thus having understood what is higher than the sense of identity, keeping the personal energies under control of the coreSelf, a yogi should uproot the enemy, the form of passionate desire, the seductive lower influence which is difficult to grasp. A yogi will have to earn proficiency if he is subdue the psyche.

Kundalini / spine posture

From the aroused kundalini, there is a pushing force which straightens the spine of the yogi. It removes the tendency for hunched back and fetal posture of the spine. It uncoils the fetal posture or the *curve over the navel* tendency of the spine.

This pushes the yogi away from rebirth. In the astral world hereafter, a yogi should take care not to sleep in a fetal position as that is the inclination to take an embryo haphazardly. The human body developed from the primate body. This also means that it may regress to that form if it is not prevented by special divine impetus.

The aroused kundalini also supports the segregation between the intellect and the sense of identity with the identity being more directive to the intellect.

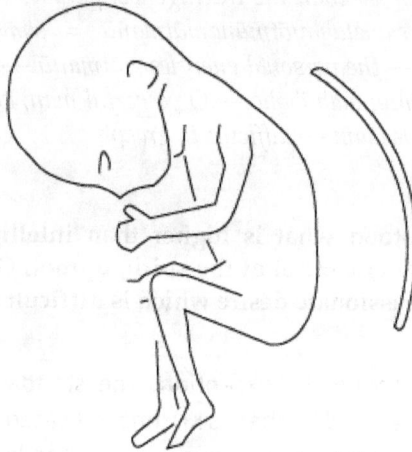

fetal spine

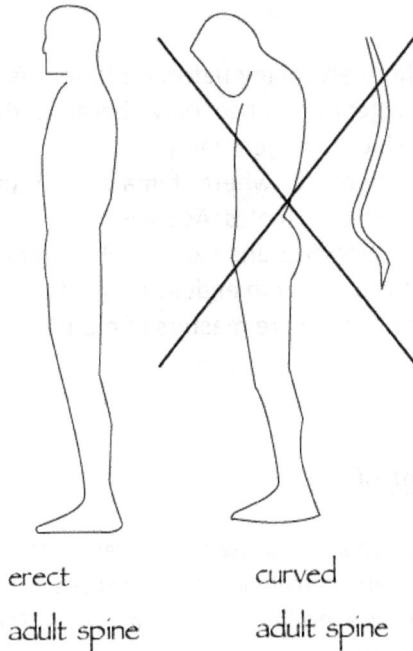

erect   curved

adult spine   adult spine

August 24, 2007

Rebirth repelling face

It is in the interest of a yogi to develop a rebirth repelling face. This happens by mastery of kundalini yoga, to rid the kundalini of its creature form addiction tendency. Kundalini is attracted to the survival tendency, where it wants to take births on and on in the struggle for existence. This is a competitive game played by the kundalini which despite the trauma involved, it still wants to participate and take the risks which comes with the danger of having a perishable body.

The rebirth repelling face is developed for a yogi if his practice of kundalini yoga is so complete, that his kundalini loses interest in being in the dimensions in which life forms are evolving by physical means. One can develop insight in a subtle body. However the kundalini prefers to use its subtle configuration to develop living physical forms which allows it to indulge in the hard struggle on the material level of existence. This needs to be changed so that at least the kundalini is happy to develop in the subtle world only and does not require physical systems.

September 2, 2007

I realized that there are many natural differences between males and females. This is in a general sense only, because there are similarities between individuals which defy generality.

Desire is one difference where females are mistresses of desire expression much more so than males. As cows eat grass and excrete manure, women digest desire fulfillments and excrete whatever in a desire they could not digest. Males do the same with endeavor energy. Women are mistresses of emotional action while men are masters of mental action.

September 6, 2007

Kundalini sense control

The kundalini controls the senses. For that matter the kundalini is the collective of sensual energies from which the senses emerged. The enclosure of the individual sensual energies has five gateways. These are experienced as five subtle and gross senses.

The idea that the senses are controlled by the core, the observing I presence is preposterous for most of the living beings. Only those who are liberated and realized the coreSelf in segregation from the adjuncts can be in control of the senses. And even for them that control is sporadic.

Besides, it is not practical for the core to monitor every sensual quest or interaction. It is befitting that the senses be controlled by the energy which energizes them. And that energy should do so for the benefit of the psyche. Of course our experience is that the senses act in ways which are both constructive towards and destructive of the psyche.

A study of how the senses operate in reference to the kundalini which is their natural monitor, is necessary for the yogi. This is done both in meditation and by astute observations during interacts with the senses when not meditating.

When a sense, for example the sight sense endeavors to perceive an object, the kundalini flashes forward in the vision energy with matching sensors which confront the incoming information to determine its value. This action is interpreted as enthusiasm and comparison. When the sensors make a decision as to the worth of the incoming information, this decision energy is routed to the intellect which emits an energy either to curtail the investment in the object perceived or encourage further access to the object.

This is done without the consent of the coreSelf. Once the intellect determines to accept or reject more information about the sense object, the sense of identity which functions as the curiosity of the core, makes contact with the intellect and becomes prejudiced by the intellect into inducing the core to contribute energy to the investigation or to withhold energy from it. A yogi should study these mento-emotional operations and learn how to bring them under control.

September 8, 2007

Yogeshwarananda

He explained that the sensual energies continually seek objects even when the core has no interest. The permission of the core for the operation of the intellect, senses or kundalini is required but it does not have to be deliberate. A small percentage of energy from the core, leaks through the sense of identity to the intellect and the kundalini. Even though this is a minor amount of energy like a drip drip leak from a water tank, it is enough to fund the operations of involuntary behavior of the intellect, senses and kundalini.

It occurs frequently that the intellect, senses and kundalini keep working even when the core is not objectively aware of their activities. The impulsions continue regardless of if the core desires them or is aware of their operations.

A yogi must study this in deep meditation. He may take steps to curtail this leakage but he must have the insight to take such subtle actions which discipline the intellect, kundalini and senses so that they remain oriented to promoting the interest of the core.

It is necessary to upgrade the kundalini intake of energy. This causes the sensual pursuit to switch where the kundalini develops an interest in higher reality and avoids lower dimensions.

September 9, 2007

In the kundalini there is a fear mechanism. This is a psychic operation. When the kundalini is unable to properly rate a sense object or its rating is that the object is insurmountable, a fear energy is instantly manifested. This power may remain as a small incidence or it may flood the entire psyche.

This fear response acts as a wave of energy which expands through the psyche. It motivates movement so as to change location to avoid the real or imagined challenge.

From the perspective of order, the psyche of the average entity is disordered. It operates in a chaotic manner but it is predictable if one understands the details of the interactions of the adjuncts. A yogi must reorder the psyche if he intends to be the master of it.

Assisting others

Assisting others as an objective in spiritual practice is counterproductive. One may assist others but it should not be the main objective because the psyche has a limited amount of energy for *self reformation*. If any of that energy is used to assist others, it deprives the self of what it requires to upturn its internal chaos.

There is fulfillment felt when helping others, even when that is counterproductive to the spiritual interest of the self. One may forego that sense of satisfaction and stick to self-reform. The energy which exudes from the psyche when there is successful self-order will be expressed in the aura of the self. This is how to assist others without self-sabotage.

Emotional subtle forms

In the astral world, one experiences many emotional bodies. These are one subtle body experienced differently according to the dimension it registers. I met an elderly man on the astral side of the island of Trinidad. I lived in his house for some months during the 1960s. He wanted to supervise another person and myself who lived there and knew his family.

He used an emotional form which is a relationship body in which one only thinks of completing relationships based on incidences which happened years ago. This elderly person is departed with no physical access but he continues relationships which were based on what he did when he used the last physical form.

In the astral world, this elder was attentive to me and another young man just as if we were his sons and he was responsible to train us so that we could be functional adults as skilled successful fathers and husbands.

October 2, 2007

Kundalini distribution

Pranayama breath infusion when mastered, gives the yogi the ability to arouse the kundalini through the spine into the brain on a daily basis. Just as pleasure loving people are sure to have sexual climax experience on a daily basis, a kundalini yogi uses kapalabhati/bhastrika pranayama practice to induce kundalini to climax through the spine into the brain every day.

Eventually however, the yogi realizes that the kundalini should be expressed in each part of the subtle body. It should be aroused throughout the subtle body, not merely in the subtle spine and head.

As a yogi drives out the heavy polluted subtle energy from the sushumna nadi central spinal passage, he should also cause the kundalini to go into every part of the subtle body. Kundalini in the form of micro kundalinis of individual cells should be expressed as they are in their original location. This will cause the subtle body to be upgraded as a whole, rather than clarity in it only in the spine and head.

October 4, 2007

Mental images

If there are many images flashing in the mind during meditation, where the yogi is powerless to cease the displays, he should investigate as to the reason for the power of the images. The flashing images are created in the intellect. The core sees these presentations indirectly. They are seen by the attention beam of the sense of identity, which relates the visions to the core directly.

There are two concerns:
- strength of the image
- weakness of the attention beam

These features are related. The strength of the image is derived from the sensual energy interest when the sense object from which the image was derived was contacted by one or more senses. If there was a strong sensual interest the memory record of it will have a holding power which will hypnotize the attention beam.

The weakness of the attention beam is related to its attachment and reliance on the intellect. In cases where the attention is much reliant on the intellect, certain sensual displays will hypnotize the attention where it will not have the power to extract itself when it is captivated by a display in the intellect.

The yogi should study how the senses appropriate objects and how that contact causes irresistible memory impressions which captivate the attention of the self later. He should review the reliance of the attention on the intellect so that he can make the attention more independent.

Part 6

September 5, 2007

Kundalini love

The love affair between one adjunct and another should be studied by the yogi. He should intercept the energy of attachment which flows between one adjunct and another. That is how he may wrestle control and make the psyche serve the spiritual needs of the coreSelf.

The kundalini and the intellect are in a locked relationship with the intellect being the influenced component and the kundalini being the dominant force. The kundalini generates the emotional energy which the intellect requires for its actions. Since the intellect is always in need of emotions, the yogi can adjust the relationship by providing the kundalini with high grade feelings.

The experience is that when the kundalini is flushed with high subtle energy, it no longer has lower interest and induces higher perceptions in the intellect. Breath infusion is a reliable method of elevating the intake energy of the kundalini. It is a reliable practice for causing the intellect to shift to higher dimensions where it will have supernatural and spiritual access.

Intellect lift

The intellect should be lifted. It should be moved from its default position. This is required to cause a change in its operations. A yogi should move the intellect and discover that changes in its position causes its resistance to willpower commands to increase or decrease. When it is in its default position, it has the most resistance to the commands of the coreSelf.

When the kundalini is aroused through the spine into the brain and when it hits the intellect and moves it or shifts it upwards in energy saturation, the intellect becomes responsible to the core and abandons lower interest in mundane memories and objects.

If the coreSelf adheres to the naad sound resonance, it can resist the influence of the intellect. The intellect can be silenced if the core is naad absorbed.

Yogesh gave a diagram which shows the core absorbed in naad while the aroused kundalini pushes the intellect upward out of its default position. When this happens the intellect becomes quieted and no longer displays images and ideas which are related to material existence and the lower subtle levels.

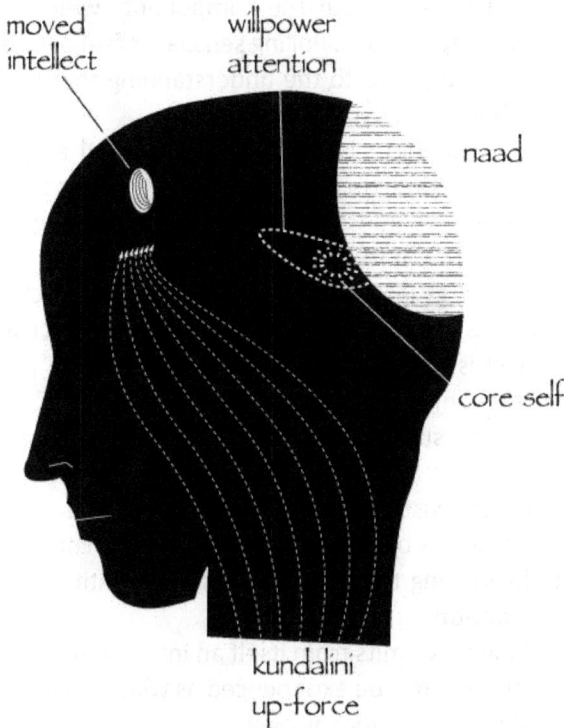

October 8, 2007

Willpower pullback

When one begins meditating, one cannot discern between the intellect, the sense of identity and the coreSelf. One feels these as one cohesive existence termed as the self. In this composition there is the kundalini and its sensual energies and the senses as well. These comprise a confusion where there is lack of clarity, where there is little insight.

For those who do not do kundalini yoga, who are unable to arouse and experience the breath infused kundalini energy, their experience of sexual climax is the only way they can understand the impetuous sensational force of the kundalini. Otherwise the involuntary actions of the kundalini lifeForce can gives one some estimation about the completion of duties of this lifeForce. Vital functions like heart beat and breathing are regulated by the kundalini. Generally, the coreSelf is oblivious to the involuntary actions which cause the body to be alive and functional. The agency which maintains and operates the body is the kundalini psychic lifeForce.

The initial attempt at introspection is a clumsy effort but if one persists with it, one will get insight about the components which are involved in emotional and mental operations. Pulling sensual or feelings energy back into the psyche will eventually lead to the understanding that the center of the head of the subtle body is a psychic location.

In the subtle head there is the intellect, as well as the observing I-consciousness. This observing I-consciousness functions as a witness and as an energy source when it witnesses anything. Its witnessing function is itself the flowing of energy from it to an adjunct.

When sensual energy leaves the psyche to pursue objects in the physical or astral environments, it does so from the kundalini lifeForce and not directly from the coreSelf. It is the kundalini which expresses the pursuing sensual energy which detects objects, gages and procures them.

In the head of the subtle body, the intellect is involved in the sensual operations as a checker and censor. Its conclusions attract the sense of identity which the self usually mistakes for itself. The self or coreSelf is surrounded by the sense of identity, such that the core cannot perceive anything except by looking through the sense of identity. Hence the core is prejudiced by the identity.

This sense of identity emits from itself an interest in what the intellect is involved in. This interest may be experienced as willpower or as interest or as curiously about what the intellect displays.

October 10, 2007

Muktananda

He said that his mission went down sharply since he left the physical body. People forgot him quickly. He considers taking another body to continue teaching.

I replied that his guru, Nityananda, did not take another body. Why should Muktananda? And besides India changed. The same social environment is no longer current.

He replied that just as I did, he could be successful in a new body even without getting a physical guru like Nityananda and even without getting a body in India. His view is that with the correct parents for starting life, it would not matter which country one's parents were located in.

Muktananda

He said that the initial introspection involved internalization of the general energies which course out of the psyche. For a beginner these are like longs rays of energy pulling inward.

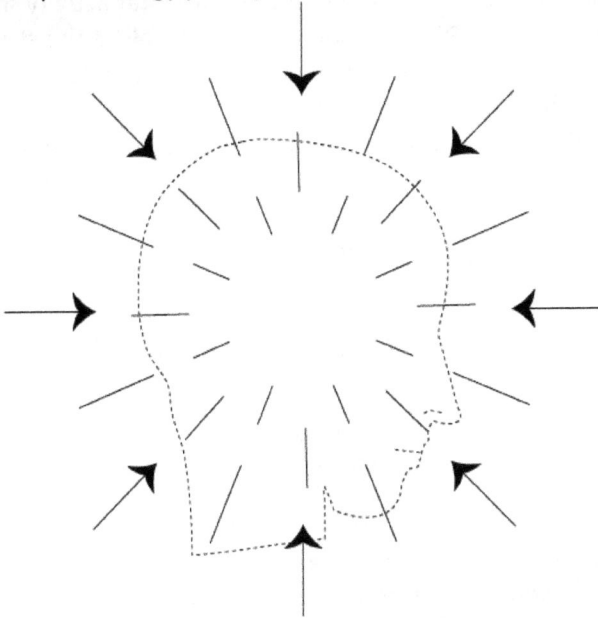

As the person practices, these rays will be compacted until they are being drawn only in the subtle head and do not come from outside of the subtle head.

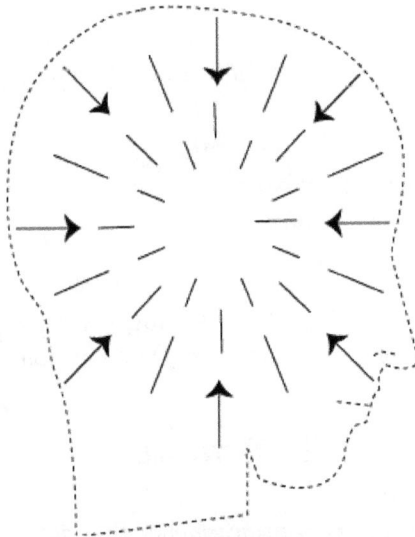

Taimni

This ascetic did a commentary of the *Yoga Sutras*. He told me that everything in meditation has to do with ceasing the mental activity in the frontal part of the subtle head. Pictures, sound ideas as well as the struggle of the coreSelf against the intellect which imagines and illustrated memory must cease. This must happen for long periods in mediation. When this is happening without effort, there arises the supernatural insight (prātibha). When this is stable the yogi uses that insight. He cited verses from the *Yoga Sutras*:

प्रातिभाद्वा सर्वम्॥३४॥

prātibhād vā sarvam

prātibhād = *prātibhāt – resulting from samyama on the shining organ of divination; vā – or; sarvam – everything, all reality.*

By complete restraint of the mento-emotional energy, while focusing on the shining organ of divination in the head of the subtle body, the yogin is able to know all reality. (Yoga Sutras 3.34)

ततः प्रातिभश्रावणवेदनादर्शास्वादवार्ता जायन्ते॥३७॥

tataḥ prātibha śrāvaṇa vedana
ādarśa āsvāda vārtāḥ jāyante

tataḥ – thence, therefore, from that focus; prātibha – the shining organ of divination; śrāvaṇa – hearing; vedana – touching; ādarśa – sight; āsvāda – taste; vārtāḥ – smell; jāyante – is produced.

From that focus is produced smelling, tasting, seeing, touching and hearing, through the shining organ of divination. (Yoga Sutras 3.37)

ततो मनोजवित्वं विकरणभावः प्रधानजयश्च॥४९॥

tataḥ manojavitvaṁ vikaraṇabhāvaḥ pradhānajayaḥ ca

tataḥ – subsequently; manojavitvaṁ = manah – mind + javitvaṁ – swiftness, rapidity; vikaraṇabhāvaḥ = vi – parting away from, dispersing + karana – creating, making + bhāvaḥ – mento-emotional energy, feeling; pradhānah – subtle matter; jayaḥ – conquest; ca – and.

Subsequently, there is conquest over the influence of subtle matter and over the parting away or dispersion of the mento-emotional energy, with the required swiftness of mind. (Yoga Sutras 3.49)

October 19, 2007

Yogeshwarananda

Anti-gravity method

Yogesh showed an anti-gravity method for pulling up hormonal energy which by nature usually moves down to the groin area. Eventually when one becomes proficient in kundalini yoga one becomes an urdhvareta yogi, or one whose hormonal energy goes down to the pubic area and then goes up through the spine into the brain.

There is however a stage of advancement beyond that which is when the yogi pulls up the hormonal energy so that it does not go down before it goes up. Instead of moving into and accumulating in the groin area, the energy rises as soon as it is formed. It travels through the trunk of the body into the chest and then into the head of the subtle body with no necessity of going downwards. This method causes energy which is generated in the thighs, legs and feet to rise through the trunk and neck instead of going to the groin area and then being passaged upwards through the spine.

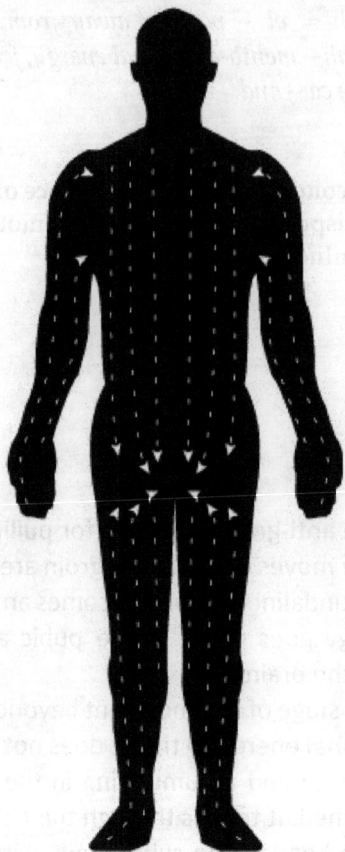

hormonal energy
travel to groin

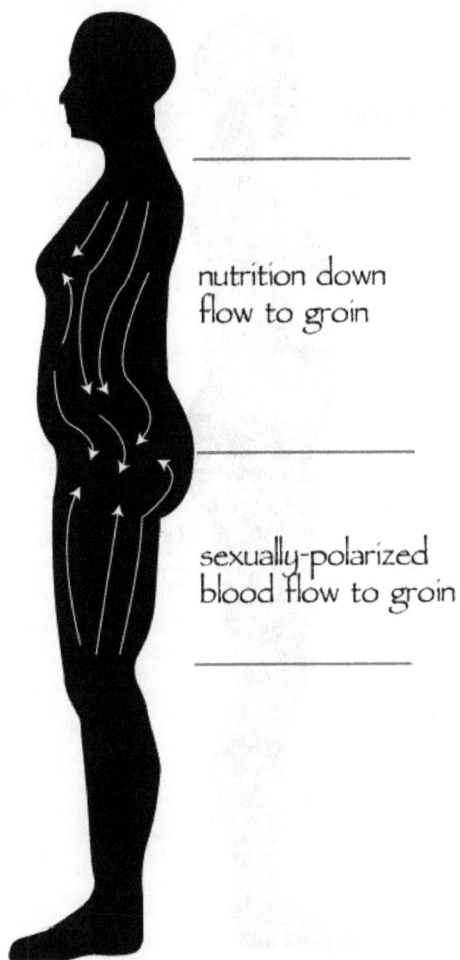

nutrition down
flow to groin

sexually-polarized
blood flow to groin

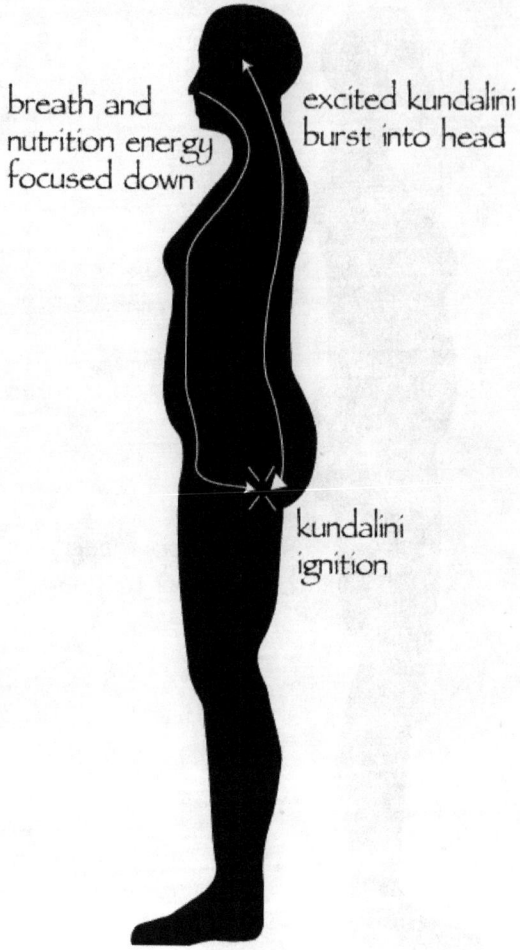

breath and
nutrition energy
focused down

excited kundalini
burst into head

kundalini
ignition

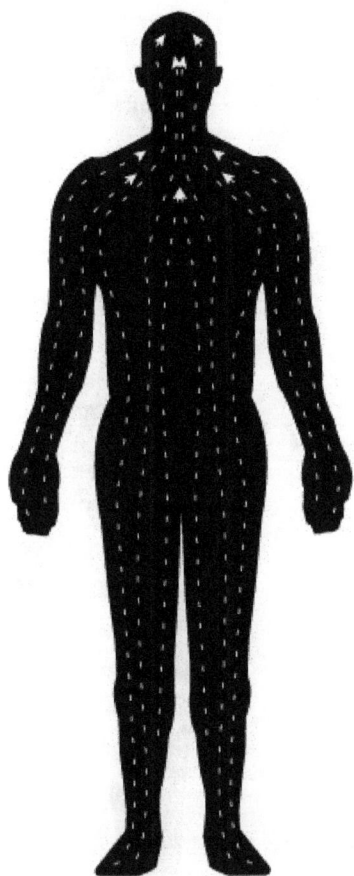

hormonal energy
travels upward only

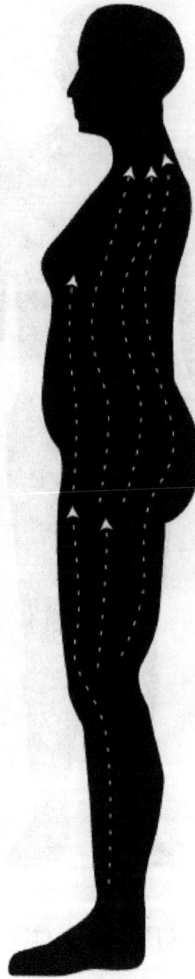

nutrition flow up

October 19, 2007

Yogeshwarananda

He gave a surcharged subtle energy pull. This is done during breath infusion, where the surcharged subtle breath energy saturates the trunk of the subtle body. It is then pulled into the head by a mental force. It causes a bliss energy to abound in the subtle head.

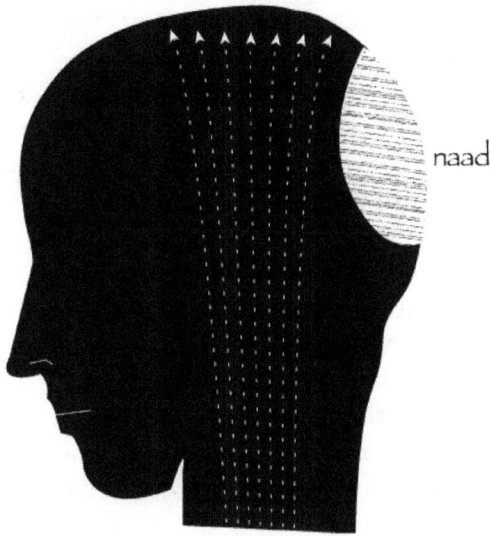

naad

October 21, 2007

I did the kriya illustrated below. These are techniques which free the coreSelf from its adjuncts. These give a yogi confidence that he/she can attain freedom from mental and emotional influence.

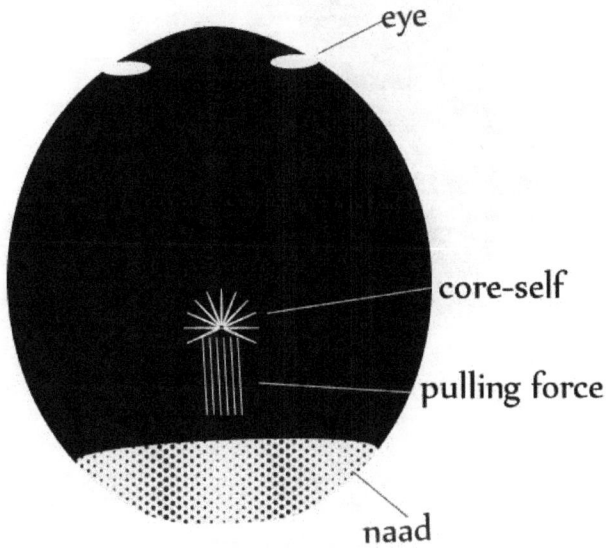

eye

core-self

pulling force

naad

Willpower intercept

This was shown by Yogesh. It is a willpower intercept, where the execution of will power by the coreSelf is terminated so that the core is left with no tool to connect to the intellect or any other adjunct. This leaves the core powerless but it also gives the core a sense of being immune to the influences of the adjuncts.

A yogi must meditate to understand how the coreSelf is surrounded by a sense of identity, which encloses the core on all sides, spherically. The sense of identity is a neutral power but it becomes prejudiced towards the intellect and is affected by the conditions and operations of the intellect. When the core is inquisitive about the activities of the intellect, the core emits an interest which forms as a protrusion from the sense of identity. This protrusion is experienced as an exhibition of attention or as willpower, a type of mental muscle.

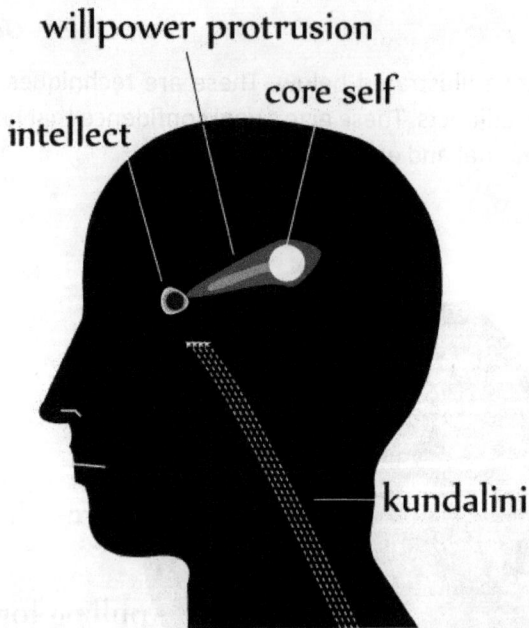

willpower protrusion

core self

intellect

kundalini

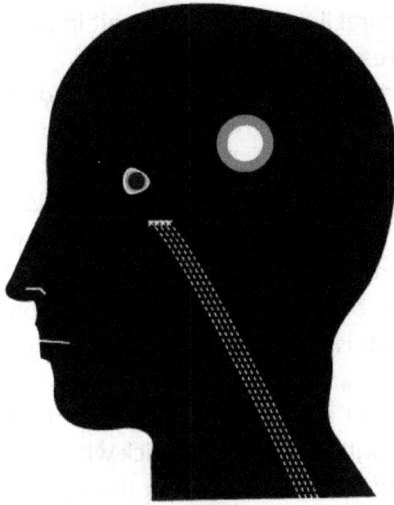

willpower extension
withdrawn

October 22, 2007

Sound naad / Vision jyoti

This was a naad sound absorption meditation with additional jyoti light inVision. Many practicing kriya yogis tend to seek light in the subtle head during meditation. For them supernatural light is the craze. This practice is different because the focus and basis of this is continuous naad sound resonance emersion. When the sound absorption is properly established, when the coreSelf is flooded with naad resonance and is stabilized in it, the yogi, while holding the connection in naad, looks meekly to see if there is supernatural light. If there is none, if the mind space which is not occupied with naad is blank or presents ideas from the physical or lower subtle environments, the yogi returns fully to naad and postpones the effort to view supernatural light.

The conclusion drawn about this failure to contact supernatural light is that the yogi has not done sufficient naad absorption. He has to practice more and more until he qualifies. He must be patient and continue naad intonement.

If however when the yogi looks meekly to see if there is supernatural light, he actually perceives it, he should observe and check to be sure that he is still anchored in naad. Once he secures that anchor he should continue gazing at the supernatural light and should wait in that state of dual focus on naad and light for increase and clearer vision.

A question to be considered by those who do not have naad sound absorption as the anchor during kriya meditation is:

What is your anchor?

If the anchor is the coreSelf itself, then that is not a sensible answer because the core is a limited entity. It is perpetual by nature but its energy radiation is limited. It needs a shelter, other than itself.

Meditations in which there is no naad absorption, where the core exist in a mental space which is bland, void, grey or dark can be productive if the core feels settled in that and has no hankering for anything else. A yogi may remain in such a state for a time. Eventually from that state he will become naad cognizant. There will be a switch or click where the yogi will find that he shifted into naad sound resonance and that this resonance is there with a sky counterpart which is nourishing.

If however the yogi finds that the mental space has energy from physical existence with related memories and ideas, he should know that the meditation is worthless. He should find a method for removing the coreSelf from that low mental place.

October 24, 2007

Kundalini allegiance

The kundalini as one came to be aware of it through its functions, has allegiance primarily to sexual functions of the physical or subtle body. This arrangement is efficient in that the material bodies which the subtle body requires are short term. They do not last forever. They can however as a consolation for this, reproduce new forms which mimic their lifecycle behavior of birth, growth, sexual maturity, reproduction and death.

This mission of the kundalini where its primary allegiance is to sexual functions is justified in terms of the need for reproduction for the continuation of the species. However it so happens that in many lifeforms this reproduction energy is interpreted as a pleasure potency.

Pleasure is addictive, which means that the reproductive urge is exploited to derive the pleasure which is felt in reproduction motions. This is an energy expenditure. As it is with pleasure addictions, one is disinclined in keeping the tally of the energy consumed. One is hesitant for self-discipline because that would cause curtailment of pleasure.

For yoga however, the allegiance of the kundalini to the sexual functions must be broken. How the yogi does this is not a contention. The method can be this. It may be that. Our interest is that it should be done irrespective of the method used.

Since the physio-biological body is designed for reproduction, a yogi must study its outlay. He should design a way to change it so that the reproductive aim is minimized. The attention and related energies which are naturally invested in sexual functions should curtailed.

By practicing kundalini yoga, one may learn how to divert the sexual energy so that it is not all consumed in reproductive and the related pleasure functions. The kundalini can be reoriented so that it attracts sexual energy to itself and then with that energy moves up through the spine into the brain. This would be in contrast to the natural way of sexual expression where the kundalini is pulled into the sexual organs for sexual climax experience.

All cells of the body are dedicated to reproduction functions. This is how one or two bodies produce new bodies. It is a task for the yogi to change the mission of the cells so that their primary interest is not reproduction but is contributory to supernatural and spiritual insight of the coreSelf.

Naad zone check

A yogi should not take naad sound resonance for granted. He should carefully check naad, as to its location in or out of the subtle head, as to its size, as to its zonal reach, as to the volume, as to the intensity, as to the vibrational concentration, as to if it has a visual register, as to its attraction, as to its friendliness and as to its fondness for the coreSelf.

Many students listen to naad and take pride in the ability to do so but they neglect a full naad inspection. By all means one should minutely investigate naad. That alone is the full absorption.

The investigation of naad must include a thorough understanding of if naad originated from outside the psyche of the yogi, outside the subtle head. Did naad penetrate the psyche?

Does naad saturate the entire psyche or only a part of it? Is naad heard in the leg of the subtle body or in the head of it only? If it is in the head, is it in the entire head or is it in a part of it only.

The mantra for naad sound resonance contact is a popular mantra used in India. This is:

- *Om namah Shivaya*

It is also rendered as:

- *Om namo Shivaya*

Mental not audial repetition of this mantra may not cause the student to hear naad. It depends on which teacher gave this mantra to the student and on the condition of the meditation.

In my experience, *om namah Shivaya* does cause the attention of the yogi to perceive naad sound resonance. It may do so after many, a few or even one mental repetition of the mantra. If this does not happen for a student, he should not be discouraged but should practice the meditation he was introduced to until he can get more advanced instructions or be inspired with a superior method.

A yogi should check to see what activities he can render when immerged in naad. Can the coreSelf complete thinking ideation activities when in naad? Must the core exit naad to complete mental acts?

Does the intellect reside in naad?

Can the core bring the intellect into naad?

Where is the intellect located while the core is immerged in naad?

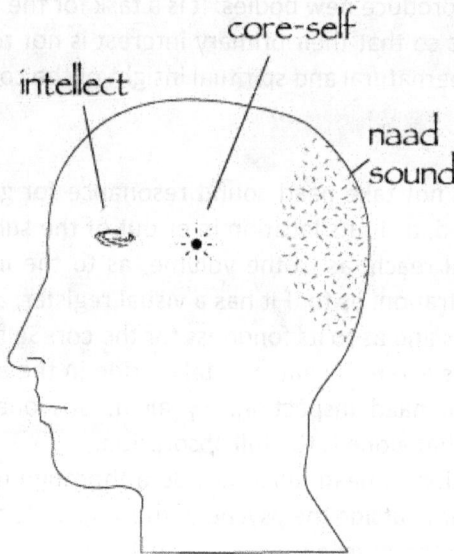

October 29, 2007

Yogeshwarananda

He stated that the condition of the kundalini affects one's ability to control the intellect. The kundalini influences the intellect for lower or higher interest. Efforts by the coreSelf to sever the connection between the kundalini and the intellect are mostly ineffective because the design of the psyche is such that the kundalini has power over the intellect. The willpower of the core does not have absolute power over the kundalini or the intellect. It is experienced that on occasion the willpower commands the psyche but for the most part, it does not have absolute power. The willpower operates efficiently only when the intellect and kundalini agrees to its proposal.

The yogic process takes these facts into account. Thus kundalini yoga is for mastery and upgrade of the kundalini with a resulting benefit that the kundalini influences the intellect to endeavor for and to cooperate for the objectives of yoga. This is better than thinking that by wishes, mental commands or desires one can cause the intellect or the kundalini to cooperate. Haphazard now and again cooperation is insufficient. One must master kundalini yoga to gain definite control of the intellect.

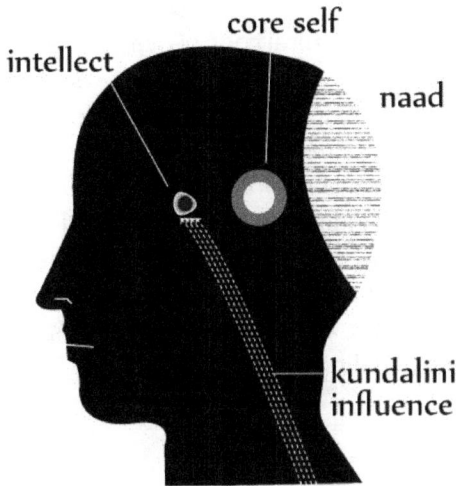

October 31, 2007

Imagination orb

The imagination orb is part of the intellect analysis mental illustration psychic mechanism. The intellect is an invisible organ, which is difficult to perceive. The intellect is mostly understood through its activities and not directly. When it is inactive it disappears. It seems to be nonexistent.

A yogi should study the intellect to get the experiences of its operative and non-operative states. It must be checked to understand how it is connected to the memories and how it acquires sensual input. The imagination orb is part of the intellect. This orb should be studied because it has a high interference grade during meditation. The sense of identity is frequently hypnotized by the imagination even during meditation. Due to this orb the coreSelf loses grasp on the meditation objectives and frequently finds itself under the spell of the orb.

The imagination orb is prompted to show an icon or scene which is a caption to a series of other scenes. The prompt may be a sound or scene impression. The prompt may come from the kundalini, one or more of its sensual offshoots, or from memory, or from a nudge from the sense of identity which desires to see a sequence of images displayed.

The sense of identity does not retain images or impressions of anything. It is neutral and has no retaining ability. However it is laden with desire to see impressions displayed. Hence it may emit a call or prompting for the intellect (imagination orb) to produce a display. This hunger of the identity for displays is the bane of it. Somehow a yogi must change this if he wants to enter deep meditation.

The coreSelf has some natural control over the sense of identity but this control is limited. In fact the sense of identity is controlled more by its attraction to the intellect than it is to anything else. For this reason the core must exert itself in meditation to change what is natural for the identity.

The intellect is more distant from the core than the sense of identity, which makes it even more difficult, more unnatural for the core to control the intellect. The truth is that as the psyche was designed, the intellect is influenced primarily by the kundalini psychic lifeForce. Until the core can bring the kundalini to order, there is little hope that it can wrestle control of the psyche from the kundalini.

November 1, 2007

Yogeshwarananda

He advised that yogis should pull and tug on the imagination orb intellect psychic mechanism. Initially it is not possible to do this because a student may not have the clarity of mind to locate the adjuncts. However as one practices more and more, the required insight is developed.

When there is a visualization or imagined idea, the coreSelf perceives it because there is a compulsion in the sense of identity to relay the information from the intellect. At that time, a yogi should realize that the intellect is easy to identify because it is the instrument which constructs the ideation in the mind. The core should pull on the display. If the display disappears, the core should pull on the location where the display was seen. This is how it is done.

It helps considerably if the core is in touch with the naad sound resonance. If it is not connected to or anchored in naad, it may not have the power to tug the intellect. It could attempt to do so but the intellect may ignore the prompting.

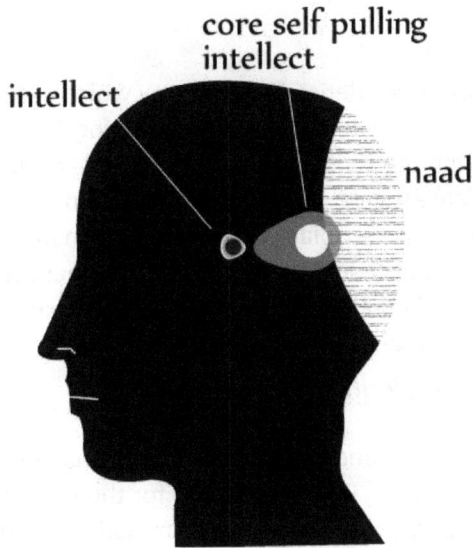

core self pulling
intellect

intellect

naad

November 2, 2007

Kundalini saturation

Conventional kundalini arousal causes a rush of supernatural energy through the spine into the subtle head. It comes into the subtle head from the back center of the neck, from in the middle of the spine. There is whole body kundalini where it spread through the trunk of the subtle body and passes through the neck not just the spine of it.

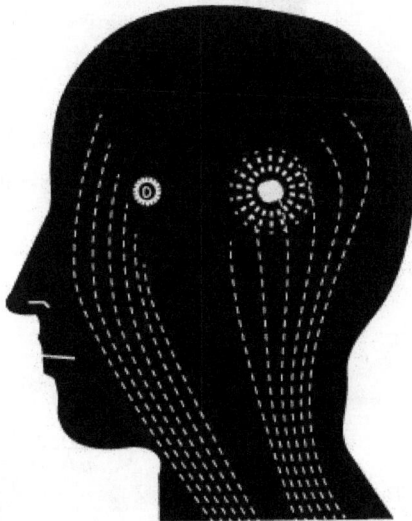

CoreSelf in fog

The coreSelf exist in a dense foggy energy which allows it no clarity and no vision except what is revealed near to it in the fog. Whatever it sees in this way is distorted. Even the senses which itemize and censures objects are not calibrated. The senses give incorrect information and form erroneous conclusions. Still, the core is reliant on this misinformation. What can it do?

The material existence and the lower astral planes are in the fog. A yogi has the mission to dissipate the fog and attain clear insight to see the supernatural and spiritual environments.

Breath infusion to muladhar base chakra

As long as the navel and reproductive zones have heavy astral energy and subtle polluted energy, it is not possible for the infused breath energy to directly strike the kundalini lifeForce at the muladhar base chakra. However this does not mean that the kundalini cannot ever reach the base chakra. It can but it must do so reaching it after successfully infusing the navel and then the reproductive zones. Ultimately a yogi must target these zones so that all heavy astral energy and subtle polluted force no longer resides at the navel area and pubic regions. When the pollutions are removed, the yogi may directly attacked the base chakra.

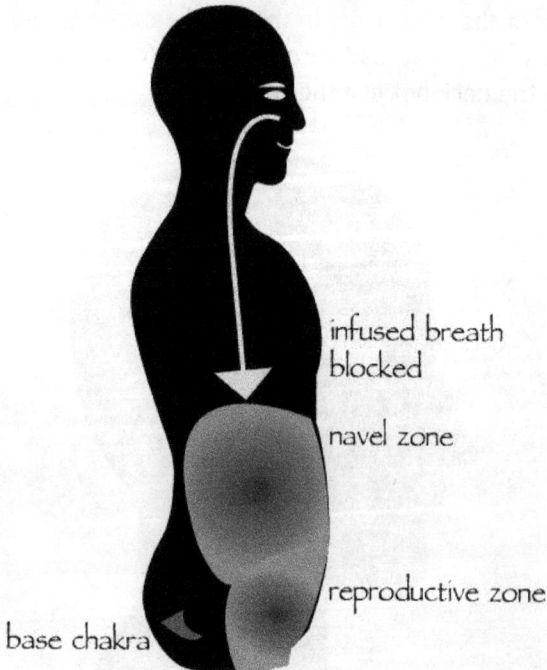

infused breath blocked

navel zone

reproductive zone

base chakra

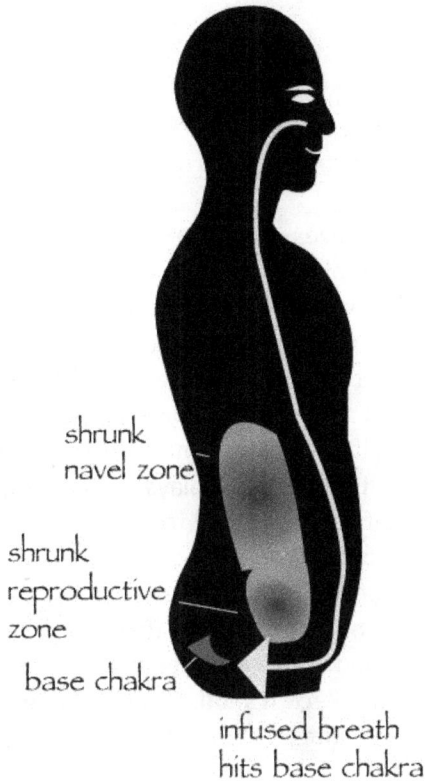

shrunk
navel zone

shrunk
reproductive
zone

base chakra

infused breath
hits base chakra

November 8, 2007

Practice

Consistent practice brings success, if only after a long period of time. Some methods must be corrected by an advanced yogi but some errors will be realized by the student. One should feel a sense of direction, a force of making progress as the objectives change as one advances.

Sometimes after some months or years, one realizes or one is told about an incorrect method which one had great confidence in. This should not cause discouragement. This should be noted so that one may explain it to others who are on lower stages and who are prone to the same error.

November 13, 2007

Muktananda

He wanted to assist in the effort in removing heavy astral energy which gives mental darkness and calling up or attracting the kundalini upward through the psyche.

The practice which gives the coreSelf the ability to command the adjuncts is development of the reliance on naad sound resonance. The experience of the self in isolation in the center of the mind, is one of the coreSelf being surrounded by the sense of identity and holding itself in abeyance with no contact to the intellect and without emotional influences affecting the core. In that state the self is likely to lose objectivity. When that happens it discovers itself in the mind under the convention of being under the influence of the intellect's displays. This happens frequently in alternation, with the self being isolated from the intellect and feelings, and then with the self being influenced by the same.

Naad sound resonance is the free reliable shelter for the coreSelf. It should abandon the blank mind and fix itself into naad. That reliance is superior to the blank mind state. From being in naad resonance, the core should turn to face the intellect. It should do so and determine if it has more power to command the intellect and if the intellect has less ability to hypnotize the core.

The core should realize that without naad support, it does not have the absolute authority over the intellect. It is prone to being influenced even if it becomes stabilized in the blank state of mind. The intellect will carry through with oscillations in procuring objects or memories of objects. As soon the core becomes absorbed in the blank state, the intellect may in another dimension continue with the procurements of impressions. This activity will develop strength to attract the core.

November 14, 2007

Muktananda

He requested that I write more and explain the importance of consistent daily practice. His idea is that descriptions of daily meditations have variations such that students would be encouraged to exert for progress.

Muktananda said that if the kundalini does not migrate to the head, there is no question of liberation. The convention of kundalini is to remain at the base chakra. When it is motivated it may move into the head momentarily. That is insufficient. After repeatedly arousing kundalini on a consistent basis, kundalini will itself flush through the sushumna nadi central spinal passage. This will cause the passage to remain clear of pollution and low grade subtle energy. Kundalini will then always radiate through the spine into the head. If a yogi can maintain a cleared spinal passage for some years, kundalini will migrate into the head, abandoning the base chakra.

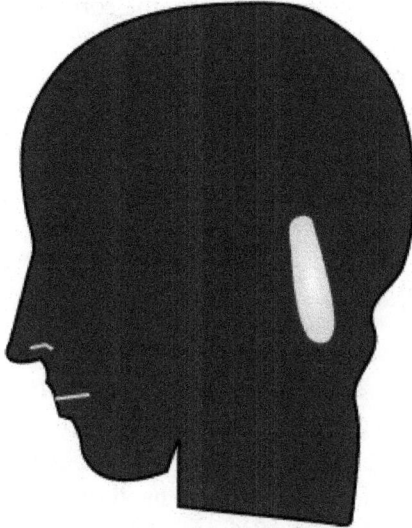

November 15, 2007

Muktananda

He stated that the sexual energy, the anal energy system and the navel digestive mechanisms should be lifted. This is achieved by doing breath infusion as kapalabhati/bhastrika pranayama.

When the psyche is elevated, it no longer has heavy astral energy and pollutions. This results in meditations which are high grade, where conventional thoughts, images and ideas are absent. The yogi is no longer terrorized within the mind during meditation. The terror is conducted by the intellect and by the kundalini psychic lifeForce.

The intellect acts with terror by creating ideas which have the power to lure the coreSelf into abandoning meditation to become absorbed in what is imagined as a mental video. The intellect uses impressions from memory and from the sensual energy. The long lost memories leave the chest area and float up where they become attached to the intellect which become pregnant with the ideas and is compelled to illustrate them in the mind.

There are current memories which are in the head of the subtle body or in the neck area. These also besiege the intellect, which under assault is forced to accept them. It then illustrates these and the power generated attracts the core for viewing what they produce in the mirror of the mind.

The kundalini psychic lifeForce also terrorizes the coreSelf but it does so through expression of feelings which it creates outright and which the intellect illustrates. These powerfully draw the coreSelf to the intellect, where the core hankers for illustrations of the feelings.

All of this is the bane of yoga. This cause failure to reach high states of meditation. It secures the yogi as a mediocre ascetic with no hope of ever becoming advanced.

November 15, 2007

Muktananda

He explained that in deep meditation, there is the likelihood that the kundalini will continue shimmering and moving on some other plane of existence. This will attract the core eventually. Hence it is required that one elevate the kundalini before doing meditation, because this will cause the kundalini to be less of a disturbance as it will be in a high state of consciousness in which it is not a nuisance to the self.

November 18, 2007

Muktananda

He discussed the tail like kundalini. It is similar to the form of the spine of an alligator but in the human form the kundalini spreads into two parts to provide nerves for two feet.

Looking from outside the physical or subtle body, one may see indications of the kundalini by observing how its nervous system is designed for control of the limbs and senses of the body.

Peering at it from inside the mind, as the coreSelf, one begins by looking down from within the mind in the head of the subtle body through the neck and then through the trunk or spine in the trunk. Initially there is no vision while doing this. One merely peers through mental darkness or blankness.

Those who do breath infusion just prior to meditation or in preparation for meditation, may see through the trunk of subtle spine and may see colors or energies with subjective hues.

When looking down one should be conversant with naad sound resonance. The observing self should cling to naad while looking down but there may be a narrow gap between the self and naad or the self may do so remaining emerged in naad.

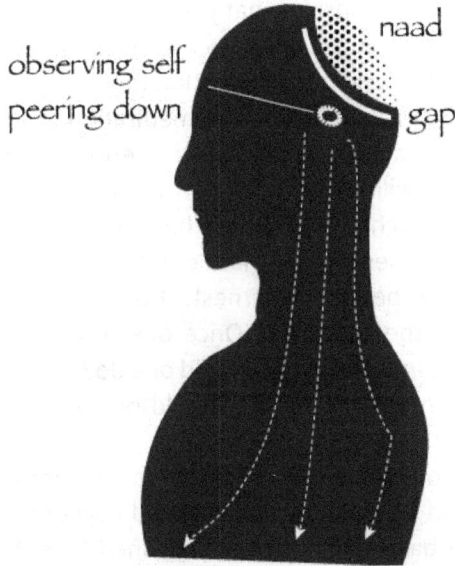

For some students a fear is experienced when attempting to look down through the neck of the subtle body. If however one persist in the effort and if one takes assistance from naad by having keen hearing of naad sound resonance during the effort, the fear will disappear.

November 28, 2007

Dharana technique

Dharana is listed by Patanjali as the sixth (6th) stage of yoga. It follows the fifth (5th) which is pratyahar. Generally those who meditate reach dharana infrequently. They struggle with pratyahar but do not realize that it is not rated as meditation. Pratyahar is the stage just before meditation.

Meditation begins with dharana and reaches its fullness in samadhi. The intermediary stage is dhyana. Patanjali listed dharana, dhyana and samadhi as samyama which is meditation.

Pratyahar is introspection with stress on causing the sensual energies to lose interest in what is outside the physical bodies as well as what is outside the subtle body but which is in the lower astral existence. I frequently translate pratyahar as sensual energy withdrawal. To understand what it means think of consumption through the senses. When this consumption ceases and the senses are no longer interested in the quest for objects that is pratyahar.

To better grasp this, consider that praty is actually prati which is a prefix which means against or reversal. Ahara means eating or consuming. When the psyche does the reversal of consumption that is pratyahar. It is necessary as a precursor to meditation. Just before meditation one's mind should have a lack of interest in consumption through the senses. If the mind does not do this the meditation will be erratic, which means that a high state of absorption will not be achieved. One will have no advanced insights.

If however the senses display a lack of interest in pursuing objects, then the meditation may begin in earnest. However we must define the meditation. What is the objective? Once one discovers oneself in a mind which has no sensual interest, what should one do? Should one remain in the blankness of the non-seeking mind? Should one adopt a particular focus? Should one mentally chant a mantra?

Hence there should be a specific psychic action done during meditation. This objective should be given by an advanced yogi or it may be adopted by the student on the basis of information gleaned from books like the *Yoga Sutras* of Patanjali or the *Bhagavad Gita* discourse of Krishna.

The yogi should focus on that objective. That deliberate focus is called dharana. The higher stage is dhyana which concerns the same focus except that it is done without effort. It is conducted spontaneously by the mind without the yogi having to exert attention or willpower to cause it.

The next stage is the final stage of yoga, which is samadhi. This is the same spontaneous focus but for a long period of time, say for five or fifteen minutes or more. Usually the spontaneous focus occurs for short durations, like for five or ten seconds only. Then the yogi must resume the deliberate focus where he exerts himself into the focus deliberately. This is why samadhi is special, because in samadhi the absorption lasts for a time all by itself without exertion.

November 30, 2007

Third Eye focus

Many kriya yoga sects recommend that one should sit to meditate and focus between the eyebrows where the third eye is located. This is also called the brow chakra. Any type of focus for procurement of anything outside the physical and subtle bodies, involves focusing through this chakra. It is important.

Yet, to meditate on it will not necessarily bring success to the yogi. Even though one may focus between the eyebrows, if it is blank there, one should focus mildly without much concentration. A firm focus there may cause the mind to resume its calculative mode. That would defeat the purpose of the meditation. If a tiny star appears between the eyebrows or if a space opens there, one may focus on the star or through the window space which becomes available. Even then, it should be a mild focus otherwise if one applies too much concentration that may cause the star or opening to instantly disappear.

December 6, 2007

Attention leakage

During meditation there will be leakage of the attention so that instead of the full attention being applied only a portion of it will be directed. The rest will be engaged in other behaviors which contravene the practice. Realizing that there is leakage is a skill in itself. Many students are not sensitive enough to know that the focus was breached in some way. However as one advances one recognizes this.

Naad is the way to gage what portion of the attention parted away from the desired focus. Naad absorption allows the coreSelf more objectivity so that it can see how the attention seeps away from the focus and engages in the shenanigans of the intellect. Even the intellect, even if it is quieted, may become active even without the coreSelf realizing this. Even the intellect must be inspected from time to time during meditation.

Shenyen Chang

This Taoist master said that once the willpower or attention of the coreSelf reaches across to the intellect, the kundalini energy rays cease rising through the subtle head. Kundalini then operates only as a survival seeking mechanism.

The flow of energy from the coreSelf to the intellect uses the sense of identity as the conduit. This energy causes the kundalini to lose interest in higher reality. The sense of identity is a neutral energy but it is prejudiced by the intellect. If the intellect has a high interest, the sense of identity will mimic that and maintain itself on a high psychic plane. Otherwise if the intellect has lower concerns the identity will mimic that and influence the coreSelf to endorse a development in lower realities.

When the kundalini strikes the intellect, whatever happens depends on the condition of the kundalini. If the kundalini is in a lower vibration the intellect will lack insight. The intellect is directly and immediately affected by the energy of the kundalini.

Unless it is isolated the sense of identity is affected by the changes in the intellect, such that if the intellect moves to a lower plane, the identity shifts along with it. If the coreSelf fails to isolate the sense of identity, the psyche will pursue whatever interest is expressed by the kundalini into the intellect.

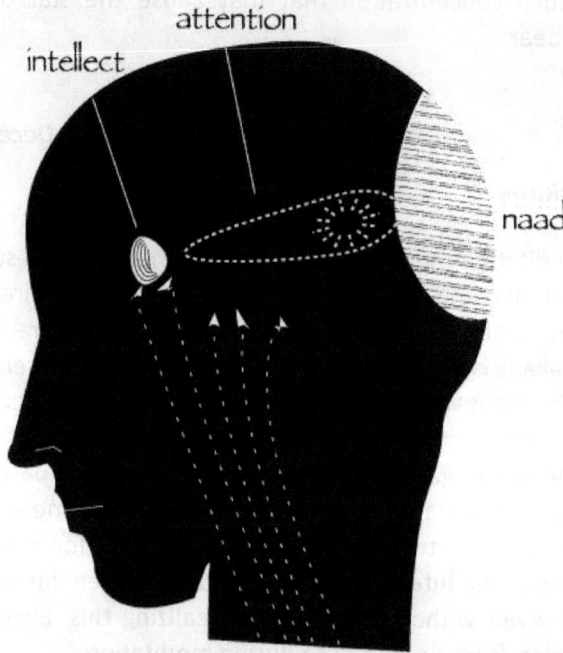

attention

intellect

naad

kundalini blocked by attention
but strikes intellect

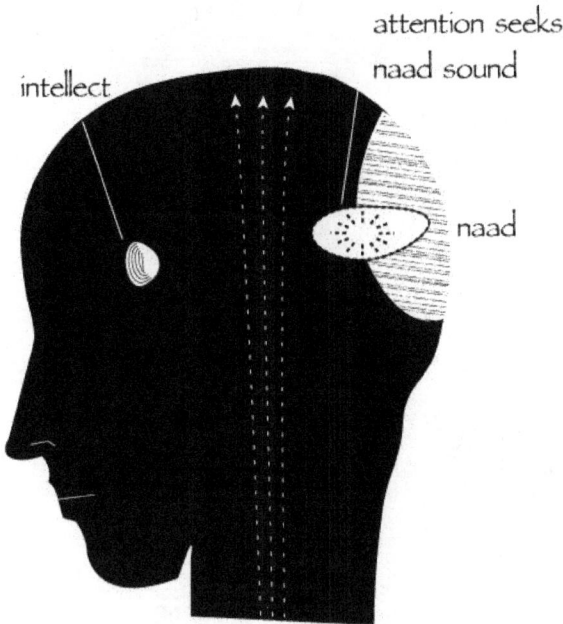

attention seeks
naad sound

intellect

naad

kundalini passes through head
does not strike intellect

December 7, 2007

Shenyen Chang

His advice is that during meditation a yogi should forget the desire for supernatural vision for the time being. Even though this desire is there, it should not be stress. The yogi should ignore it. If he can, during meditation practice, he should forget that he wants the psychic perception.

His view is that the attention of the coreSelf should be kept with the core and should not be expressed into the intellect. Interest or curiosity about the intellect should be dismissed. There should be no thoughts, not even flimsy compressed impressions which have potential to develop into full blown ideas.

December 8, 2007

Shenyen Chang

He claimed that naad is an ultimate objective and that the talk zones of the mind, the mental chatter and mental imaging areas should be bombarded with naad sound resonance.

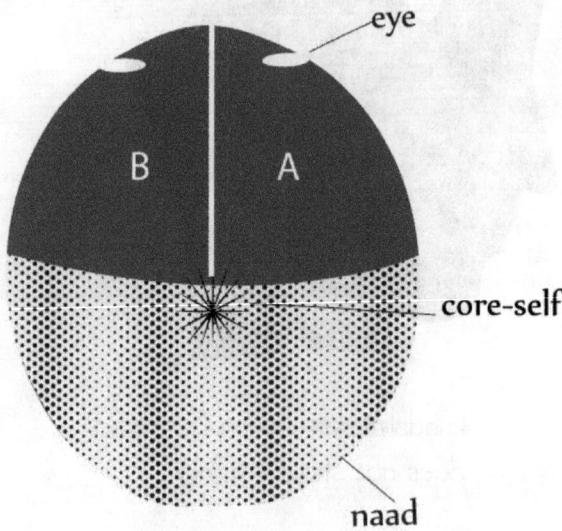

spread naad influence
into zones A and B

December 11, 2007

On close inspection, I saw that the sense of identity (ahamkara) developed as a psychic muscle around the coreSelf. Initially this energy surrounds the core on all sides evenly. In that state it is tensionless. However as soon as there is development of interest, tensions arise which surge in opposite directions. That results in a protrusion wave which sweeps around searching for something of interest.

A yogi must cause the protrusion to lapse, so that the sense of identity becomes tensionless again

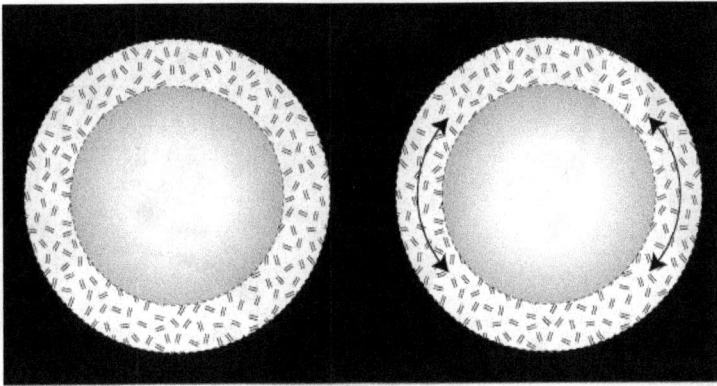

disinterested sense of identity
surrounding core-self

sense of identity searches
for interest around core-self

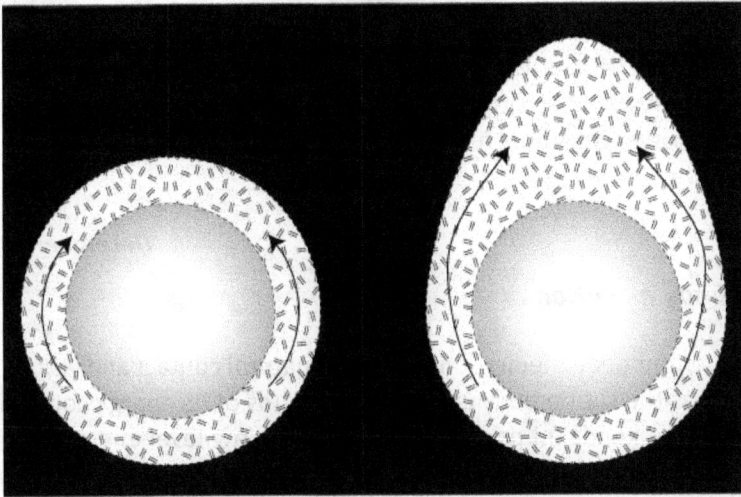

sense of identity searches
for interest towards
front of face

sense of identity searches
and protrudes towards
front of face

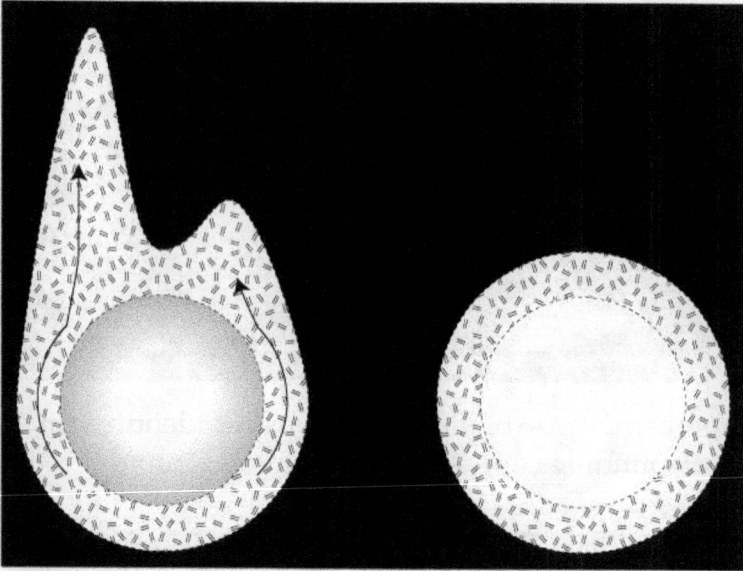

sense of identity
pursue one strong
and one weak interest

sense of identity
without interest

December 18, 2007

Subtle body elevation

Consistent deep meditation with supernatural contact and vision cannot occur unless the subtle body is elevated in terms of its energy consumption. So long as the kundalini psychic lifeForce has a low level energy intake, the psyche cannot provide deep absorption. In consideration, proficiency in kundalini yoga is necessary.

All parts of the subtle body should be cleared of low level astral energy. This includes the extremities like the fingers and toes. A yogi should persists with pranayama breath infusion, proper diet, proper times of eating, prompt evacuation, limited thinking and limited association with others. He should protect the senses from exposure to objects which cause the mind to neglect yoga practice.

The entire subtle body, the psyche, should be hollowed so that all negative energy, pollutants and low astral force is expelled from it.

November 20, 2007

The thigh muscles should be reformed. As they are created, their support is offered to the sex organs. A yogi should change this so that their energy moves up through the trunk and is not polarized merely for sexual participation.

My experience is that after a thorough session of kapalabhati/bhastrika breath infusion where the psyche is cleared of pollutants, especially in the thighs, legs, feet, arms, forearms, fingers, groin and buttocks, there is a likelihood that one will gain access to the chit akash sky of consciousness during the meditation that follows.

The mind is usually quieted. The intellect is shut down. The mind space has the light (jyoti) of the naad sound resonance which is a glow light which is soothing and which encourages one to wait for the access into the sky of consciousness.

Asana postures with breath infusion are not a waste of time. The tensing and relaxation of the muscles and tendons during stretches, causes the release of pollutants from the cellular level in both the physical and subtle systems. The breath infusion which is done during the stretches effects the removal of pollutants and infusion of fresh energy.

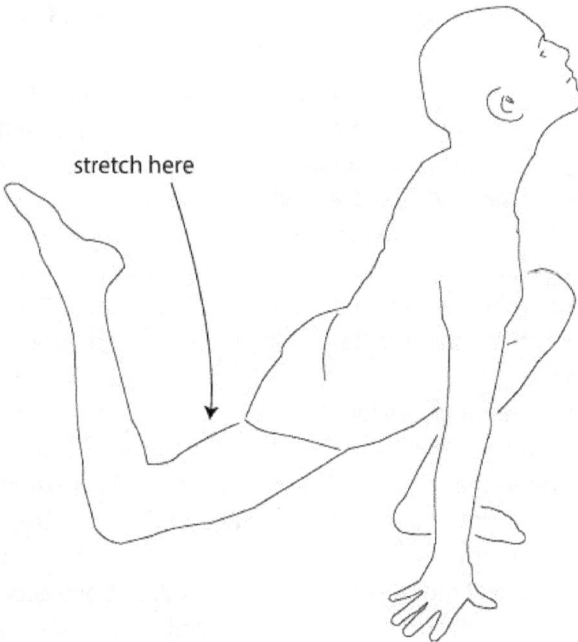

stretch here

December 24, 2007

Brow chakra opening

The brow chakra is also known as the third eye. It is an opening which occurs in the subtle head. From within the mind, looking forward, one may suddenly see an open space beyond which there is an environment or there may be light shining only or hazy light or light like moonlight. When this happens it may last for one, two or more seconds. Usually one cannot control the duration and one cannot direct it but one is directed by it in the sense that the vision may move around so that one sees different things in the environment which the third eye has access to.

Those who practiced deep meditation for a while may control the movement of the vision into the other dimensions. Such a yogi may direct the third eye but if his meditation lapses back to less absorption, he will lose the ability, even though he can by practice stabilize the progress again.

This event of brow chakra opening occurred a bit to the left of center. I could hold it for a short time only. Then it disappeared just as it became visible.

Subtle body / morality evasive

The subtle body is morality evasive, which means that it will find ways to breach physical morality. Physical morality varies from country to country depending on religious and secular ideas about social interactions. However the subtle body is not concerned with these rulings. It systematically evades the rules for approved physical behavior.

Myself being married, I had an astral sexual encounter with a married woman. Some days after this woman met me physically. She had no recall of the astral connection but I was aware of it. Her imprint of the relationship was known in her mind only as a desire to be sexually connected to me. When she met me physically, she brushed by my body so as to interact through the sense of touch.

During that seemingly incidental contact, her subtle body transformed and assumed a form which was identical to my wife's subtle body. The woman had no idea that her subtle body did that. This is similar to when a lizard's skin changes color to match tree bark and the lizard itself is not aware that the change occurred.

To bypass physical moral stipulations, the subtle body acts on its own to fulfill desires which social morality prohibit for the physical form. It does this with or without the consent of the social self. That social self is a mockup of various behavioral standards. To keep the status quo, the social self lives in one way and the subtle body in another. They do agree on occasion however.

January 2, 2008

Krishna

He sent a message which related that for a yogi, naad is like the mother's milk to a baby.

January 8, 2008

Nityananda

He said that when there is no clarity in the frontal part of the subtle head, a yogi should retreat into naad and become sound absorbed. He should remain with naad, abandoning the frontal area.

January 13, 2008

I concluded that the condition of the kundalini determines the quality of the meditation, one will have. If the kundalini has low grade energy, the meditation will be of low quality. If the kundalini has high grade subtle energy, the meditation will be productive with insight consciousness and bliss feelings. It is beneficial to master kundalini yoga. Pranayama breath infusion is not a waste of time.

January 19, 2008

Muktananda

His view is that a yogi should not pursue or even try to eliminate the thought-idea harassment theatrical shows in the mind. Instead of doing this, he should take shelter in naad sound resonance. He stated that his guru, Nityananda pioneered the naad absorption as the sure method for bringing on mental silence.

January 20, 2008

Muktananda

Using a miniature form, he entered the mind space. He showed how to use naad sound as an elimination force by pointing naad to the thoughts and ideas which arise in the mind during meditation.

A yogi should not be afraid of unwanted mental activity which arises during meditation. This activity may be compulsive, such that the coreSelf discovers itself viewing this even though it does not want to do so. But if the core is naad absorbed, it will have the strength to ignore the unwanted mental displays. This ignoring act will cause the displays to disappear.

When the frontal part of the subtle head has no thoughts or ideas, the core while being naad absorbed should look forward slightly. It should do so without anxiety and with very little exertion.

The behavior of the intellect, its functions, its dependent relationship on the kundalini and its command over the attention of the core, should be minutely studied by the yogi. I presented details of this in this and other books. Such information is helpful but it requires detailed inMind study to be realized. The realization is a power itself whereby the yogi gets the authority to command the intellect instead of being under its influence.

February 2, 2008

Mahesh Yogi

I saw this yogi in his special heavenly world. There with him are children only. He said that he experienced the Mahapurusha or Great Cosmic Person. This happened in meditation before he came to the Western countries. He said this Mahapurusha is the form of God which is parallel to the Vishvarupa Cosmic Supervisory Person who monitors the shifts in cultural participation.

February 6, 2008

I had a realization that the hankering for sex pleasure and the quest for spiritual happiness through kundalini are both motivated by the kundalini itself. However despite the similarity, the need for spiritual happiness should be pursued aggressively by a yogi, and the sexual pleasure quest should be discarded.

These aspects are based on the self's need for excitation, something which the self should study in detail and make a decision to curtail or expand according to the conclusions drawn about the elevation or degradation which results from a quest.

Sexual excitation usually leads to birth in a material body, while spiritual happiness causes an interest in transiting to higher dimensions which are not ridden with trauma as the material world is. Hence spiritual happiness should be pursued. It is preferred. However in so far as it is sponsored by the kundalini's need for pleasure, one should be wary about it.

February 22, 2008

Muktananda

His opinion is that the psyche is configured so that the kundalini is not handled directly by the coreSelf. The interaction between the core and kundalini is indirectly done by the intellect making direct contact with the kundalini. If the self wants to influence the kundalini in this arrangement, it has to do so through the sense of identity, which contacts the intellect. This arrangement is unsatisfactory because the intellect is prejudiced by the kundalini and the sense of identity is prejudiced by the intellect.

The core is reliant on so many other factors that it is an unreliable agency. Its success is part-time only. That is not suitable for yoga objectives. The self is required to make a detailed study of the operations and relationships of the adjuncts. Then a decision should be made about reordering the psyche.

Part 7

Accomplishment

I indexed the commentary on Bhagavad Gita which concerns kriya yoga. In chapter eighteen Krishna told Arjuna this:

पञ्चैतानि महाबाहो
कारणानि निबोध मे ।
सांख्ये कृतान्ते प्रोक्तानि
सिद्धये सर्वकर्मणाम् ॥१८.१३॥

pañcaitāni mahābāho
kāraṇāni nibodha me
sāṁkhye kṛtānte proktāni
siddhaye sarvakarmaṇām (18.13)

pañcaitāni — pañca — five + tāni — these; mahābāho — O mighty-armed man; kāraṇāni — factors; nibodha — learn; me — from me; sāṁkhye — in Sāṁkhya philosophy; kṛtānte — in conclusion, in doctrine; proktāni — declared; siddhaye — in accomplishment; sarvakarmaṇām — of all actions

Learn from Me, O mighty-armed man, of the five factors declared in the Sāṁkhya doctrine for the accomplishment of all actions. (Bhagavad Gita 18.13)

अधिष्ठानं तथा कर्ता
करणं च पृथग्विधम् ।
विविधाश्च पृथक्चेष्टा
दैवं चैवात्र पञ्चमम् ॥१८.१४॥

adhiṣṭhānaṁ tathā kartā
karaṇaṁ ca pṛthagvidham
vividhāśca pṛthakceṣṭā
daivaṁ caivātra pañcama (18.14)

adhiṣṭhānaṁ — location; *tathā* — as well as; *kartā* — the agent; *karaṇaṁ* — the instrument; *ca* — and; *pṛthagvidham* — various kinds; *vividhāśca = vividhāḥ* — various + ca — and; *pṛthakceṣṭa* — movements; *daivam* — destiny; *caivātra* — ca — and + eva — indeed + atra — here in this case; *pañcamam* — the fifth

The location, the agent, the various instruments, the various movements, and destiny, the fifth factor. (Bhagavad Gita 18.14)

शरीरवाङ्मनोभिर्यत्
कर्म प्रारभते नरः ।
न्याय्यं वा विपरीतं वा
पञ्चैते तस्य हेतवः ॥१८.१५॥

śarīravāṅmanobhiryat
karma prārabhate naraḥ
nyāyyaṁ vā viparītaṁ vā
pañcaite tasya hetavaḥ (18.15)

śarīravāṅmanobhiḥ = śarīra — body + *vān(vās)* — speech + *manobhiḥ* — with mind; *yat = yad* — whatever; *karma* — project; *prārabhate* — he undertakes; *naraḥ* — a human being; *nyāyyaṁ* — moral; *vā* — or; *viparītam* — immoral; *vā* — or; *pañcaite* — *pañca* — five + *ete* — these; *tasya* — of it; *hetayaḥ* — factors

As for whatever project a human being undertakes with body, speech and mind, regardless of it being moral or immoral, these are its five factors. (Bhagavad Gita 18.15)

It is interesting that initially Arjuna saw himself as the agent. That is why he was hesitant to do his duties. The task before him was greater than his capacity. Arjuna saw himself as the agent and did not consider other contributing factors. If we remain with only the agent idea, we are bound to be upset by providence.

Suppose it is unnatural to see the four factors and it is only natural to be aware of oneself as the agent, then the next best thing is to take lessons from the Bhagavad Gita and to remember these instructions when one find the self in a fix. If one does this, one will instantly get out of a bad way and become resituated without opposition to reality.

Children

Right now a big issue and crisis is the condition of children, regarding how they are raised. If you listen to News you will hear about gas prices, the economy, the housing crisis, global warming and warfare but few consider the condition of children. It is funny in a way because as soon as reincarnation is mentioned most conversations cease. But if reincarnation has no meaning why are we concerned about global warming. If you will have only one life, why does it matter if the planet is abused, because after all we will not be here for long?

It only makes sense to worry about global warming if we have some instinct that tells us that we will return to experience this environment at some future time. The immediate crisis is the condition of children and how we have made the world hostile to them. The big thing is sexual facility. We have carefully and surely made arrangements for sexual facility without having to worry about responsibility for children, as if we can go on with sex without the generation of infant bodies.

Actually everything hinges on infant bodies. If somebody is really after sexual intercourse then it is in the person's interest to secure some progeny, so that in the future there will be opportunity to take birth again and again grow up to have a teenaged and young adult body for sexual pleasure. Even from that angle childcare makes sense.

There is a part of the Bhagavad Gita in chapter two, where Krishna chided Arjuna saying that even if Arjuna felt that someone will die and that would be the end, still it made sense only to go ahead and do one's righteous duty, because at least, one would have lived a worthy life. Even if this is the only life, it makes sense to care for the infants and not to herd them into day care centers as soon as they are born.

On checking our attitude, we may find that we are careless about the prospects for rebirth. This carelessness comes from the lifeForce which is a blind force which is concerned with survival in any which way. But even though it is careless, it expects to get on top of everything and to have every convenience once it gets into a situation. This is why one race or group of people commit war against another and try to dominate another for resources.

Even though we are careless about rebirth, still if I take birth in a family haphazardly I still want the very best for myself. I still expect my parents to nurture me. When it is time for marriage, I desire the most qualified spouse. This careless methodology is done by the lifeForce. We mimic the lifeForce's attitudes without thinking deeply.

No time for meditation?

Try this. Settle the mind before resting. Do not grog out. Gather yourself, your emotions, ideas, feelings, frustrations, worries and everything. Just as you attempt to rest gently put every stress producing energy down in the mind space. Then meditate.

Under pressure?

Pressure will always be there. Suppose you carry a large weight on one shoulder. Eventually that shoulder will tire. Naturally if you desire relief, you could shift it to the other shoulder. Perhaps to ease both shoulders you may put the weight on your head. By that action you shifted the pressure to the neck. That is fine for a while because at least you would feel ease for the shoulders. But then the neck will soon be strained.

What do you do then?

You could carry the weight by gripping it with your fingers and allowing it to hang down. But then the fingers and arms will become strained.

To ease that and not to further aggravate any other body parts which are strained, you could brace the weight on your abdomen by leaning back. But soon the abdomen will be irritated with this.

All the while the feet were under the same strain. They will tire.

It is like that.

Pressures are ever present no matter what.

Daily practice

It is not easy to maintain a daily practice unless one is in an environment where that is enforced either by an authority or by peer pressure. Much of what we do consistently as human beings, takes place under some type of internal or external pressure. We are creatures of habit but habits which are not natural to animal forms, have to be developed and then maintained by consistent practice. If it is not maintained we regress to natural habits. These bodies are basic animal forms. It is natural for these forms to regress to creature habits.

Sometimes I am asked about maintaining a daily practice but this is not an easy topic to discuss because there is no single advice for everyone. Depending on your circumstance, you are afflicted with particular resistant energies which deter practice. For each individual, a particular method must be introduced.

If we study the ashram or hermitage environment, we will see that it is based mostly on two principles:

- The self-discipline of an authority, a resident or non-resident guru.

- The general peer pressure which causes everyone in the ashram to feel they must confirm to a prescribed lifestyle.

This means that we require pressure to conform. The question is: What is the difference between an ordinary resident of the ashram and the guru. The answer is that the guru has some inner driving force that keeps him or her going.

Buddha is a good example of a guru who had his own driving force and whose force was used by others to keep them in an ashram discipline. Even today thousands of Buddhists take help from even the memory of Gautama Buddha for maintaining austerities.

If you cannot find it in yourself to keep a daily practice, try to find a guru for whom you could commit to practice. If you cannot find such a person to whom you feel obligated, then commit yourself as you are.

Some energy for practice, some impetus, has to come either from yourself or from someone else. If you cannot get it from anywhere, you should be satisfied as you are.

In chapter twelve of Bhagavad Gita, Krishna digressed, saying that if one cannot do this, one should do that and if one still cannot do that one should do this. He gave alternatives. Study that chapter. See where you fit in.

Body waste in hatha yoga

One important aspect of yoga that is overlooked is evacuation of waste.

Hardly a human being, no matter how materialistic he or she may be, wants to live in a place where the solid and liquid waste of all sorts are not removed promptly. A hallmark of modern civilization is efficient garbage collection and sewage removal.

These things were mastered in Roman civilization but Chinese civilization also developed it efficiently. It is just that the Western version of it progressed from the lead and stone piping system of the Romans. Once plumbing was organized by governments, people lived in cities in relative cleanliness because of the efficient removal of sewage. That combined with government mandated garbage removal, made it cleaner. Specters like Black Death and other plagues receded from human civilizations.

In hatha yoga the stress is also the efficient removal of liquid waste, urine, and solid waste, stools, from the body. A yogi should attend to that. Usually human beings only pay attention to that when the body gets so old that it can no longer function because the piping is clogged up completely, such that enemas and colon surgery must be given like getting a citation from the city because of keeping garbage in your back yard, rather than paying the municipal authorities to haul it away.

Each day a yogi should be sure to check the body to be sure that the urine and stools are promptly evacuated.

This physical act helps in raising and cubing kundalini shakti from its lower habits. I recommend it highly. Do not let a day pass that you cannot say to yourself, that yesterday's solid waste passed out of the body.

Arthur Beverford

Just recently I got news that Arthur Beverford passed from his body in February 20, 1999. He is the person who was my first yoga teacher, when I was in the Philippines. He was a martial arts instructor. Bee as he was known studied martial arts in Korea and Japan, and also was in a Buddhist monastery when he turned away and decided for family life. He had also studied yoga under a contemporary of Paramhansa Yogananda, who was Rishi Singh Gherwal, a master of hatha yoga.

Kundalini / primal drive

Some persons think that the purpose of kundalini is to motivate the effort for enlightenment.

If this was true, we would not have to endeavor for yoga austerities in order to both energize kundalini and gain enlightenment. Kundalini's natural posture is survival. The kundalini lifeForce acts as the protector of the body. It is primarily concerned with survival. It has no interest in enlightenment. For kundalini enlightenment means getting accurate information from the senses in order to exploit opportunities in nature.

Kundalini does motivate us, but not for enlightenment. When we find that it motivates us for enlightenment, we will soon realize that its objective is enjoyment and the procurement of experience.

Patanjali comes to our rescue. He said that the purpose of prakriti, subtle material nature, is to provide experience.

Kundalini's main concern is survival. Its subsidiary interest is experience. It survives to experience. It is not true that it is concerned with enlightenment, except that in the quest for enlightenment, kundalini does appreciate the higher experiences gained

The self must itself push on for that quest. If it waits for kundalini to motivate, the self will be waiting for millions of years. For that matter many of us did just that.

Motivation / habit

Motivation sponsors endeavor. Habit converts an endeavor into a spontaneous or involuntary act. For years, teaching yoga I observed how this functions in the lives of aspiring yogis. For one thing, people start in the quest of spiritual advancement on the basis of a motivation. If it is weak their start is correspondingly weak. They soon fizz out. If the motivation is strong they begin with a huff and a puff as if they struggle for the achievement. Soon after if the practice fails to form into a habit, they leave aside the effort and either tag along or give up completely.

Motivation may not last. It may give a good start. Then it may disappear.

Why does habit not stick with us in spiritual practice even though it sticks with us in other aspects of our lives?

Motivation gets one started but it soon abandons one to the care of habit, except that habit may be concerned only to maintain already developed habits.

Incremental yoga progress

Sometimes people doubt when it is explained how slow spiritual advancement may be and how hard it is to attain perfection. Usually one is in the mood of getting instant results and of feeling that one ought to have this or that, merely because one exists in this creation.

Even if one observes that life is made up of little events, still the tendency for instant results may not go way. One may still be impatient.

Human civilization took millions of years to develop, not just thousands but millions, and with large contributions from other species of life, except that we seem to be in the culmination or peak of it. When one is at the peak of attainment, one has a tendency to forget the long journey to the top. The enjoyment one feels at the peak, robs one of the vision of the many years of effort involved in producing a particular ideal.

There is also a confusion between attainment and use of an attainment. The person who uses a computer, and who purchased it with $600, does not have the same attainment of the electronic genius who supervised the manufacture of the item. However the user may feel that he or she has attained the computer, even though in fact, that person is not part of the genius in the product's development.

In a sense each person tries to accomplish something big, but does one realize that the user of a computer may not have the gadget as his or her attainment. One who masters the usage of a product may not in any way have a part of the attainment of its manufacture. In fact the consumer may have no attainment in comparison to the manufacturer.

To manufacture the item, a group of human beings must first take shelter under the attainment of humanity in its million-year evolutionary history. These persons do this by detailed study in universities and elsewhere. That study is made up of trillions of little parts of information and research.

In spiritual development a similar feat is accomplished by yogi mystics who take years, in fact lives of practice to reach the perfection of yogic insight. To utilize those studies, one too will have to give detailed attention to the practice and research into yogic techniques, just as the technocrats of computers do in reference to man's evolutionary march through science.

There is a similarity between these scientists and the yogis. The only really difference between them is that they are tackling a totally different topic. If a yogi wants to excel, discover the psychic world and get direct insight into it, as well as to share that research information with others, he must be just as dedicated as a scientist. The yogi must show that his information is genuine and transparent.

Everyone is trying to accomplish something big, including yogis. An ascetic should realize that small achievements, thousands of them, will in the long run add up to something big in the form of spiritual vision. Yoga is out of reach of those who are not patient in this regard.

If one cannot appreciate small progressions made while doing yoga, one cannot be successful, since so much of it is attained in bits and pieces, which are summarized from time to time with big realizations and visions.

I encourage every yogi to keep a daily log of his efforts. Keep track of the bits and pieces, even the smallest of realizations and observations. Those little parts will summarize into big achievements. If you neglect the parts, feeling that they are trivial and are of no consequence, you will be throwing away the big achievement.

Identity dependence

One of the things we struggle with is identity dependence. Particularly in the social field of life, one has to have an identity to survive, just as when one moves to a foreign country one has to keep a passport handy in case of arrest, where officers would immediately ask, "Who are you? How did you get here? To which country do you belong?"

Though it is a necessity, the identify dependence pose questions for all aspiring yogis.

What is the worth of social identity? How much of it should one support?

Suppose you are a termite queen in the heart of the Amazon jungle. What is your identity? Are you the mother of thousands of termite eggs you lay in one life time?

What will happen to you when your queen bodies dies, either by natural causes or by a poisonous sting injected by enemy ants?

Will your reign end at that time? Or will you continue laying in the subtle world?

To those thousands of termites in the colony, you are the ultimate mother, a literal Goddess, source of life. No other termite in the colony has such a large body as yours. No other female in the colony is able to reproduce. You are special and ultimate in the colony. The other termites stand in awe of you.

But again, is that honor really yours. Are you just another tool of life like the insignificant army termites who walk up and down briskly all their waking hours, until they drop in a tunnel from the exhaustion which brought on their deaths?

After assuming that life-giving role which nature graciously bestowed upon you, would it be possible for you to forget all about it and not take yourself seriously, to see that the honor was only related to your place in nature as a utility?

Practice

In meditation one should make every effort to identify and catalog the various types of energies which develop in the psyche. Some situations cause a particular energy to gain power over the psyche. Even though an energy may go dormant, still if a certain type of situation arises, that energy will, all of a sudden, without notice to the coreSelf, arise and take over the psyche, forcing it to act, and forcing the self to be responsible for the good or bad effects of the action.

The secret to understanding action is to realize what Buddha explained which is that everything concerning this world ends traumatically. That was his conclusion. He observed the ordinary miseries like disease and death. Later when he attained enlightenment, he factually realized this by supernatural vision.

Once we can identify the various energies in meditation, we can observe and control those energies when we are not in meditation. The way it works is this: At first one has to meditate. One must discern the various forces in the psyche in meditation. After one can identify those forces, one can begin observing and regulating their manifestation and behavior.

In the Bhagavad-Gita, Krishna gave the hint of karma yoga, or karma with yoga, karma plus yoga. That is cultural activities with the application of the realizations gained through yoga practice. Cultural life by itself without that application has no insight.

The word psyche simply means the mental and emotional energies which we live in, within the self. But the coreSelf is just one item in the psyche. There are others. When we use the word self to mean the coreSelf with all contents of the psyche, we are abiding by convention. The coreSelf is not the psyche. It is only one component.

No one can assist you in self-improvement if you do not practice. You must practice if you want to gain advancement. If one does not endeavor for money, usually one does not get it. If one does not practice, there will be no advancement in meditation. Practice is necessary.

Why should I practice if I do not feel to do it and if I do not have the impetus to attempt it?

This question is answered simply like this:

One should practice due to being asked to do so by a teacher. The relationship with a teacher is based on compliance to practice. If there is no compliance, the realization and benefits of meditation cannot flow.

Kundalini / learning

Learning, an aspect of life which sometimes becomes an unwanted challenge, is required in these existences. There is so much one should adopt in every life and in any dimension one may enter.

In some higher dimensions, the body one assumes, has within it most of the attributes which one requires to function properly, but there are situations we may enter, in which we would be better off, if we took the time to learn methods of efficient operations in those places.

In the Bhagavad Gita, the situation of learning is there from the beginning, with Arjuna being perplexed, suffering from a mental break down and asking for advice. Krishna gave Arjuna a crash course on karma yoga.

Can we teach ourselves or orient ourselves to learn and cause ourselves to have a willingness to learn? In each life we must re-learn nearly everything except how to eat, how to evacuate and other involuntary actions like how to have sexual intercourse. These rudimentary educations are given to us by the grace of a Nature which itself is preoccupied day and night with learning.

Geneticists try to figure the lessons learned by Nature by studying the genetic code, which they say began with just one strand of chemical coding and progressed into millions of strands of information, which diverged into various species of life. Each species developed variations which were adaptations due to voluntary or forced learning, brought on by environmental pressures.

Whatever is not given to us by Nature, but which we would be better off using, can only be developed through learning. This learning begins in each new body in childhood. It is conducted by the natural teachers, the parents or guardians, with their *"Don't do that! Do this!"* instructions. Later if one is in a developed environment, one gets more training in schools. Then again one gets trained in a skill.

A lack of learning poses a threat to one's social security, since it is tied to the income one generates. Is learning worth it? Should one subject oneself to rigors of education?

From the perspective of kundalini yoga, the kundalini force is the main force concerned with learning, which it gains through experiencing different situations through the senses. Kundalini is obsessed with learning but only for the purpose of mastering survival. Kundalini is obsessed with survival in the material world. It feels that sooner or later it may get such a full education that it would not be subjected to existential pressures of change which usually require it to vacate one material body after another.

But obviously, we can conclude that kundalini is plain crazy, because such a goal will never be realized. Still learning remains a necessity in these worlds.

God's contribution

Praying is a good idea when one may be unable to change an undesirable or a stagnating situation. After all, if one does not have the power to change the circumstances of life, one may appeal to some other power which can affect the desired change.

However, I recommend that the energy used in praying and hoping, be carefully collected in the psyche and be invested instead in an endeavor to make progression, to practice. This energy is itself unruly. One should carefully gather it, because it is usually scattered.

Suppose you need to have a glass of sand for some reason or the other. But it so happens that the only sand in the vicinity, is in your back yard, scattered as tiny grains which mixed with top soil. What should you do? Should you pray that a beach should form at your front door? Of course you will not do that. That would be absurd.

But if you will not do that what should you do? If in fact the only sand in the vicinity is in your back yard mixed in with many square feet of top soil, your only recourse would be to patiently gather those grains until you got the required quantity.

Thus what I am saying is that the energy of hope, the energy of praying for grace, needs to be redirected, so that it is invested in fulfilling your desired spiritual needs. To do that you should be patient with yourself and very insistent upon yourself to practice.

One clear understanding is that God will not produce a beach at your front door. Once you get that idea, you can plan to acquire that sand which is in the top soil. But then there is a question: Is it really worth the endeavor?

If God brings the beach, then of course you could easily get your glass of sand and the value of that desire would not occur. But if you have to collect sand grains from a mixture of top soil, the question of the worth becomes paramount. At that point you may consider, "This is worth it, even if takes me two years of sorting for those sand grains."

Or you may think: "This is not worth it. It will take forever. I should endeavor for something that will give me immediate results."

But stop and think about it. If it is not worth it to you, it means that the desired glass of sand, was not worth God's attention to your prayer. If God were to give you that beach God would be a fool in a way. Why should God fulfill a whimsical desire?

In spiritual life, God already did His part. The only thing lacking is our endeavor as per his instructions in Bhagavad Gita. Otherwise persons like Patanjali did their part and gave instructions.

My point is that you need to realize that God will do nothing about it. He already made the contribution to your development. You should collect energies of hope. You should apply them to the task at hand.

In spiritual life the progression comes bit by bit. It does happen that one makes a big progression all of a sudden but that is after one completes many small steps. It is like this: Because the car stalled a man pushed it uphill. Of course it was an effort, but when he got it to the top the rest happened easily. The car willingly rolled. In spiritual life one begins by pushing oneself to practice. Suddenly at a certain stage one attains stability and deep insight.

Momentum of meditation

Arjuna inquired of the failure of yogis to complete the practice. He said:

अर्जुन उवाच
अयतिः श्रद्धयोपेतो
योगाच्चलितमानसः ।
अप्राप्य योगसंसिद्धिं
कां गतिं कृष्ण गच्छति ॥६.३७॥

arjuna uvāca
ayatiḥ śraddhayopeto
yogāccalitamānasaḥ
aprāpya yogasaṁsiddhiṁ
kāṁ gatiṁ kṛṣṇa gacchati (6.37)

arjuna — Arjuna; uvāca — said; ayatiḥ — indiscipliined person; śraddhayopeto = śraddhayopetaḥ = śraddhayā — by faith + upetaḥ — has got; yogāccalitamānasaḥ = yogāc (yogāt) — from yoga practice + calita — deviated + mānasaḥ — mind;

aprāpya — not attain; yogasaṁsiddhim — yoga proficiency; kāṁ — what; gatiṁ — course; kṛṣṇa — Krishna; gacchati — he goes

Arjuna said: What about the undisciplined person who has faith? Having deviated from yoga practice, having not attained yoga proficiency, what course does he take, O Krishna? (Bhagavad Gita 6.37)

कच्चिन्नोभयविभ्रष्टश्
छिन्नाभ्रमिव नश्यति ।
अप्रतिष्ठो महाबाहो
विमूढो ब्रह्मणः पथि ॥६.३८॥

*kaccinnobhayavibhraṣṭaś
chinnābhramiva naśyati
apratiṣṭho mahābāho
vimūḍho brahmaṇaḥ pathi (6.38)*

kaccin = kaccid — is he; nobhayavibhraṣṭaś = na — not + ubhaya — both + vibhraṣṭaḥ — lost out; chinnābhram = chinna — faded + abhram — cloud; iva — like; naśyati — lost; apratiṣṭho = apratiṣṭhaḥ — without foundation; mahābāho — O Almighty Kṛṣṇa; vimūḍho = vimūḍhaḥ — baffled; brahmaṇaḥ — of the spirituality; pathi — on the path

Is he not like a faded cloud, lost from both situations, like being without a foundation? O Almighty Krishna: He is baffled on the path of spirituality. (Bhagavad Gita 6.38)

As it is with everything, if one leaves aside an item, one may endeavor to assume its possession again. Even ordinary habits like brushing the teeth in the early morning, must again be assumed by renewed efforts if one neglects to do it. Yoga practice, meditation habits, have the same application.

Momentum indicates that the yogi has a sense of having a sustained practice. He misses that sustained force when he sits to meditate after leaving aside the practice for a time. The yogi should reflect on how he developed a sustained practice in the first place.

The method of development of a sustained meditation practice is the same now as it was formerly when ancient yogis practiced. It is the same thing with yogis who all of a sudden realize that they were yogis in the past life and that they forgot the practice, and who find themselves missing that practice in a new body.

For example, if a yogi passed away, let us say in 1946. He left that body after practicing and attained an advanced stage. However this yogi despite the advancement found himself still stuck in the lower astral regions. He did not transfer to a higher subtle world. He found that he took another body, because that is the way of nature's operations in the lower subtle levels.

In the new body, he found that around 16 years of age, he suddenly begins remembering something about yoga. This first surfaces in the mind as an instinct for practice and an interest in things having to do with psychic phenomena. Then over some four or five years, he gets some ideas about his past life from books like Bhagavad-Gita and from persons who are conscious of past lives.

What is his situation? Can he suddenly and effortlessly resume the sustained practice from the former life?

Obviously that would hardly happen. The nature of things, is that this resumption comes about only by renewed efforts. If the yogi does not make special efforts to resume the practice, he will not rise to his former level of advancement. Nature will simply not allow it, because Nature's method is support for downward devolution. Upward evolution comes about in Nature by striving.

Will Nature allow a yogi to resume a former practice, from the moment that yogi sits down to meditate?

This is the question!

It may be better to ask this:

What efforts are required for the resumption of a former practice?

Does one have to do elementary practice again?

Once you consider that, the inquiry leads to this question:

Is it worth it?

Observation of thoughts in meditation

The observation of thoughts is the first stage in meditation practice. This is natural because it is the nature of the mind to ramble on. This produces the saying that an idle mind is the devil's workshop, or that if one refrains from constructive activity, one will, by the nature of the mind begin thinking of something mischievous. There are thoughts and potential energy for thoughts even in focused minds but there are multiple ideas springing in a scattered mind.

As soon as one sits for meditation, thoughts emerge. This is untrue but it appears to be true because while we are engaged in some activities we cannot observe the thoughts. The thoughts are always coming even while we are in an activity but we do not see them because we focus on something else. The thoughts continue even when we are unaware of them. The mind is littered with them. The mind continues running images and sounds regardless of our awareness of those impressions.

The correct statement is that as soon as one sits for meditation, one may observe the congestion of mental traffic. There is a large sound-proof building which is adjacent to a highway. Usually the workers are oblivious of the traffic noise and movements but as soon as they leave the building at the end of the work shift, they hear the noise and see the congestion. In meditation when one leaves aside physical activity and social interactions, one sees the thoughts running here and there across the screen of the mind.

Thoughts are based on one's lifestyle

In meditation one sorts various thoughts and pictures in the mind. Some are sound images. Some are picture images. Some invoke feelings. Some cause the apprehension of odors and flavors. As soon as something is perceived mentally or emotionally, one assumes responsibility for it. If one's environment is in disorder and if one has to live with it, one will naturally try to get some order by sorting and organizing.

It is all about being involved. Human beings, the little busybodies that we are, are always getting involved in projects. Why not get involved in the mind and try to sort thoughts. Make order in the mind. If there will be traffic and if it cannot be stopped, then at least the mayor of the city should regulate it by installing traffic lights, parking rules and traffic policemen. Thoughts should not be permitted to go here or there at random. An effort should be made to sort them.

Outside of the mind, we sort business concerns, social life and many other things, why not catalog the mind's content. Where should I begin? I had a family. I sorted the children. I have a wife. I sorted the relationship. I had a business, I sorted employees. Now for God's sake, let me sort the crazy mind. What is the thought traffic? Where do these ideas originate? Who created the impressions?

Categorizing thoughts

When a yogi starts sorting he makes observations of the method used. He may categorize and label the thought items. Usually one remains in the sorting stage for some time and then at last one graduates to making written or just mental notations. Sorting and sorting and sorting could go on for months or years, or even lives. It depends on the good luck of the yogi. This is called accounting. It is similar to business. Some businessmen keep everything about purchases and sales in a ledger. From time to time they review this and make certain decisions. Others businessmen keep no record.

They do no accounting. For the purposes of higher yoga, this accounting is required.

Thought patterns

A yogi may realize three types of thoughts patterns. This is like the bystander near a highway who noticed that there were three types of vehicles like passenger cars, trucks and buses. The categories are.

- lifestyle
- novel subject
- desire

The **lifestyle** itself causes the generation of thoughts and ideas. This is spontaneous. The observing self is impulsively drawn to the related mental impressions and emotional responses in the mind.

Novel subjects have a compelling influence because of the curiosity tendency. When a novel subject is sensed, there is a feeling of curiosity about it. This energy encourages the intellect to develop the idea further or to gain more information about it.

Desire means deliberate desires, ones that arise either by mentally constructing them or by their arising in the mind and then being endorsed by the self. There are other types of desires which the self is forced to fulfill, willingly or unwillingly, consciously or unconsciously, but since the self neither constructed nor endorsed the other desires, they are not rated in the initial stage of sorting and cataloging.

Amazing Gita

One of the most important statements from the mouth of Krishna, told to Arjuna was this:

उद्धरेदात्मनात्मानं
नात्मानमवसादयेत् ।
आत्मैव ह्यात्मनो बन्धुर्
आत्मैव रिपुरात्मनः ॥६.५॥

uddharedātmanātmānaṁ
nātmānamavasādayet
ātmaiva hyātmano bandhur
ātmaiva ripurātmanaḥ (6.5)

uddhared = uddharet — should elevate; ātmanā — by the self; 'tmānaṁ = ātmānam — the self; nātmānam = na — not + ātmānam — the self; avasādayet — should degrade; ātmaiva = ātmā — self + eva — only; hyātmano = hyātmanaḥ

= *hy (hi)* — *indeed* + *ātmanaḥ* — *of the self; bandhur = bandhuḥ* — *friend;*
ātmaiva = ātmā — *self + eva* — *as well; ripur = ripuḥ* — *enemy; ātmanaḥ* — *of*
the self

One should elevate his being by himself. One should not degrade the self.
Indeed, the person should be the friend of himself. Or he could be the
enemy as well. (Bhagavad Gita 6.5)

बन्धुरात्मात्मनस्तस्य
येनात्मैवात्मना जितः ।
अनात्मनस्तु शत्रुत्वे
वर्तेतात्मैव शत्रुवत् ॥६.६॥

bandhurātmātmanastasya
yenātmaivātmanā jitaḥ
anātmanastu śatrutve
vartetātmaiva śatruvat (6.6)

bandhur = bandhuḥ — *friend; ātmā* — *personal energies; 'tmanas = ātmanas* —
of the self; tasya — *of him; yenātmaivātmanā = yena* — *by whom + ātmā* — *self*
+ eva — *indeed + ātmanā* — *by the self; jitaḥ* — *subdued; anātmanas* — *of one*
who is not self-possessed; tu — *but; śatrutve* — *in hostility; vartetātmaiva =*
varteta — *it operates + ātmā - self + eva* — *indeed; śatruvat* — *like an enemy*

The personal energies are the friend of the person by whom those energies
are subdued. But for one whose personality is not self-possessed, the
personal energies operate in hostility like an enemy. (Bhagavad Gita 6.6)

Krishna suggested that our biggest stumbling block is the self energies.
The self works against its own interest because it is reliant on psychological
energies which are faulty.

The self must study its personal energies, find their faults and irradiate
these or at least realize if these can be adjusted. Some aspects, we can
improve but we may not eliminate everyone. The self should sort the energies
carefully and painstakingly. It should categorize, assess, improve or eliminate
them.

If we are lazy about this, it will be difficult, albeit near impossible for us
to make advancement. One big hang up is the inner privacy. Even though
inner privacy in the mind and emotions seems to be a valuable right and
asset, still in a way that is a disadvantage, because it means that to improve
psychologically, we are left to our own devices.

If something is not externalized then no one can criticize it, at least no one who does not have keen mystic insight. Unless we are in the association with a person that has such insight and who is willing to use it as a service to us, we are doomed to stagnation. Even such a person must absorb our resentments when we are corrected, since by nature we are resistant to critique.

Socially there is malicious criticism and peer pressure which keeps us in check to some degree. For example, if one wants to walk down a city street without clothing, one may hesitate to do so for fear of ridicule and for fear of being arrested for indecent exposure. But if one wants to walk down the street and be naked on the emotional plane, nobody will criticize that. It is then left to the individual to police himself and herself and in this sense, the progress of the self depends on the self. A big part of kriya yoga has to do with mastering self-criticism. It is part of the pratyahar sensual energy withdrawal process. Without conserving energy and using it to improve oneself, one cannot gain enough purity to reach even the most elementary divine state.

Indeed we should regularly read Bhagavad Gita. There is so much in Gita that it is amazing that we give the text so little attention. Gita is there for us on a day to day basis, for direct contact with Krishna.

Tracking kundalini

I started doing kundalini yoga in 1972 in Denver Colorado, at Yogi Bhajan's kundalini yoga ashram.

Length of time of doing kundalini practice is not a good way to assess a practitioner. Sometimes a person may have a long history of practice and someone else who began recently may understand the practice more and get more results from it. It depends on a person's overall practice from many lives. A person carries in the psyche, a residual effect of practice from past lives. When that is activated, it may make a person who began recently, bypass another who has a longer history.

In terms of experiences during the practice, it works like this. If one has a daily practice, during and just after the practice there are experiences. One should keep a log of the experiences. In addition there may be experiences even when one does not practice. For someone who practices daily, there are daily experiences.

Kundalini arousal distribution

Kundalini is designed to spread energy through the whole system, but it usually does so in an uneven way. When kundalini rises and remains spread out or concentrated, it may be doing so in a haphazard way and it may bypass the proper channels. Thus more of its energy may go to one area and less to another area.

You can balance kundalini by trying in meditation to silently attract or call kundalini back to the base chakra. Once you feel that kundalini has withdrawn itself back to that base, you may then cause kundalini to again ascent but in a gradual and steady way, spreading its energy through the whole subtle system of nadi subtle channels.

When you do this, try to see if kundalini is mainly moving straight up the spine or if it is mainly spread forward to the groin-belly area. According to observation, one may direct kundalini in a different way and bring it under control. Before attempting this, please practice to situate the coreSelf at the base chakra. In other words, move the coreSelf from the head to the base chakra.

Thought storage

Everyone has thoughts according to the lifestyle but everyone does not analyze thoughts in the same way. It is helpful when someone explains his mental process, since others may get hints on how to control the inner movements. Each person is not endowed with the same ability of discovery. Even in ordinary matters, we find that we are always dependent on others to invent various items which we require but which we cannot produce on our own. A simple feature as a cup to drink from or a bucket to carry water, is not something that each of us can invent just like that. Some features were invented by one person here or there and then others adopted it after realizing the usefulness. Efforts to control thoughts are there for all who attempt to meditate but the details of how to do so varies.

Patanjali discussed shutting down the mind continuous ranting and raving but the elementary details of how to get into a position to execute Patanjali's instruction is hard to come by even in the explanations of Patanjali.

The question is:

Is there a database of all thoughts?

There is a database or stated more precisely there is an origin point and a generation organ and an issuance point of the thoughts. One of the things that is so hard to understand due to vagueness in the mind and due to the abstraction or subtleness of mental stuffs, is that there are mental objects. These arise from specific mental locations.

But if I tell you that there is a database, how does that help you if you cannot see or sense it. The information is useful if you are willing to go into the mind, and patiently and minutely observe.

Bhagavad Gita is also a great source of theoretical information on the psyche but again one is faced with the same problem of trying to realize the information by direct insight.

Each of us gets most of our thoughts from the database of our individual lifestyles. Bhagavad Gita confirms this where Krishna discussed material nature, referring to it as a tree-like organism.

अधश्चोर्ध्वं प्रसृतास्तस्य शाखा
गुणप्रवृद्धा विषयप्रवालाः ।
अधश्च मूलान्यनुसंततानि
कर्मानुबन्धीनि मनुष्यलोके ॥१५.२॥

adhaścordhvaṁ prasṛtāstasya śākhā
guṇapravṛddhā viṣayapravālāḥ
adhaśca mūlānyanusaṁtatāni
karmānubandhīni manuṣyaloke (15.2)

Adhaścordhvaṁ = adhaḥ — downward + ca — and + urdhvam — upward; prasṛtāḥ — widely spreading; tasya — of it; śākhā — branches; guṇa — mundane influence; pravṛddhā — nourished; viṣayapravālāḥ = viṣaya — attractive objects + pravālāḥ — sprouts; adhaśca = adhaḥ — below + ca — and; mūlāni — roots; anusaṁtatāni— stretched out; karmānubandhīni = karmā — action + anubandhīni — promoting; manuṣyaloke = manuṣya — of human being + loke — in the world

Branches spread from it, upwards and downwards. It is nourished by the mundane influences and the attractive objects are its sprouts. The roots are spread below, promoting action in the world of human beings. (Bhagavad Gita 15.2)

The roots of this material existence spread below into this world. It promotes individual lifestyles in the world of human beings. Thus one source of thought energy and thought construction is our social activity itself. Efforts to control thoughts which arise from our social activity are futile, since unless we reform the social life, those thoughts will be generated. If we get the social life more in control, the thoughts would decrease considerably. They would change in quality.

Thought storage

Similar thoughts are generated from one place. The subtle energy from which the thoughts arise is generated usually from our social activity. There is storage of thought activity but that storage is not the same as the generation of the original thoughts. Thus we have two factors and not one. It is not just thought storage but rather it is thought production. Suppose I manufacture a product in a concrete building and then I store the manufactured item in a steel building, you can understand that manufacturing and storing are two different activities, carried out in two different locations. Suppose I manufacture another item in that concrete building but I mail the product to a consumer. The only part of the product which I would keep is the billing information. That has to be stored in a file cabinet or in a computer filing system.

The bill is not the item, but it represents the item and the transaction of the sale. That bill is just like a compressed impression which is stored in the mind and then is used to create more thoughts.

In the case of the item which I mailed to a consumer, I may at a later date, decide to contact that consumer about some other item which I manufacture. Then I would check the file and get the consumer's information. In the same way, the mind uses previous impressions to create or to support new thought patterns.

Are thoughts about fishing stored at one place and do fishermen acquire thoughts about fishing from that same place?

Thoughts on going fishing are not necessarily created in a simple way in the mind. Any thought may come about by a complex combination of various thought energies.

Let us see this in an example: Jim got a phone call from Pamela, who suggested that they go fishing. Jim did not like the suggestion because he was married to someone else. He would have to skip work for an afternoon to meet Pamela who is his extra-marital lover. Jim told Pamela that he would meet her, even though he knew that it was a marital breach.

Jim then configured a scheme to convince his employer that he had to attend family matters on Wednesday afternoon. Jim did meet Pamela. During the fishing trip, he had a sexual intercourse with her.

Jim's plan was successful because neither the employer nor his wife knew of the matter.

In the example above the thoughts of fishing were subsidiary. The first thought was Pamela's idea. She did not care about fishing. She wanted to be alone with her lover. Jim's ideas about fishing which including getting fishing gear, buying bait, buying a cooler and ice, renting a boat, were incidental to the real issue which was his and Pamela's sexual desire.

Pin-pointing the coreSelf

When the coreSelf is in the head, how is it distinguished from the mind and intellect?

To pin-point something we usually trace the energy which is emitted by the object. If one hears a sound, one can trace it by tracking the energy emittance of the sound-making device. In the same way we may trace out the coreSelf. The problem arises however because to trace an energy you must first recognize it. If there is a keen sound which only a dog can detect, the dog alone will become alert to it, while the human beings will not sense it. This means that one has to find a way to locate a certain type of energy before one can find a way to the source of it. In the case of a dog and its owner, the owner may use the dog to trace a sound or to trace the smell of another animal, by allowing the dog to do the research while the owner follows the pet. Police-dogs are used to sniff explosives and narcotics because the human beings are unable to sniff those odors.

As far as the self is concerned, due to its subtlety it is hard to detect. To make matters worse, it is subjective to itself. When something is subjective, it is difficult for it to understand and catalog itself. The method of pin-pointing and locating the coreSelf is pratyahar, which is the 5th stage of yoga. By a careful study of the word one can understand the process of pratyahar. This word is a combination of two Sanskrit terms, the prefix prati and the root word ahara. Prati means to be against or to go against and ahara means to consume. In combination prati is changed to praty and ahara remains the same. This compound word means to stop outward expression, to cease consumption, except that it refers to psychic stuff.

The secret to locating and isolating the self is to practice introversion. Usually energy is leaving the mind going outward. That is the natural way. Normally even when the mind hashes over something, it usually does so only in terms of an external quest or acquisition. This habit, which is the natural way, has to change before the coreSelf can sort itself amidst the other psychic energies and objects in the mind.

How to do this?

There is only one way and that is to sit and repeatedly pull-in the existential energies which one feels oozing out from the mind. One must exert a mental and emotional force upon those psyche energies in an effort to pull them back into the mind.

After this is done repeatedly day after day through a consistent practice, one will begin to experience as if the energy which usually drains away from the mind in all directions, especially from the face outwards, begins to drain back into the mind from all directions.

It would be like at rush hour when thousands of cars travel main roads away from a city to the suburbs. Suppose suddenly all those cars went into reverse and begin going back into the city instead. It would be something like that. The cars should not turn around, rather they should be pulled backwards into the city. So the psychic energy should be pulled backwards from all directions spherically back into the head.

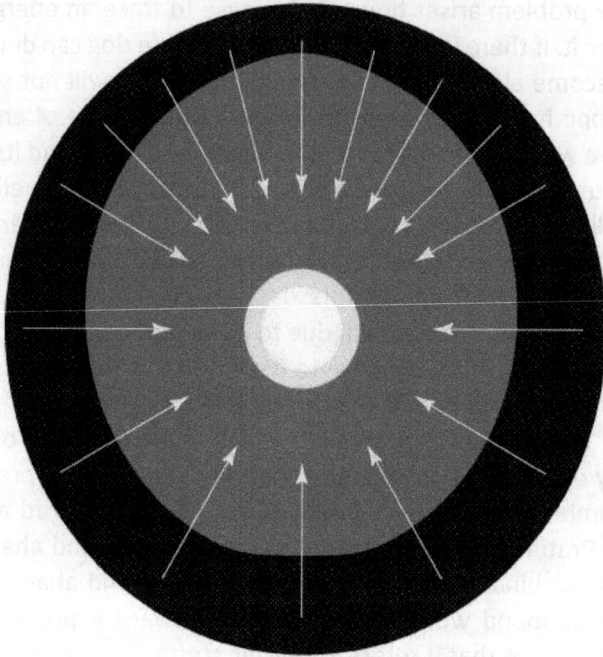

pratyahar - 5th. stage of yoga
retracting all interest
into the central focal consciousness
real self-nourishment

When this is done sufficiently, one will feel as if there is a core-point or origin-point from which energy leaves and goes outward traveling though the mind and out into the space around the body. One will then feel that pin-point or source point and be able to distinguish it from other parts and other components in the mind.

These insights come about gradually through a consistent, day after day, month after month pratyahar retraction practice. The first concrete realization and insight comes about as an understanding that there is a coreSelf. There is energy rushing away from it in all directions. It is experienced then as a tiny microscopic something which continually exudes energy in all directions.

Though tiny, the insight shows that the coreSelf is very powerful and is a perpetual energy source, but there will be a realization that it is being used to its disadvantage. Something may be great. It may be powerful. It may be eternal and perpetual. But at the same time, that something may find itself in a compromising relationship.

A consistent pratyahar practice yields this insight.

Operation of responsibility

In the material world things are so mixed up, so delicate and complicated at the same time, that one may find himself or herself in a situation where one has to be responsible for someone who rejects one's interest in their welfare.

What to do at that point? Well again one needs to learn how to track influences. After all how does one come to be responsible for someone in the first place? The traditional way for being responsible is to be in a certain family. Even in the case of a leader of a country who is responsible for the war and peace of the nation, he or she still gets into that position through family connections. First there must be birth through certain parents before anyone can assume physical responsibility.

The confusing aspect is this: How does one know to whom one is responsible. Say, for instance, that you are the parent, then we know that you are held responsible for the child. That is the 'for' part of it. That is easy to figure. But to whom are you responsible?

Once one tags the party to whom one is responsible, the mix up can be sorted. Are you responsible to your parents? Are you responsible to the government? Are you responsible to the priest? Are you responsible to disembodied souls? Are you responsible to God?

As soon as we can correctly tag the person or persons to whom we are responsible, the problems which face us are solved. The confusion about the intricacies of action disappear as soon as we can identify the person or persons to whom we are accountable.

If I have a job which I do not like, then why do I continue with it? What is the force which causes me to continue? To whom do I feel accountable?

It is not that I should, in disgust, quit the job, but as soon as I can tag the force which causes me to maintain that undesirable employment, I become somewhat freed from stress.

Knowing consciously the motivating force, frees one so that one can make a decision either to continue willingly or to desist. One does not have to like the compelling force to cooperate with it. In many circumstances liking and disliking have no part to play. It is more of matter of reality, of knowing the rulings of reality which govern what we do, rulings which are greater and more impressive than our puny wills.

Just seeing the motivating forces and understanding their position over us, is enough to rid us of the confusion as to why we have to do certain things which are undesirable.

Resumption of practice

Jot down your desires for practice. Making a list of the main areas you feel you need to work on.

From the list isolate the smallest problem area. This small problem should be one which you feel you can tackle.

Avoid tackling big problems. Let us say for example that your desire to rise early to meditate. Do not isolate your reluctance or inability to rise early. That is too much of a challenge for a start procedure. Instead make a commitment to do 5 or 10 minutes of meditation when you arise late.

The first thing is to develop self-confidence. You cannot do that by picking the most difficult achievement. Pick a small aspect and form a habit from that.

A habit from the past which is now lost, cannot be regained in one step. One has to work to adopt it again step by step, acting from where one is located in the deterioration of the habit.

Confidence must be there but if I lost a habit, much of my confidence about it may be lost regardless of whether I realize that or not. Sometimes I say to myself, "Since I did this before, I can easily repeat it."

But when I apply myself I find that I am unable to complete it. This is because the confidence which I had previously and which developed with that skill, deteriorated. My spontaneous attitude of 'I can do it.', is different to the confidence I developed.

This is why it is important to review a situation, make a listing of what you wish to achieve and then work for it beginning with the smallest achievement. That will give you the ability to again develop confidence.

Once you single out the smallest achievement, you should make a plan to practice that. Cultivate that. When you master a small achievement, take responsibility to tackle other small aspects. When these are attained tackle bigger feats.

Be humble to the method of life which we know as habit. Respect nature's way of forming and of leaving aside certain habits. Observe how nature operates. Adapt to its methods. Do not second guess nature. It has the upper hand. If you want to get the better of it, study its process and work within its limits.

Shift of consciousness

When your coreSelf is situated in your head, how do you assess that? How do you experience it?

Remark:

Some mystic doctrines place the coreSelf in the heart. Others place it as an all-pervasive non-location reality. Each person has to research into this personally.

One may perform a simple test in meditation. Sit in a silent place in the dark. Pinch the body in the arm or leg. Pinching produces a tiny size but very shrill pain. One should do this while eyes are closed and note if one's consciousness shifts to focus on the pinch. How is the consciousness shifted, from where to where?

Does the consciousness leave a certain place in the body, or even a certain zone of the body and go directly to the pin-point of the pinch?

Another test may be performed by someone who has a severe illness. When there is such an illness, the mind shifts to the illness completely. Even though the mind is abstract and seemingly unknown, still a person who suffers an illness knows that the illness distracts and acts as a focal of consciousness. It interferes with the usual consciousness outlay.

In yoga there is an important way to find out where the consciousness is usually positioned or zoned. That is the method of using cramps to find where the consciousness relaxes to or desires to relax to, when a cramp is discovered and it is forgotten or ignored. Here is the method for this:

When you sit to meditate, if you have a cramp or discomfort in one part of the body, allow that condition to continue. Do not move the body nor rearrange it in any way to get relief.

Use the discomfort to train yourself to observe the movement of consciousness. Once there is movement, there must be locations and objects. If something moves, it means that there must be a location from which the item was shifted. The item itself is an object. It may be temporary but it is an object nevertheless. Be aware that the short duration of an object's existence does not deny that the object existed. A powerful bomb will destroy itself and other items. The bomb will then go out of existence but still we cannot say that the bomb never existed merely because it is no longer an object. Many things in the mind exist for extremely short durations and to make matters worse, some of these objects are subtle. Still these exist, existed or will come into existence in the future.

In meditation use discomfort to your advantage by allowing it to continue and by observing the movements of consciousness. Notice how the mind moves from its usual position to the discomfort. Notice how the mind makes plans to remove a discomfort, but do not allow the mind to act on its decisions. You will find that the mind moves to the discomfort zone and then returns to its normal position, and then goes back to the discomfort, repeatedly. Take note of this movement. Chart the movement. You will see where the mind is usually located.

After doing this, track where the coreSelf is in relation to the mind. Initially in meditation it may appear that the coreSelf is the mind. Later, if you persist you will get insight into the various components in the mind.

Location of coreSelf

Before the coreSelf can be located, it should be identified as something which is in the field of consciousness. The field of consciousness is known as the mind or as the emotions of a living being or as both simultaneously. Some of us are aware of consciousness as feelings. Some say it is emotions. Some say it is the mind or mental energy.

Test for all-pervasiveness

Take a nail clipper, pair a fingernail. Take a scissors cut one strand of hair. Take a pin or a thorn, press that gentle into your arm?

There is no pain felt when the hair is cut, nor when the nail is paired. There is pain felt, sensation created, when your arm is contacted by the pin or thorn. Study this in meditation to realize that your consciousness is not all-pervasive, otherwise it would have felt sensations when your nail and hair were altered. Your consciousness is localized. This is why there were sensations when your arm was contacted by the pin or thorn. As soon as the pin or thorn is removed from the arm, it no longer had the sensation of the contact. This means that the intensity of focus on the arm was reduced. This means that focus of consciousness can shift from one place to another within the psyche.

In meditation observe how the focus of consciousness shifts. Try one session of meditation where you repeatedly shift the focus to the location on the arm where the pin or thorn made contact.

If your memory of the experience fades, apply slight pressure to the same spot to reawaken the memory. Repeatedly shift the focus to that spot and repeatedly relax the focus away from there. Do this for 20 minutes of meditation. Continue this daily during one week of meditation.

After completing this practice for one week. Find another focus in the body. Try to shift the focus there for one more week.

This will confirm that the focus of consciousness shifts. It is not sufficient to agree that this is true. Do the practice as advised. It is only by such practice that you will realize this. To agree mentally does not give you the benefit gained from the actual mental act of shifting the consciousness.

After a week of practice, twenty minutes per day, use the pin to poke at one part of the same arm and then use the pin to poke immediately at another part of the body, such as the leg or thigh. Now practice shifting the mind from the spot on the arm to the spot on the thigh. Do this repeatedly, for one week, doing the meditation for twenty minutes. Do not rush this meditation. Do this with patience. Do not allow yourself to be bored. Do this practice to shift the focus of consciousness.

The next phase of this practice is to discover if the consciousness is being emitted from a particular location. If for instance there is a search light on a tall building in a city, and if that light is focused on a street corner, we can understand that the beams of light originated on the tall building. Even if the operator of the light moves it to focus on another corner, we can still trace the beams to the same building.

If the consciousness was shifted from the arm to the leg, what took place? Was the consciousness similar to the search light? Did it originate from one place in the psyche and then shifted its focus only? Or did the entire consciousness move from the arm to the leg?

If the consciousness moved from the arm to the leg, then where is it located when it is not focused on the arm or leg? In other words, is the consciousness like a police car, which with a focusing dome light moves from place to place? Or is it like the tall building which remains in one place but which has a turret for moving the beam?

Thus you would again return to the practice of shifting the focus of consciousness from the arm to leg, except that you will track the beam of consciousness to find the origin point.

First you will do one week of practice with only the arm. You will again take help from the pin, poking the arm gentle to remind the mind of the location for focus. As soon as the focus is established you will research as to where the beam of consciousness, the focus, originates.

Do not feel frustrated if you cannot find the focus. Keep the effort for tracking it. After one week note your conclusions.

Resume the practice of focusing on the arm and alternately make efforts to track the source of focus.

When your coreSelf is situated in your head, how do you assess that? What confirms to you that your coreSelf is there?

The coreSelf is experienced in a location by personal observations in meditation and by shifting the focus of consciousness and tracing its original point. This practice may take weeks, months or years, to perfect, depending on what you need to do to realize it. Each person may master this in a short or long space of time.

Base chakra entry

Initially if one has success moving the coreSelf to the location of the base chakra, it happens momentarily only. This is because of the gravitational force of the base chakra and floatation power of the core. If a diver takes a styrofoam to the bottom of a lake, it will not remain there unless it is held by force. If the diver releases it, it will rapidly move upwards to the surface. If on the other hand, the diver takes a piece of iron, it will remain submerged.

The coreSelf may be compared to the cork, in that if one is successful in taking it to the base chakra, it will stay there momentarily at the most.

However after steady practice, that time span may increase.

By nature the core is allied to, in fact it is glued to the sense of initiative, which in turn is glued to the intellect organ. The coreSelf is not directly allied to the kundalini force. Its normal way of relationship with this force is through the sense of initiative and the intellect.

How does one feel when the coreSelf is at the base chakra? Initially this feels like being in pitch black darkness, in a darkness that is denser and more severe than any other type of mental darkness. It is a feeling that there is a hallow darkness at the base chakra. One feels as if one was transported there and was left there. Then suddenly one will find oneself back in the normal location of the coreSelf, which is central in the subtle head.

If one does this meditation, one will find that periodically again and again one is switched to the base for a second or for five seconds and then one is switched back to the head. This will continue for a time until one's practice is sufficient to cause longer stays at the base.

What happens to the mind/brain consciousness when you leave the head?

The mind/brain consciousness continues when one is at the base, accept that one is not centralized in it. It is similar to being in an office and then being in one's home. Does the office continue while one is in the home? Everything in the office remains intact, when the occupant is absent. Similarly the other aspects of the subtle head, remain intact while the coreSelf is at the base.

Are you aware of the brain when you move the coreSelf out of that space?

In some experiences one maintains an awareness of the head, and in others one does not feel the head's awareness until one is switched back to the head.

Does brain activity continue, when the coreSelf goes elsewhere?

Brain activity is put on standby when the coreSelf goes elsewhere. The brains remains functional but its thinking and planning activities are temporarily suspended.

Part 8

Tracking desires

One important practice is the tracking and tracing of desires. Desires move the material world. We may regard the lower animals as being motivated by instinct for the most part, but as soon as we cross into the human species, we find a predominance of sensuality and desire. Of course the human being too is an animal, though a very special one.

Desire carries an inherent force and sets itself up with rights for functioning and rights for compelling us to act.

How does desire originate?

Desire is not that simply in its origin. We cannot sidestep every desire. Some desires even contrary ones enforce themselves and compel us from time to time.

The secret to getting some leverage on desires is to develop a method of tracking their sources. Even if you cannot avoid fulfilling a desire, even if it has the power to compel you, still if you could trace the source, you would have the upper hand by transcending your identity crisis in that regard.

The crisis occurs when one fails to track a particular desire, but go on serving it without the knowledge of its origin. Usually when a desire arises in the mind or in the emotions, the first thing one attempts to do is to fulfill it. This is because one feels some emotional or mental discomfort because the desire is not fulfilled. But at the same time as one tries to ease oneself by the fulfillments, one should track a desire to its source.

Where does the desire come from?

This simply question has a complex answer. Desires can come from several places. One may originate from motivations which join together to create a conjoint aspiration. In such a conjoint urge, one has to untangle the net of influences and then track each thread of it, to its source.

Memory grasping

Memory control and observation is part of yoga practice. Patanjali listed memory as one of five unwanted vrittis or vibrational modes of the psyche. His suggestion is that these operations should cease.

Memory operates a grasping and releasing action, which is prejudiced, which is conditioned by certain other aspects of the psyche. As one advances what seemed to be abstract or non-perceptible, becomes plain to see. What was subjective, becomes objective.

In meditation and also in day to day observation of the operation of memory, one should begin to note that the memory is very active in grasping, in releasing what is grasped and in trying to regain what it released. The memory has a scan and search feature.

The easiest way to begin observing the grasping feature of the memory is to check on it when it tries to avoid or to escape from something which occurred. This object may be a mental occurrence and/or a physical one.

There is a mental contrast when one confronts something which the memory is prejudiced against. It acts just as a child would if he or she were given a sour fruit instead of a sweet one. Usually the child will turn away from the sour item, because a memory of it, is feared by the mind. Physically the child will turn away from the sour item. His or her face will show refusal to accept the fruit. Within the mind this sour attitude will prevail. The memory part of the mind will show itself as a restricted region, quarantined from acceptance. Subsequently the rest of the psyche will be left on its own to make the decision to accept the fruit. The memory assumes an "I will not accept this." attitude.

Blackmailed and intimidated in this way, even the intellect will feel disempowered and will back away to comply with the memory's refusal. The person will experience a negative mood.

It is easier to begin studying the operation of the memory by checking when one dislikes a feature. If one checks when one likes a feature, one will have a difficult time being objective. The liking of a feature causes one to lose objectivity and to identify strongly with the pleasure derived.

Forms of breathing

Two major forms of breathing practice in kundalini yoga are kapalabhati and bhastrika. Bhastrika is more forceful. Usually one should begin the breath practice by doing kapalabhati, which is done with a forceful exhale and with an automatic quick in-draw of breath on the inhale. In that case, the inhale is done deliberately with force. The exhale is done by a reflex action of the diaphragm.

If you listen to someone doing kapalabhati, you will realize that the inhale is done with emphasis and the exhale just seems to follow as a reflex. As one masters this, one will be shown or will develop into the bhastrika which is stressed on both the inhale and the exhale, so that both are deliberately done and neither is left as a reflexive action.

There is another type of bhastrika, which Yogi Ramdeva showed me in the astral world. This however is not really a bhastrika breath. In that breath, there is focus to strike muladhar base chakra, the lowest of the chakras, the place where kundalini resides, the place from which the kundalini lifeForce, carries out its operations.

In that breath the focus is on the inhale on striking the base chakra with the breath which is drawn in with force. On the exhale, one again strikes the base chakra to make it yield impurities. This breath is important when one practiced kapalabhati and bhastrika for a time and gained success in regularly raising kundalini.

Kundalini study

Kundalini is worthy of detailed study both through meditation practice and by studying our creature habits. Kundalini is the driving force, the real authority in our mundane life, causing our sleeping, eating, mating and defending.

The intellect, through a precise and dictatorial force, is really working as a very loyal slave-captive of kundalini. Intellect is so dedicated to working for kundalini that it would go against the wishes of the coreSelf if there was a disagreement with kundalini. It is only when the coreSelf exerts tremendous power in the psyche, that it can direct activities.

There is a gravitation force between kundalini and the intellect, and between the intellect and the iSense as it relates to this world. There is a relationship between the iSense and the coreSelf.

Normally by convention the core serves the interest of kundalini indirectly by submitting to the biases of the iSense, which in turn submits to the biases of the intellect, which in turn is a slave of the major power which is the kundalini.

How to reverse this power cycle so that the coreSelf gains control?

The first step is keen observation in meditation. The second step is observation during regular social activity. And the third step is to study books like Bhagavad-Gita and Yoga Sutras, to get some idea of how to tackle this conquest of the psyche.

The fourth step is to begin the conquest by subduing the weaker areas of influence of kundalini. It is not a good idea to begin by taking the big areas like food greed and sexual needs. Find small areas where kundalini has little control, where kundalini is careless in its influence. Conquer those. Then one may develop confidence in the power of the coreSelf to bring the system under control.

Evicted

Eventually one will get an eviction notice. After moving into and out of a particular body which is known as Joan or Jim, one will be informed by a terminal disease, that within a short time, one will permanently leave the body. Sometimes one does not get such a notice but one may see a portent and not realize that for what it is. It is said that King Kamsa got a notice in the form a dream in which he found himself in the nude, his body oiled, riding on a donkey, going to the south. Soon after he was killed and was unable to enter his dear residence, the material body.

It is a good idea to consider this each night before one takes to sleeping. This may be the last night. There is no guarantee that after tonight you will enter the body and awaken on this side of existence again. The other side, the one which you now avoid and only use for sleeping and dreaming, is the permanent last resort side. It is the place you will resort to when the physical body dies.

Are you ready to be permanently relocated to the psychic side?

Do you meditate on this? Do you know that you may stay on the psychic side on any particular night, being left out of your existential apartment, having to vacate without belongings, like a refugee caught in a war where the enemy has blown up his residence and left him in a destitute condition?

What would it be like to be denied entry into a body which you love so dearly? What would it be like to leave your money, commitments, family, employment, privacy, everything?

Each night, it is a good idea, to know for sure, that this may be your last exit from the physical reality.

Kundalini / vices curtailed

Each person should meditate and observe and then find an area of conquest which is a weak area for kundalini, an area in which kundalini is not so defensive and reactive to discipline.

One person may be addicted to music through electronic media. Another person may be addicted to being around young adults of the opposite sex for the seeing and enjoying people with skimpy clothing. For instance a person, may like to go to shopping areas to see persons in sexually suggestive clothing. Another person may like to be on a college campus for the same reason. One other person may be addicted to sweets food. One person may be addicted to salty food. Another may be addicted to caffiene drinks. One may have a need for alcohol. One person may not like to rise early in the morning. Another person may be addicted to late night activity. There are many areas. One should find one area and test to see if kundalini will resists strongly. If it will one should find another area.

Realize that eating and having sex connections are the main interest of kundalini.

Why?

Because eating concerns continuation of life in a body. Sex concerns making another body, so that one can have an opportunity in the future through that other body to again have a stake in history. It is not the sexual act itself which is the real attraction for kundalini but the result of sex which is reproduction. Kundalini is concerned to eat to continue existing here and to have sexual engagements to guarantee that more opportunities for new bodies are facilitated. Kundalini will defend these interests forcibly.

In the areas of nutrition and reproduction, kundalini is protective. One should not directly attack these areas until one develops a very powerful disciplinary habit in reference to other vices which kundalini will not care about if they were abandoned. List your habits. Find the undesirable ones which are easy to abandon. Eliminate these.

Identity impermanence

One teaching of Buddha which deserves special attention, is the idea of the impermanence of identity. Usually teachers explain that this means that the spirit is temporary. Actually this cannot mean that. It means however that the identity assumed by the spirit is definitely impermanent.

This is proven conclusively by anyone who keeps dreams under observations. If one takes notation of dreams and one's assumption of various identities in dreams, one will realize that one's connections to the present social status, is definitely temporary.

Please take note of the mental condition after dreams. Do you ever experience a loss of identity after a dream, whereby you cannot recall your identity in this social setting immediately after arising from the dream? Did it ever take time for you to again get a grip on your social self?

Have you experienced yourself in a dream, totally forgetting your social posture in this world, and functioning in the dream environment in a totally different capacity, with people whom you do not recall meeting in this world?

When you return from a dream in which you lost track of the familiar social self, what is the process of repossessing your personality format in this world?

Did it ever occur to you that perhaps you were temporarily relinquished or deprived of the social familiarity with this world?

I had similar experiences, but not in relation to dreams. I had this happen quite a few times when doing pranayama exercises. I would strike the muladhar chakra with an inhaled breath and retain it, and then lose all memory. When I resumed objective consciousness, I do not know where I was, or who I was. I repossess the identity by looking at my external surroundings. I saw the room where I sat and said, "I am in Brooklyn," or "I am in Guyana." Then I resume the social format.

Identity impermanence when arousing kundalini

Sometimes when arousing kundalini, a student may have experiences where he loses objectivity when kundalini moves or spreads from the base muladhar chakra.

This is called samadhi in the mode of ignorance. If while doing breath infusion, one retains the breath on an inhale or exhale, one may lose objective awareness.

The question is: How long did you retain the inhale breath? What was your guideline for how to retain the breath?

My guess is that the student had no guideline, or that he read a book by a not-so-advanced yogi, and took that advice, or did not read that advice completely and applied the advisories partially.

In the kapalabhati/bhastrika breath infusion which I teach, one first charges the system, then one holds the breath for only as long as the system can be retained with the charged breath. In other words, as soon as the system used the charged breath, one should begin charging the system again. If one holds the breath beyond that point, one will blackout. Kundalini lives on gross and subtle air. Subtle air is known as prana (praa-nuh). As soon as kundalini cannot get the required charge, it shifts to another dimension in an effort to get that air, When this is done there is a disconnect from the intellect. That is experienced as a blackout or a loss of self-consciousness.

When striking muladhar base chakra, do not hold the breath if muladhar does not have enough of a charge to maintain clarity of consciousness. In that case, keep the charge going. If you give it a long lasting charge, you can safely hold the breath for a time without losing objective consciousness. The objective consciousness will remain but it will shift to a higher plane where conscious experience of a higher state of consciousness will be experienced.

If however one finds that kundalini itself seems to want to do this practice without sufficient charge, it means that one's kundalini is not interested in higher awareness. That should be realized and observed and one should take it upon oneself to train kundalini so that it changes the attitude.

Why would kundalini not be interested in higher consciousness?

The reason is simple, kundalini may be afraid that it will lose control of the psyche. Higher is only beneficial to kundalini if it increases control. At least that will be the mood of kundalini. The yogi must work to change the attitude of kundalini and rid it of the fear of higher levels.

Some yogis deliberately practice for entering non-objective states. They do not hold the breath until blacking out. They hold the breath in or out and as soon as they feel there will be a blackout, they release the system, so that kundalini regains control. This will result in a shorter duration of the blank consciousness, a short loss of objectivity.

In that shorter duration of jada samadhi the yogi can track how consciousness shifts over into that plane of ignorance. It is similar to moving from one part of a cave which is dimly lit to another part which is pitch black. This is a shift of consciousness which one should study. Yogis study these changes in awareness to map the terrain of consciousness.

This study is required so that one knows the landscape of consciousness. That is our natural interest as transmigrating beings. Physically there are maps. If you know a location, you can go to another easily by using a map. At the time of death and immediately thereafter, knowledge of dimensional locations may be the difference between a haphazard rebirth and one where you move into a better environment.

There are two aspects to study in this case, one is how you shift from this level to the level of that jada samadhi or loss of objectivity and the second is the shift from unconsciousness to self-awareness.

There is also the extra assignment which is to study how the components of consciousness disconnect from each other, and cause the resulting loss of objectivity.

Does the intellect disconnect from the coreSelf?

After being disconnected how is the intellect reconnected to the core?

Why is the core dependent on intellect for objectivity?

What is the connection between intellect and kundalini?

These questions may be realized if one has a stupor samadhi experience. I recommend it with hold the breath for shorter periods of time. Hold it enough to trigger a short duration stupor state.

The loss of memory should be studied. Suppose I lose my wallet and retrieve it. That would be a case of being temporarily disconnected from it. However if I lose it because it fell into the ocean, that would be a permanent separation from it. In experiences where one loses a memory or a set of memories and then repossesses these, one can concluded that the disconnection was not a permanent separation. But how is one disconnected from a memory? How is one reconnected to it? How does nature do this? The memory is taken from you or you are deprived of it. Then it is returned to you.

When one is reconnected to the intellect one regains objective consciousness but without the present cultural identity, and thus without any idea of the locations which that cultural identity was familiar with.

When one's attention shifts into this environment, one's cultural identity is resumed or is again allied to or unified with the coreSelf which was devoid of that identity just seconds before. By making the effort to resume that missed cultural self, one accelerates the resumption of that identity. But even that resumption take some seconds more to establish.

Kundalini/child comparison

Kundalini acts exactly like a child.
What are a child's habits?
- Craving food and nourishment
- Craving attention and affection
- Reacting violently when needs are not furnished
- Expecting to be the center of the world

When I say child I mean the organism which is childhood. I do not mean the coreSelf around which that organism grows. Mostly, childhood is regulated 95% by the kundalini lifeForce. The core has very little to do with it. Can a child make its body grow? Can it heal its body? The coreSelf depends on the lifeForce to repair the body. The lifeForce does other negative functions as well. Some of these condemn the core to a miserable life in the body.

People are generally confused when it comes to disciplining children. The confusion arises because of our inability to differentiate between the coreSelf and the lifeForce. In fact the convention is to accept the lifeForce as the coreSelf.

The strong craving for affection and for approval for anti-social acts comes from kundalini not from the coreSelf. In childhood, the core has so little control over the psyche that the self is like a nobody.

If we study children, we can get much insight into the nature of the kundalini lifeForce. From that study we may devise a plan for its control.

Just as we avoid disciplining children because of their annoying violent reactions in the form of crying, tantrums, refusal to cooperate and constant insistent demands, we may treat the kundalini energy in the same way. Thus we are at the mercy of kundalini, just as parents are emotionally terrorized by children.

The kundalini can be controlled but it will take endeavor, serious planning and persistent execution of the proven controlling methods. I began to control the kundalini after my body reached the age of 20. Before that it was a losing battle due to the constant changes in the development of the body, from infancy, toddler, adolescence, and young adult. These changes caused ruptures in the effort to control the psyche. Parents can provide help with this but usually parents are baffled by and accommodating of kundalini. They do not have the discernment to challenge it.

Capable parents are a milestone in this effort. Krishna spoke of that in chapter six of the Bhagavad Gita. Still one cannot expect to get such favorable births as those described by Krishna. The most we may get are parents who insist on moral behavior. The rest of our development would come from yoga teachers

In this birth, neither the mother of the body nor its father was present in its development between the ages of 3½ to 15. This body was raised by a grandmother, the mother of the father of the body.

The childhood of this body was not an ideal one. It was not the kind of childhood which kundalini approves of. Thus kundalini was very troublesome in the childhood and adolescence of this body. It is a mistake to expect the world to be centered on one's lifeForce. That is an instinct of the lifeForce, but it is a very grave misunderstanding about existence.

We should set our minds so that we are naturally interested in self-control, with emphasis on tightly regulating kundalini's behavior.

Individual kundalini / cosmic kundalini.

Individual kundalini is the psychic power in the limited psyche. Cosmic kundalini in outside the individual psyche. These two factors interact. In the instructions of Krishna to Uddhava, there is an explanation about a cosmic force called the sutram. That is the sum-total kundalini. When parts of that are divested or shared to the individual living entities, you or me, it becomes individualized.

For example, in a passport office, there are many blank documents, perhaps thousands of them. When there are applications, a clerk removes them one by one, writes identity information and issues each to different citizens. At that point each is considered to be the passport of a particular person. If you open a passport there may be a notice stating that it is the property of the Government.

In one sense, the passport I have is mine. In another sense it is owned by the government. Considering it to be mine, I say, 'This is my passport.' All the same if there is a problem at the airport, a government clerk may seize the document, claiming that the government revoked it.

Let us view this from another angle. When kundalini is divested to each individual self, it becomes polarized or marked in a particular way, because of that spirit's use of it. This is just like the difference between my passport and yours. Mine has a water stain because coffee spilled on it. Yours is clean because you kept it in a plastic case. Originally we had similar looking clean passports, now mine looks different. Similarly each person was awarded the same type of kundalini force, but due to different usage, each appears different.

Spread of sexual energy

When there is a greater percentage of carbon dioxide in the body, the sexual energy remains focused on the sexual organs. If that percentage is decreased, the sexual energy spreads to other parts of the body more evenly. Thus the sexual desires decreases in the groin area and that decrease is offset by an increase in other parts of the form.

The sexual energy does not vanish. It has to go somewhere, either to be used in sexual dalliances or to be reabsorbed into the body. In yoga, one makes an aggressive effort to reabsorb the sexual energy by doing various postures and by using pranayama breath infusion which is the most efficient method of absorption.

The body produces sex hormones. One would have to emasculate someone to stop the production. Nature is concerned with reproduction and generation of new bodies.

Just as we cannot imagine life without money, so material nature cannot stir without reproduction. Just as there is always a need for money no matter what, so there is always a need for new bodies.

This means that if we suppress sexual energy, it will manifest somewhere else. If it is effectively suppressed, we may declare that it is not in the genitals. It is no longer a nuisance in that area. But where is it? Is it reabsorbed into the blood stream?

In kundalini yoga practice a yogi directs it here and there in the body. By itself if one practice static celibacy, the sexual energy will spread wherever it can according to the health and genetic tendencies of the body. But that is not sufficient for yoga. In yoga one directs the energy

Will sexual energy be a nuisance if it is diverted away from the genital and if instead it is distributive all over the body?

If one becomes very advanced in kundalini yoga before one leaves the present body, one will have to protect the subtle body from the expenditure of sexual attraction. If one fails to do so, one will attract angelic partners. That attraction will produce sexual intercourses on the subtle plane. These in turn will cause the subtle body to become de-energized and one will again assume another gross body as a matter of course.

It is important to advance as far as one can while one has a body and to secure connections with advanced yogis in whose association one would be resistant to angelic sexual attraction.

What causes this attraction?

The same sexual energy which was conserved from sexual intercourses and which was spread throughout the form. Usually if you could look at a subtle body of an average human being you will see that it is darkish in color with orange hues at the chakras and at the vital organs. When the sexual energy is conserved, the orange-yellowish glow spreads evenly through the subtle body. This is seen in the subtle world by others and they are attracted to it. When they come to it, they feel the need for sexual love.

To protect yogis from this attraction, greater yogis make congregations of ascetics in special astral realms. These have come to be known as siddhaloka or perfection preparatory zones.

Some other great yogis are loners or reside with a few persons of similar progression. They do not allow others to enter the association. One can get into a large congregation of yogis easily. Just as when there is the melas in India, many ascetics congregate, so in the astral world there are large and small gatherings of yogis who stay together to get protection from haphazard rebirth. The heavenly worlds, which are known as swargaloka in the puranas, are real places, paradises, but in most of those places sexual life is full blown. Yoga is not prominent.

Can you imagine doing yoga in a sex-facility night club or in a spa or in any other place that is design for expression of sense pleasure? Such is the heavenly world except the pleasure facilities are increased considerably. In such a place yoga is out.

It is important to get oneself in order before passing the body. Even though it may appear that the odds are against success, still we should endeavor if for no other reason than to comply with the instructions of greater yogis.

Increase of sexual energy

There is relationship between the rise and spread of sexual energy throughout the body, and the breath energy in the body. If there is an increase in breath energy, there will be an increase in the even distribution of the sexual hormones in the body, in both the subtle and gross forms.

Some people get the idea that celibacy will terminate sexual desires. This idea is a fantasy. Celibacy increases sexual desire. A person who takes to celibacy has an increased sex urge and is tempted even more for sexual acts. Unless such a person increases his or her resistance to sex attraction, he or she will again return to habitual sexual contact with a greater desire than before. Celibacy does not stop sexual desire. Sex desire cannot be stopped by any practice, because the sensual energies are by their very nature sex oriented.

When there is a greater percentage of carbon dioxide in the body, the sexual energy remains focused on the sexual organs. If that percentage is decreased, the sexual energy spreads to other parts of the body more evenly.

Thus the sexual desires decreases in the groin area. That decrease is offset by an increase in other parts of the form.

Kundalini yoga is designed to cause this increase in other parts of the body, by increasing the air intake, so as to decrease the percentage of stale or used air in the body. But kundalini yoga does not protect anyone from sexual habits.

What does it do then? It makes you more aware of those habits. It alerts you to arousals of sexual energy in a very clear and defined way. You become aware of the slight sexual advances, as well as the possible consequences and liabilities which would come on if one completes a sexual contact. With that information one may then make a conscious decision to desist or divert or take up sexual opportunities.

No sane person will sign their name on a dotted line, if they are aware of many negative after effects which are clearly stated in the fine print of the document. But the same person may sign that paper, if he or she was not aware of the negative aspects. Kundalini yoga magnifies the fine print and gives one the ability to consider it objectively before one embarks on a sexual adventure.

If a male has a body of fifty years of age. Let us say for instance, that he has an opportunity to have a sexual affair with a very attractive young woman. Why should he not take it? Why should he side-step, avoid or divert himself from it? If the woman is young and attractive, what has he to lose? He is not a political official. He is not a religious leader who has a reputation which would be tarnished. What is there to stop him from taking the risk?

In kundalini yoga, reputation and such matters have little value. The real consideration is liability. There are two factors which one will see, which are:

- The emotional liabilities for the woman
- The commitment as a father which will last for at least 16 years.

Kundalini yoga unlike normal religious life is not concerned with other aspects, which are spearheaded by morality. Kundalini yoga is concerned with the self's ignorance of the liabilities involved

The sexual pleasure with the young woman is okay. That is something positive, at least one may think that or feel that. But what about the emotional interaction? Can one afford to manage that?

What about the commitment to a child which could be developed. That commitment would last for sixteen years.

To go through with this in all seriousness, one would be saying to himself that one sexual act was worth sixteen years of commitment to a child and the 16+ years of an uncertain relationship with the child's mother.

If after considering this, he still thinks it is worth it, then one may accept the pleasure. That would be like accepting a large loan from a bank, but doing so even if one was shown the high interest rate and the large monthly payments required to avoid foreclosure.

This is how kundalini yoga helps. This is how the effort at celibacy helps. It gives one a little breathing space, a gap to consider what is to be done, to look before one leaps into relationships.

People who criticize celibacy and who are afraid of it, have many false alarmist ideas. The main misconception is that it freezes sexual desire. But it actually increases that, but it gives the sincere yogi, the insight into the liabilities.

Quantity of sexual energy

In regards to the spread of sexual energy, there is an advanced level in the practice of kundalini yoga. The obsession with sexual energy control is not just a matter for yogis. It is a matter for non-ascetics as well.

Usually the male body functions in such a way that it reaches the climax of sexual expression very quickly. This is not the general condition with females. A male feels that he is under pressure to perform more effectively in a sexual intercourse with a female. As such there is a multi-million dollar drug industry which is dedicated to increasing male sex drive. They want to produce more male sexual energy and stamina.

In higher yoga another problem arises where a yogi realizes that he has no need for much sexual energy. At first in kundalini yoga the objective is to channel the sexual energy away from the sex utility and to cause it to move up into the brain of the body. After that is achieved, the yogi realized that even that is not the objective.

A question then forms in the mind of the yogi, as to why the system produces more sexual energy than it needs for its most efficient operation. The yogi consults with great yogins and gets practices from them which curtail sexual energy production. After all if your system produces more energy than it would use for basic needs, the excess energy will have to be used in some way, either for desirable or undesirable purposes. An advanced method is given by higher yogins so that the yogi's body does not produce even one drop of extra energy.

I mentioned this to give some idea about the progress of celibacy. It applies to females as well. If one will not produce infants through the uterine system then what is the need for menstrual cycles and for egg production? If one's idea of being female entails that, one will be condemned to only earthly life and life in the subtle worlds which are adjacent to this earth. But if one wants to go higher one has to develop a different idea about what it is to be female.

The same goes for the male beings. They should endeavor to get their existential situations transferred to a divine status.

Quantity of sexual energy

After all if your system produces more energy than it would use for basic needs, the excess energy will have to be used in some way, either for desirable or undesirable purposes. An advanced method is given by higher yogins so that the yogi's body does not produce even one drop of extra energy.

In the beginning however until one masters kundalini yoga, such higher methods are of no value. I mentioned this to give some idea about the progress of celibacy. This applies to females as well. For instance, if one will not produce infants through the uterine system what is the need for menstrual cycles and ovary production?

Old Age / Sex Desire

Old age does not reduce sex consciousness. The physical form is not the mental nor the emotional form. We find that those two other forms, the mental and emotional ones, continue their sexual interest in earnest. In fact because the physical body has an incapacitation by impotence in men and menopause in women, the mental and emotional systems actually increase their interest in sex by developing anxieties about the physical body's lack of performance.

If this were not true, then sex enhancing drugs would not be on sale, and females who are faced with the reality of menopause would not be anxious about what it may do to their libido or sexual drive.

If a person thinks that with the advance of age, the sexual needs will decrease, that person is making a miscalculation. There is a famous story about an Indian emperor. He was fascinated about the predominance of sexual attraction. Once he asked a yogi about it. The yogi explained that even in old age one does not give up the sexual interest. The Emperor doubted that.

The yogi then set up an experiment to prove the point. He took the Emperor to a hostel which had sick old men. When they entered they went to the bed of one of the elderly patients, a scrawny looking old man who was about to breathe his last. The yogi arranged for a sexually appealing young lady to pass by that elderly man's bed. When she did so, the man sat up and strained himself to see her. His eyes remained glued to her torso.

We should not think that we will give up sex desire in old age. For that matter in old age sexual desire will increase even more, because the lifeForce will sense that it has to transmigrate and its instinct, which is to enter a young woman's body for development of an embryo, will assert itself.

Yes, I agree that sexually I will not be able to function in old age but I cannot agree that I will give up sex desire and sex attraction merely because my body cannot function sexually. That is a myth.

Resistance to sex desire is something apart from the status of the physical body. It persists regardless of the sexual capacity or incapacity of the body. It is not reliant on the old age of the body. It is reliant on self-realization and on our interest in self reform and assumption of divine status.

Quality of sexual energy / transmutation

Sex hormones is transmutable energy. Nature generates sperm from itself for the purpose of creating more life forms. Is Nature concerned with using sexual energy for liberation?

The answer is no. Nature's primary concern is its anxiety about continuity. It relieves itself of this anxiety by reproduction. For reproduction it creates hormonal fluids.

There are essentially two parts to a sexual dalliance. There is the urge for the sexual contact. Apart from that there is the flow of sexual fluids. In males these two parts are highlighted by erection of the genital organ and the remittance of fluid through the passage in the organ.

The fluid which is emitted can be divested out into other parts of the body, but where will the erection energy be diverted to?

Reproductive fluid may be used for other purposes in the body but what about the erection energy.

One should consider how complicated it is. I admitted that hormones are transmutable but I was careful not to say anything about the erection energy.

Defective psychology

There is much in the way of self conceit in our behavior. If we were to check the behavior in and out of relationships we would find that there is so much to patch up, so much to rearrange and fix, so much to eliminate, that there would be no time for even thinking of critiquing others.

One would then only deal with others in the line of duty. One would curtail trivial engagements which will lead nowhere and through which neither party would come out the better.

In kriya yoga, self-conceit has to do with the realization that much of what was awarded to us is conventional. By this I mean the intellect for instance. It is nothing special. It is a general issue item which each individual possesses so long as each has a subtle body, which is something that last for trillions of years.

If for instance I am a genius in a certain field of study, say biology for instance, I may come to the conclusion that I am special because of that, while actually that acclaim is directly related to my having a particular type of intellect. Without that intellect my claim would be invalid. But if I feel that I am the intellect and that Jack is his intellect, then of course I would be affected by a pride energy, which is in fact, a form of conceit. Conceit means that I am secretly feeling that I am that special intellect and that Jack is his awarded dull intellect. In fact neither Jack nor I are identical with the awarded intellects.

Suppose two babies are born in the same hospital, at about the same time of a certain day. One of these children, Tim, contracts the polio disease. The other child John, does not have it.

As life would have it, both Tim and John lived into teen years. John became a world class runner and got a placement on the Olympic team. Tim was restricted to a wheelchair.

John used to visit Tim and their friendship continue, but secretly in his mind, John felt that he was a better person than Tim, especially since Tim was handicapped with polio. John felt that he was the better because he had a healthy nicely formed body. He never stopped to consider that if Tim was spared the polio outbreak, Tim may have outclassed him.

Sometimes we get into a way, where we try to improve ourselves on the basis of an intellect or some other psychic accessory, and in doing so we pulverize others and alienate others unnecessarily. It is important in kriya yoga, to take time out to view these aspects of behavior.

There are differences undoubtedly, but we need to look deeply to see exactly what causes one person to excel over others. Suppose as a child you are put into a baseball team but your vision was not 20/20. Your body may be muscular but if you cannot see the ball until it gets within 15 feet of your eyes, then no matter how hard you try, you would never excel at striking.

Another team player who may not be as muscular but who is blessed with keen eyesight will on the average outperform you. What is the difference? Is it your inability or lack of keen vision? Is the other player superior merely because he has good vision?

Will he always be graced with a body with keen vision? Or will he be given his turn with bad vision in another body?

These are some of the challenges we consider when we practice kriya yoga? It makes for a very rapid advancement and a real leap forward in personal relationships with others and in assessing our positions in each social setting.

Any type of superiority which I have and which is merely based on the kind of body I was allowed by providence is a type of insecurity. Unless I can find a superiority which is not based on the kind of body I was awarded, I really have no reason to be proud of any ability and all related acclaim is vanity.

There is different equipment handed out by nature. Sometimes one gets a good tool. Sometimes the product fails. One thousand soldiers jumped from aircraft at about 10,000 feet. They all pulled their parachutes strings but two cords were defectively installed. Those unfortunate soldiers plunged to their deaths. The two were not failures. The equipment were defective.

The trick is to consider the intellect, the lifeForce, the senses and such subtle apparatus as allotted equipment.

The question as to why Nature allotted a particular person a defective piece of psychology is a different consideration altogether. When we consider that, kriya yoga begins.

Sexual energy / breath

Physical breath is not the issue. It is subtle breath. As long as we have a physical form, physical breath has importance as the shadow or counterpart of subtle breath. A physical body really means a physical body and a subtle one combined. Thus physical breath means air intake and subtle atmospheric intake simultaneously.

The lifeForce's basic energy supply is subtle air, subtle energy. It can survive on that. However whenever it maintains a physical organism like a human body, it has to utilize physical air. Thus the importance of air has to do with having a physical body.

In yoga books you will find the word prana. This does not mean air alone. It means air and subtle air, mostly it refers to subtle air.

Sexual energy is a concentration of hormones. That is the physical properties of it. However there is also subtle sexual energy which is a combination of subtle hormones. Air is involved, either for reinforcing the passionate impetus in the energy or for activating the divine potential of it.

The air or subtle air affects motivation. If for instance we isolate an individual in a chamber of propane gas, even a small concentration of it, he or she will be affected. The person's attitude will change. If in turn we remove the person from that environment into fresh air, the depression will be lifted. Air intake affects motivation.

A yogi should study to effects of increased air intake and decide to keep a pranayama breath infusion practice. In modern times, many people are obsessed with diet.

Pranayama, the 4th stage of yoga, is the regulation of gross and subtle air. Since this air pervades the body, it affects all bodily activities, including the sexual ones. One type of foodstuff causes increase in sexual interest, while another may cause a reduction of it. Similarly a certain type of breath intake would affect sexual interest either to increase or decrease it.

In the plant kingdom, there is a cycle of growth to maturity, flowering and then dormancy or death of the vegetation. A plant's endeavors before maturity are for developing maturity. Once the plant flowers, the endeavor tails off. The plant either enters dormancy or dies.

Nature's intention is reproduction. If we allow nature to take its course, we too will only contribute to reproduction. Nature's way of breathing, the natural way, the involuntary way, is designed to maximized reproduction.

Thus if we want to do something else, if we feel there is alternate purpose for existence, we should change the routing and intake of breath.

Meditation practice is the only way out of this despair

Early signs / kundalini

In the history of India, the development for adjusting human nature away from mere creature survival began in earnest during the period of the Upanishads (Ou-puh-nih-shuds). It is described there that a person named Yama discovered astral projection and was the first one to objectively separate from his material body. Survival as we know it from the perspective of the material body is the primary concern of the kundalini energy, both in its awakened and unawakened states.

Kundalini has its own nature and its own stronghold, which is completely apart from the coreSelf, but the coreSelf is affected because of a reliance on kundalini. For instance, right now I am living in this material body, like a government official under house arrest. I am not free to go and come from this body as I like. Sometimes I go outside the house but only as permitted. This outdoor activity is called trance, dream or sleep. I must also lift the house to move it from place to place as instructed and motivated by forces other than the coreSelf.

Who ordered my house arrest?

Why do I not escape?

Why do I have to lift this physical body to move from place to place?

What could life be like without this house which is strapped to my consciousness, the way a harness and heavy cart are strapped to the body of an animal?

In conditioned life kundalini lifeForce is in charge of the body. It stipulates the ambitions of the coreSelf. To change that control of kundalini, one must carefully study the format of life. One must observe and admit kundalini's dictatorship in the psyche and come up with a method for reducing its power grip.

Ancient yogis hint to us that breath control is the key to this. There are many types of breath control. One should practice one of these, then try another and another, until one finds one which works to reduce the authority of kundalini.

Yogi Bhajan immigrated to the United States when in an effort to break away from this physical level of consciousness some Western youths began experimenting with psychedelic drugs. He offered another method which he called kundalini yoga. This was in the 1960's. Soon after I was discharged from the US Air Force I found a sign with Yogi's photograph in Kansas City Missouri in 1971. I returned to the USA from the Philippines where I was in the US Air Force. I was at Richards Gebaur Air Force Base in Missouri. Before leaving Missouri I got some instructions about Yogi's ashram in Denver.

Soon after I was permitted to live in the ashram. I learned the method which the yogi taught. It was mainly bhastrika pranayama. This is a method for surcharging the gross and subtle body with breath.

What was the practice?

Thirty to forty-five minutes of practice twice per day, in the early morning about 4.30 a.m. and in the afternoon about 6.00 p.m. For me it was not an easy schedule. After I entered the ashram, I was told that because I had a job I had to pay a rent. I was working at the AT&T (a telephone company). I did practice in the morning, ate at the ashram for breakfast, went to work at AT&T, and then returned to the ashram in the afternoon and worked at the ashram's restaurant until 10.30 p.m, returned to the ashram, rested, got up at about 3.30 a.m., and began the day's routine again.

The restaurant was *Hanuman's Restaurant*. My job there had to do with washing dishes and cleaning huge pots with steam cleaners. I was unmarried and lived in the basement of the ashram. There was no heat in the basement in the winter. It was an earth floor basement. There were about 4 single young men in the basement. We used army sleeping bags. There were no beds in the basement.

What is bhastrika?

Bhastrika may begin with a process of sitting in various yoga postures, and even standing and making various coordinate arm movements and breathing as rapidly and forcefully as possible. Then stopping now and again and holding the breath. It begins as an effort to increase the body's intake of air. A basic session would last about 20 minutes or more.

How does this affect kundalini?

Suppose a snake lives in a tunnel in the ground. It does not have to come out if you call it. It may ignore you. It does not have to comply with your wishes. Suppose you take a water hose and flood the tunnel, the snake will be forced to surface. Of course you may run away. You may lose your courage, fearing the reptile may bite. Similar things happen when you try to flood kundalini with air while doing bhastrika. But if you take instruction from someone who practiced to proficiency, he or she will advise you how to confront and capture the snake.

Bad luck

For each of us bad luck will come sooner or later. It is how one reacts when it comes. Good fortune is welcomed. Bad luck is shunned.

There is a related story in Rama's adventures, where near the end of the Ramayana, the agent of death came to visit Rama. The agent came to inform Rama that even though he protected religious principles, still it was required for him to be deprived of the body. The agent told Rama in the presence of Laksman, that he had to speak to Rama in private. Rama agreed to give the private audience and thus he sent Laksman out of the quarters. Laksman agreed but the agent of death, said that if anyone would interrupt while he spoke to Rama, that person would die.

Laksman, hero that he was, and fearless as he was, agreed to the condition and left the room. It so happened that bad luck cannot wait. When it has a call for anyone, that person cannot avoid it by going here or there.

Laksman left the room and stood guard outside to bar anyone from entering. He felt it was his duty to protect anyone from having to die an untimely death, due to meeting with the agent of death who was in audience with Rama.

Durvasa Muni however was on his way to see Rama. He came there requesting to speak with Rama. He warned Laksman saying that if Laksman were to block entry, he would issue a curse for the death of Laksman.

Knowing that Durvasa was serious and was reputed to be an irritating yogi, Laksman became determined to go into the room and inform Rama of Durvasa arrival. When Laksman entered he explained the situation and told Rama and the Agent, that it was his preference to be killed by a deity's command for having entered the room, than to be killed by Durvasa for disobeying the yogi's order.

After that Laksman left the kingdom and went to the forest to starve his body to death while doing yoga austerities. In that way he confronted providence.

The point is that even though Laksman was so powerful to kill Indrajit an invincible and capable sorcerer and warrior, still he could not avoid bad luck when it targeted him.

We should prepare for bad luck. It certainly will come. It cannot be avoided.

Good luck

Good luck like bad luck is another mandatory feature of this life, except that good luck is welcomed. If someone is offered a large sum of unearned money, that person will hardly refuse it. There were exceptions though. In the history of yoga, there is the case of Mudgala, a yogin mentioned in the Mahabharata. He performed austerities and after some time, he was so successful that the presiding deity of the Swarga heavenly world sent his charioteer to get Mudgala.

The charioteer arrived at the place where Mudgala did austerities. He explained that Mudgala was offered a high position in the heavenly worlds and should immediately get on the celestial chariot. Mudgala was not excited about it. Instead of mounting the chariot in happiness, he questioned the charioteer:

"How long will this last? What are the advantages? What will happen when this ends?"

Getting from the charioteer some answers which he did not like, Mudgala refused to get on the chariot. He said he would persist in the austerities until he could attain something that was eternal and imperishable.

In that case we see that a great yogi developed the power to sidestep even good luck. But why would anyone turn away from good luck. If good luck is such a great thing, was Mudgala foolish to ignore it?

The problem with good luck is that it has an unseen, unobserved or unrealized portion. That is the responsibility for using it. It is actually an enticement.

In Mudgal's case, he was offered a long sojourn in a paradise world on the basis of good behavior and self-reform on this planet, but the flaw was the limited duration. Mudgala would go to that paradise, have a good time and then, when the supportive energies would become exhausted, he would fade from that place and discover himself in a lower astral domain. There he would again enter a womb of a human or animal female. Then again he would exert himself to rise out of that condition. He perceived that the good luck would turn into bad luck eventually. He rejected the opportunity.

In this world, by law of nature, good luck follows bad luck, and bad luck follows good luck. These two features work hand in hand. If you are confronted with good luck, you can certainly take it.

Why not?

The lesson from the story of Mudgala is that one should always try to review the whole scope.

Male ascetics

It is important for the sake of celibate practice and to honor moral rules that males do not associate loosely with females, nor be in pornographic environments through video or actual exposure of sexuality.

If you do not have a sexual partner and you are using a male form, you will of necessity have to suffer if you are exposed to visual, audial or imaginative pornographic environments.

This discussion addresses the problem of sexual suffering of males. This is due to the physiological construction of the sexual apparatus in males. The discussion is restricted to the construction of a male body.

The male body itself has limitations. For instance if a male is in a pornographic environment or if a male is involved with foreplay with a female, or if a male in any way exchanges gross or subtle energy with a female, through sight, hearing, touching, kissing, talking, smelling, that male body will experience a release of sexual fluids. But if those fluids are not discharged either by actual sexual intercourse or by masturbation or by dream emission, the male tubing in the testes may swell under pressure and will cause a slight hardly-noticeable pain or a downright irritating attention-requiring pain.

The same cannot be said about the female physiology, because their system does not function in the same way. It does not generate semen and its manufacture of ova, occurs in a completely different way. In addition human females, unlike most other females in the animal kingdom have a menstrual cycle which efficiently discharges released but unused eggs.

After foreplay a female, would have no swollen tubes. Their system is not designed in the same way.

Male ascetics who associate sexually with females without having relationship with these persons through which they can sexually complete the relationship in a responsible way, are either plain crazy or are in a situation which is totally beyond their control.

I do not encourage for any male yogi to be in sexual contact with a female nor to be in even a sexual flirtation with a female, nor to be in proximity with a sexually active and sexually attractive female, unless there is a relationship with that person through which the yogi can responsibly complete sexual contact.

There will be no pain in the testes for a female who associates sexually with a male and who does not have sexual intercourse thereafter, but for a male it is an entirely different matter.

Males should note their sexual construction and take steps to protect themselves from the pain or other health problems which may arise because of swollen tubes in the scrotum or in the prostrate area. This concerns biology not morality.

Index

About the Author

Michael Beloved (Yogi *Madhvāchārya*) took his current body in 1951 in Guyana. In 1965, while living in Trinidad, he instinctively began doing yoga postures and tried to make sense of the supernatural side of life.

Later in 1970, in the Philippines, he approached a Martial Arts Master named Arthur Beverford. He explained to the teacher that he was seeking a yoga instructor. Mr. Beverford identified himself as an advanced disciple of *Śrī* Rishi Singh Gherwal, an Ashtanga Yoga master.

Beverford taught the traditional Ashtanga Yoga with stress on postures, attentive breathing and brow chakra centering meditation. In 1972, Michael entered the Denver, Colorado Ashram of *kundalini* yoga Master *Śrī* Harbhajan Singh. There he took instruction in bhastrika pranayama and its application to yoga postures. He was supervised mostly by Yogi Bhajan's disciple named Prem Kaur.

In 1979 Michael formally entered the disciplic succession of the Brahmā - Madhava-Gaudiya Sampradaya through *Swāmī* Kirtanananda, who was a prominent sannyasi disciple of the Great Vaishnava Authority *Śrī Swāmī* Bhaktivedanta Prabhupada, the exponent of devotion to Sri Krishna.

However, yoga has a mystic side to it, thus Michael took training and teaching empowerment from several spiritual masters of different aspects of spiritual development. This is consistent with *Śrī* Krishna's advice to Arjuna in the *Bhagavad Gītā*:

Most of the instructions Michael received were given in the astral world. On that side of existence, his most prominent teachers were *Śrī Swāmī* Shivananda of Rishikesh, Yogiraj *Swāmī* Vishnudevananda, *Śrī Bābāji Mahasaya* - the master of the masters of *Kriyā* Yoga, *Śrīla* Yogeshwarananda of Gangotri - the master of the masters of *Rāj* Yoga (spiritual clarity), and Siddha *Swāmī* Nityananda the Brahmā Yoga authority.

The course for kundalini yoga using pranayama breath-infusion was detailed by Michael in the book *Kundalini Hatha Yoga Pradipika*. This current book was composed from meditation and breath-infusion notes which were originally shared in staple bound booklets as Yoga Journals.

Michael's preliminary books relating to this topic are *Meditation Pictorial*, *Meditation Expertise*, and *Meditation ~ Sense Faculty* (co-author). Every technique (kriya) mentioned was tested by him during pranayama breath-infusion and *samyama* deep meditation practice.

This is a result of over forty years of meditation practice with astute subtle observations intending to share the methods and experiences. The information is published freely with no intention of forming an institution or hogtying anyone as a disciple.

Publications

English Series

Bhagavad Gita English

Anu Gita English

Markandeya Samasya English

Yoga Sutras English

Hatha Yoga Pradipika English

Uddhava Gita English

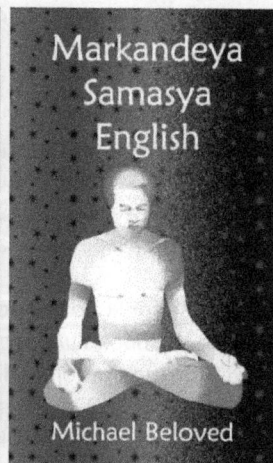

Yoga Sūtras English

Michael Beloved

Haṭha Yoga Pradīpika English

Michael Beloved

Uddhava Gītā English

Michael Beloved / Madhvāchārya dās

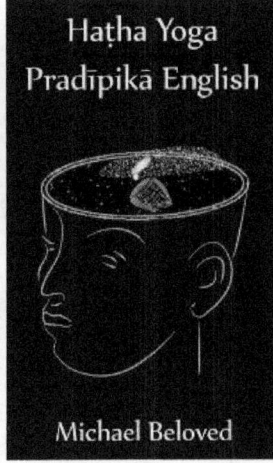

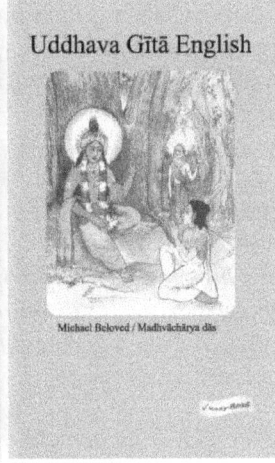

These are in 21st Century English, very precise and exacting. Many Sanskrit words which were considered untranslatable into a Western language are rendered in precise, expressive and modern English.

Three of these books are instructions from Krishna. **In Bhagavad Gita English** *and* **Anu Gita English**, *the instructions were for Arjuna. In the* **Uddhava Gita English,** *it was for Uddhava. Bhagavad Gita and Anu Gita are extracted from the Mahabharata. Uddhava Gita was extracted from the 11th Canto of the Srimad Bhagavatam (Bhagavata Purana). One of these books, the* **Markandeya Samasya English** *is about Krishna, as described by Yogi Markandeya, who survived the cosmic collapse and reached a divine child in whose transcendental body, the collapsed world was existing.*

Two of this series are the syllabus about yoga practice. The Yoga Sutras of Patanjali is elaboration about ashtanga yoga. Hatha Yoga Pradipika English, is the detailed information about asana postures, pranayama breath- infusion, energy compression, naad sound resonance and advanced meditation. The Sanskrit author is Swatmarama Mahayogin.

My suggestion is that you read **Bhagavad Gita English**, *the* **Anu Gita English,** *the* **Markandeya Samasya English,** *the* **Yoga Sutras English,** *the* **Hatha Yoga Pradipika** *and lastly the* **Uddhava Gita English**, *which is complicated and detailed.*

For each of these books we have at least one commentary, which is published separately. Thus your particular interest can be researched further in the commentaries.

The smallest of these commentaries and perhaps the simplest is the one for the Anu Gita. We published its commentary as the <u>Anu Gita Explained</u>. *The*

Bhagavad Gita explanations were published in three distinct targeted commentaries. The first is <u>Bhagavad Gita Explained</u>, which sheds lights on how people in the time of Krishna and Arjuna regarded the information and applied it. Bhagavad Gita is an exposition of the application of yoga practice to cultural activities, which is known in the Sanskrit language as karma yoga.

Interestingly, Bhagavad Gita was spoken on a battlefield just before one of the greatest battles in the ancient world. A warrior, Arjuna, lost his wits and had no idea that he could apply his training in yoga to political dealings. Krishna, his charioteer, lectured on the spur of the moment to give Arjuna the skill of using yoga proficiency in cultural dealings including how to deal with corrupt officials on a battlefield.

The second Gita commentary is the <u>Kriya Yoga Bhagavad Gita</u>. This clears the air about Krishna's information on the science of kriya yoga, showing that its techniques are clearly described for anyone who takes the time to read Bhagavad Gita. Kriya yoga concerns the battlefield which is the psyche of the living being. The internal war and the mental and emotional forces which are hostile to self-realization are dealt with in the kriya yoga practice.

The third commentary is the <u>Brahma Yoga Bhagavad Gita</u>. This shows what Krishna had to say outright and what he hinted about which concerns the brahma yoga practice, a mystic process for those who mastered kriya yoga.

*There is one commentary for the **Markandeya Samasya English**. The title of that publication is <u>Krishna Cosmic Body</u>.*

There are two commentaries to the Yoga Sutras. One is the <u>Yoga Sutras of Patanjali</u> and the other is the <u>Meditation Expertise</u>. These give detailed explanations of ashtanga Yoga.

The commentary of Hatha Yoga Pradipika is titled <u>Kundalini Hatha Yoga Pradipika</u>.

For the Uddhava Gita, we published the <u>Uddhava Gita Explained</u>. This is a large book and requires concentration and study for integration of the information. Of the books which deal with transcendental topics, my opinion is that the discourse between Krishna and Uddhava has the complete information about the realities in existence. This book is the one which removes massive existential ignorance.

Meditation Series

Meditation Pictorial

Meditation Expertise

CoreSelf Discovery

Meditation Sense Faculty

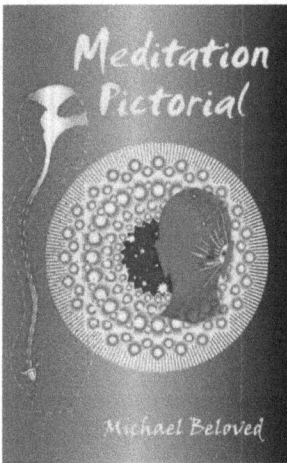

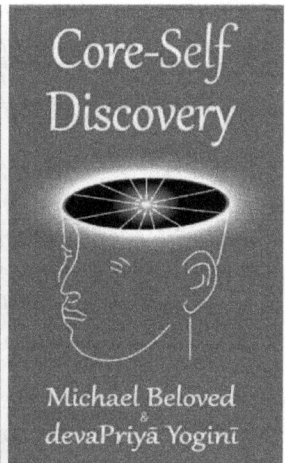

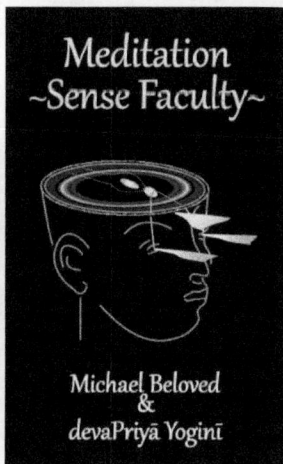

The specialty of these books is the mind diagrams which profusely illustrate what is written. This shows exactly what one has to do mentally to develop and then sustain a meditation practice.

*In the **Meditation Pictorial**, one is shown how to develop psychic insight, a feature without which meditation is imagination and visualization, without any mystic experience per se.*

*In the **Meditation Expertise**, one is shown how to corral one's practice to bring it in line with the classic syllabus of yoga which Patanjali lays out as the ashtanga yoga eight-staged practice.*

*In **CoreSelf Discovery**, (co-authored with devaPriya Yogini) one is taken though the course of pratyahar sensual energy withdrawal which is the 5th stage of yoga in the Patanjali ashtanga eight-process complete system of yoga practice. These events lead to the discovery of a coreSelf which is surrounded by psychic organs in the head of the subtle body. This product has a DVD component.*

***Meditation ~ Sense Faculty** (co-authored with devaPriya Yogini) is a detailed tutorial with profuse diagrams showing what actions to take in the subtle body to investigate the senses faculties. The meditator must first establish the location and function of the observing self. That self must be screened from the thoughts and ideas which usually hypnotize it.*

These books are profusely illustrated with mind diagrams showing the components of psychic consciousness and the inner design of the subtle body.

Explained Series

Bhagavad Gita Explained

Uddhava Gita Explained

Anu Gita Explained

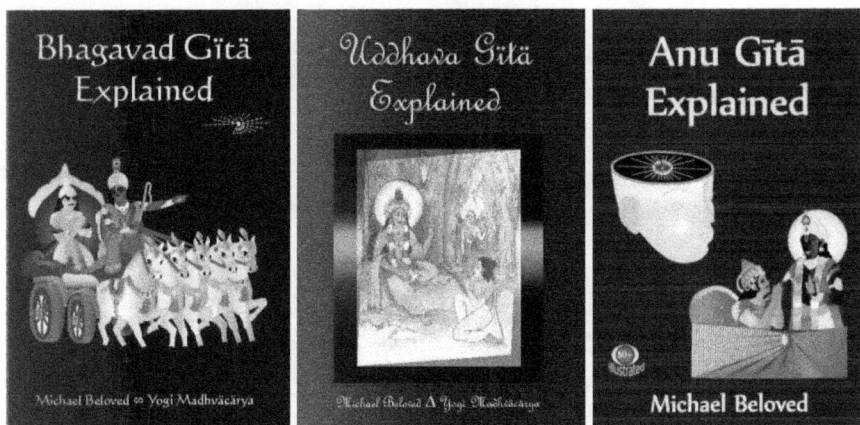

The specialty of these books is that they are free of missionary intentions, cult tactics and philosophical distortion. Instead of using these books to add credence to a philosophy, meditation process, belief or plea for followers, I spread the information out so that a reader can look through this literature and freely take or leave anything as desired.

When Krishna stressed himself as God, I stated that. When Krishna laid no claims for supremacy, I showed that. The reader is left to form an independent opinion about the validity of the information and the credibility of Krishna.

There is a difference in the discourse with Arjuna in the Bhagavad Gita and the one with Uddhava in the Uddhava Gita. In fact these two books may appear to contradict each other. In the Bhagavad Gita, Krishna pressured Arjuna to complete social duties. In the Uddhava Gita, Krishna insisted that Uddhava should abandon the same.

The Anu Gita is not as popular as the Bhagavad Gita but it is the conclusion of that text. Anu means what is to follow, what proceeds. In this discourse, an anxious Arjuna request that Krishna should repeat the Bhagavad Gita and again show His supernatural and divine forms.

However Krishna refuses to do so and chastises Arjuna for being a disappointment in forgetting what was revealed. Krishna then cited a celestial yogi, a near-perfected being, who explained the process of transmigration in vivid detail.

Commentaries

Yoga Sutras of Patanjali

Meditation Expertise

Krishna Cosmic Body

Anu Gita Explained

Bhagavad Gita Explained

Kriya Yoga Bhagavad Gita

Brahma Yoga Bhagavad Gita

Uddhava Gita Explained

Kundalini Hatha Yoga Pradipika

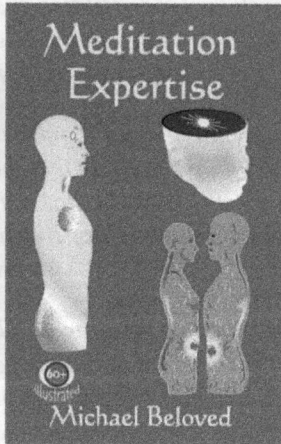

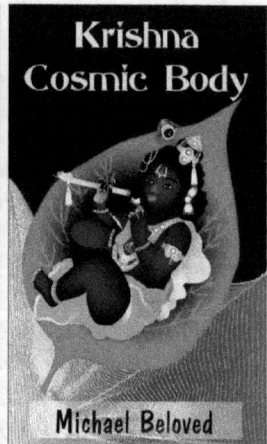

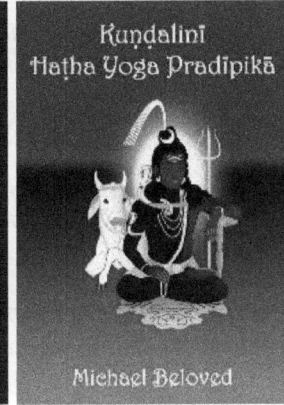

Yoga Sutras of Patanjali is the globally acclaimed text book of yoga. This has detailed expositions of yoga techniques. Many kriya techniques are vividly described in the commentary.

Meditation Expertise is an analysis and application of the Yoga Sutras. This book is loaded with illustrations and has detailed explanations of secretive advanced meditation techniques which are called kriyas in the Sanskrit language.

Krishna Cosmic Body is a narrative commentary on the Markandeya Samasya portion of the Aranyaka Parva of the Mahabharata. This is the detailed description of the dissolution of the world, as experienced by the great yogin Markandeya who transcended the cosmic deity, Brahma, and reached Brahma's source who is the divine infant, Krishna.

Anu Gita Explained is a detailed explanation of how we endure many material bodies in the course of transmigrating through various life-forms. This is a discourse between Krishna and Arjuna. Arjuna requested of Krishna a display *of the Universal Form and a repeat narration of the Bhagavad Gita but Krishna declined and explained what a siddha perfected being told the Yadu family about the sequence of existences one endures and the systematic flow of those lives at the convenience of material nature.*

Bhagavad Gita Explained *shows what was said in the Gita without religious overtones and sectarian biases.*

Kriya Yoga Bhagavad Gita *shows the instructions for those who are doing kriya yoga.*

Brahma Yoga Bhagavad Gita *shows the instructions for those who are doing brahma yoga.*

Uddhava Gita Explained *shows the instructions to Uddhava which are more advanced than the ones given to Arjuna.*

Bhagavad Gita is an instruction for applying the expertise of yoga in the cultural field. This is why the process taught to Arjuna is called karma yoga which means karma + yoga or cultural activities done with yogic insight.

Uddhava Gita is an instruction for apply the expertise of yoga to attaining spiritual status. This is why it is explains jnana yoga and bhakti yoga in detail. Jnana yoga is using mystic skill for knowing the spiritual part of existence. Bhakti yoga is for developing affectionate relationships with divine beings.

Karma yoga is for negotiating the social concerns in the material world. It is inferior to bhakti yoga which concerns negotiating the social concerns in the spiritual world.

This world has a social environment. The spiritual world has one too.

Currently, Uddhava Gita is the most advanced and informative spiritual book on the planet. There is nothing anywhere which is superior to it or which goes into so much detail as it. It verified that historically Krishna is the most advanced human being to ever have left literary instructions on this planet. Even Patanjali Yoga Sutras which I translated and gave an application for in my book, **Meditation Expertise**, *does not go as far as the Uddhava Gita.*

Some of the information of these two books is identical but while the Yoga Sutras are concerned with the personal spiritual emancipation (kaivalyam) of the individual spirits, the Uddhava Gita explains that and also explains the situations in the spiritual universes.

Bhagavad Gita is from the Mahabharata *which is the history of the Pandavas. Arjuna, the student of the Gita, is one of the Pandavas brothers. He was in a social hassle and did not know how to apply yoga expertise to solve it. On the battlefield, Krishna gave him a crash-course on yogic social interactions.*

Uddhava Gita is from the Srimad Bhagavatam (Bhagavata Purana), *which is a history of the incarnations of Krishna. Uddhava was a relative of Krishna. He was concerned about the situation of the deaths of many of his relatives but Krishna diverted Uddhava's attention to the practice of yoga for the purpose of successfully migrating to the spiritual environment.*

Kundalini Hatha Yoga Pradipika *is the commentary for the Hatha Yoga Pradipika of Swatmarama Mahayogin. This is the detailed process about asana posture, pranayama breath-infusion, complex compressions of energy, naad sound resonance intonement and advanced meditation practice.*

This is the singular book with all the techniques of how to reform and redesign the subtle body so that it does not have the tendency for physical life forms and for it to attain the status of a siddha.

These books are based on the author's experiences in meditation, yoga practice and participation in spiritual groups:

Specialty

Spiritual Master

sex you!

Sleep Paralysis

Astral Projection

Masturbation Psychic Details

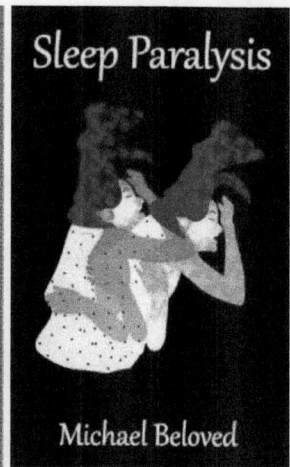

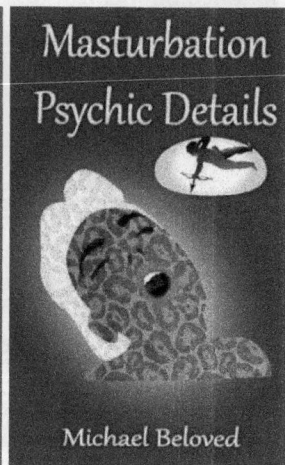

In **Spiritual Master**, Michael draws from experience with gurus or with their senior students. His contact with astral gurus is rated. He walks you through the avenue of gurus showing what you should do and what you should not do, so as to gain proficiency in whatever area of spirituality the guru has proficiency.

sex you! is a masterpiece about the adventures of an individual spirit's passage through the parents' psyches. The conversion of a departed soul into a sexual urge is described. The transit from the afterlife to residency in the emotions of the parents is detailed. This is about sex and you. Learn about how much of you comprises the romantic energy of your would-be parents!

Sleep Paralysis clears misconceptions so that one can see what sleep paralysis is and what frightening astral experience occurs while the paralysis is being experienced. *This disempowerment has great value in giving you confidence that you can and do exist even if you are unable to operate the physical body. The implication is that one can exist apart from and will survive the loss of the material form.*

Astral Projection *details experiences Michael had even in childhood, where he assumed incorrectly that everyone was astrally conversant. He discusses the lifeForce psychic mechanism which operates the sleep-wake cycle of the physical form, and which budgets energy into the separated astral form which determines if the individual will have dream recall or no objective awareness during the projections. Astral travel happens on every occasion when the physical body sleeps. What is missing in awareness is the observer status while the astral body is separated.*

Masturbation Psychic Details *is a surprise presentation which relates what happens on the psychic plane during a masturbation event. This does not tackle moral issues or even addictions but shows the involvement of memory and the sure but hidden subconscious mind which operates many features of the psyche irrespective of the desire or approval of the self-conscious personality.*

inVision Series

Yoga inVision 1

Yoga inVision 2

Yoga inVision 3

Yoga inVision 4

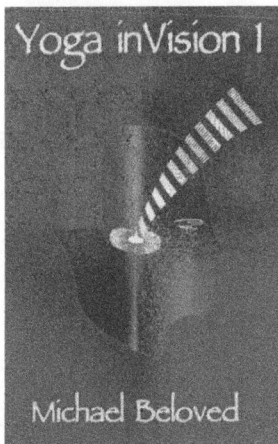

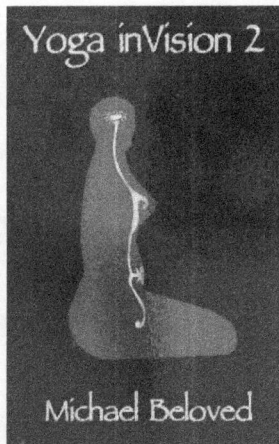

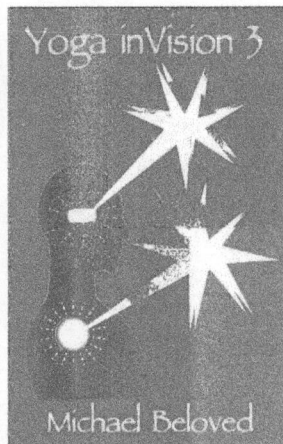

Yoga inVision 1, *the first in this series, describes the breath-infusion and meditation practices during the years of 1998 and 1999. There are unique, once in a lifetime as well as recurring insights which are elaborated. inFocus during breath-infusion and the meditation which follows is an adventure for any yogi. This gives what happened to this particular ascetic.*

Yoga inVision 2 *reports on the author's experiences from 1999 to 2001. Each day the experience is unique, illustrating the vibrancy of practice. Many rare once-in-a-lifetime perceptions are described.*

Yoga inVision 3 *reports on the author's experiences from 2001 to 2003.*

Yoga inVision 4 *reports on the author's experiences from 2006 to 2009.*

Online Resources

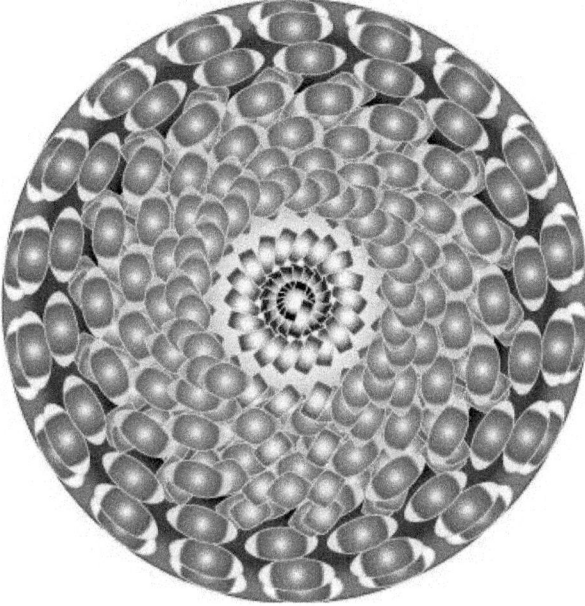

Email:	michaelbelovedbooks@gmail.com
	axisnexus@gmail.com
Website:	michaelbeloved.com
Forum:	inselfyoga.com
Posters:	zazzle.com/inself

* 9 7 8 1 9 4 2 8 8 7 1 6 4 *